# ERICH FROMM AND THE QUEST FOR SOLIDARITY

# ERICH FROMM AND THE QUEST FOR SOLIDARITY

LAWRENCE WILDE

First published in 2004 by
PALGRAVE MACMILLAN™
175 Fifth Avenue, New York, N.Y. 10010 and
Houndmills, Basingstoke, Hampshire, England RG21 6XS
Companies and representatives throughout the world.

PALGRAVE MACMILLAN is the global academic imprint of the Palgrave Macmillan division of St. Martin's Press, LLC and of Palgrave Macmillan Ltd. Macmillan® is a registered trademark in the United States, United Kingdom and other countries. Palgrave is a registered trademark in the European Union and other countries.

ISBN 1–4039–6141–7 hardback

Library of Congress Cataloging-in-Publication Data
Wilde, Lawrence.
    Erich Fromm and the quest for solidarity / Lawrence Wilde.
        p. cm.
    Includes bibliographical references and index.
    ISBN 1–4039–6141–7
        1. Solidarity. 2. Humanistic ethics. 3. Fromm, Erich, 1900– I. Title.
HM717.W55 2004
302'.14—dc22                                      2004046072

A catalogue record for this book is available from the British Library.

Design by Newgen Imaging Systems (P) Ltd., Chennai, India.

First edition: November 2004

10 9 8 7 6 5 4 3 2 1

Printed in the United States of America.

*For Frances Catherine*

# CONTENTS

# ACKNOWLEDGMENTS

I am indebted to Ian Fraser and Vincent Geoghegan for their meticulous and invaluable comments on the entire manuscript, and to Tony Burns for his comments on an early version of chapter four. Special thanks to Rainer Funk for his wonderful hospitality at the Erich Fromm Archive in Tübingen, and for granting permission to quote from the works of Erich Fromm. Many thanks to participants who commented on papers presented on Fromm's work at the University of Sussex, Edge Hill College, Lancashire, and Nottingham Trent University. I am grateful to Nottingham Trent University for granting me a sabbatical at the beginning of the project, and to the library staff there for helping me with interlibrary loans. Thank you to Joan Melia for her tireless and skillful work in helping to knock this book into shape, and to her and our daughter Frances Catherine for creating the loving environment in which it has been produced. I am grateful to Anthony Wahl of Palgrave, New York, for his enthusiastic support for this project.

# Principal Events in the Life of Erich Fromm

1900    March 23, born in Frankfurt-am-Main, Germany, the only child of an Orthodox Jewish middle-class family.

1914    Outbreak of War causes Fromm to question the irrationality of nationalism.

1916    Begins Talmudic studies with Rabbi Nehemia Nobel, until 1921.

1918    Graduates from the Wöhler-Schule and begins studying law at the University of Frankfurt.

1919    Moves to the University of Heidelberg and studies Sociology and Economics.

1920    Talmudic studies under Salman Rabinkow, a socialist, until 1926.

1922    Awarded a doctorate from Heidelberg for a dissertation on the sociology of three communities of the Jewish diaspora.

1924    Psychoanalyzed by Frieda Reichmann. They set up a therapy center for Jewish patients in Heidelberg.

1926    Marries Frieda Reichmann. Rejects theistic religion.

1928    Further psychoanalytical training in Berlin.

1929    Returns to Frankfurt to help found the South German Institute for Psychoanalysis. Seeks a new social psychology combining Marx's sociology and Freud's psychoanalysis.

1930    Publishes *The Dogma of Christ*. Joins the Institute for Social Research (the Frankfurt School) as head of psychoanalysis and social psychology. Commences work on an empirical project on the personality structure of the German working class. Completes psychoanalytical training in Berlin and opens his own practice.

1931    Parts from Frieda Fromm-Reichmann.

1932    Contracts tuberculosis and recuperates in Davos, Switzerland.

1933    Accession to power of Hitler and the Nazis forces the Institute for Social Research to move to Geneva, Switzerland. Death of father. Begins relationship with the psychoanalyst Karen Horney.

1934    Emigrates to the United States and continues work with the Institute at its new home in New York. Sets up psychoanalytical practice.

1935    Cooperation with psychoanalysts Harry Stack Sullivan and Clara Thompson.

1937    Rejects Freud's drive theory.

1938     New outbreak of tuberculosis. Convalesces in Switzerland.

1939     Leaves the Institute for Social Research.

1940     Becomes a citizen of the United States.

1941     Publication of *Escape From Freedom*. Teaches at the New School for Social Research in New York. Divorces Frieda Fromm-Reichmann. His mother comes to live in New York.

1943     Ends relationship with Karen Horney.

1944     Marries Henny Gurland. Teaches at Bennington College, Vermont.

1946     Responsible for the training of teachers at the New York branch of the William Allanson White Institute of Psychiatry.

1947     Publication of *Man For Himself* in which he sets down a normative conception of human essence.

1948     Teaches Psychoanalysis and Religion at Yale University.

1950     Moves to Mexico City to secure a better climate for his sick wife.

1951     Founds the Mexican Institute for Psychoanalysis in the National Autonomous University of Mexico.

1952     Death of Henny Gurland-Fromm.

1953     Though still resident in Mexico City, begins annual three month-long visits to New York to work at the New School for Social Research and the William Allanson Institute. Marries Annis Freeman.

1955     Publication of *The Sane Society*.

1956     Publication of *The Art of Loving*, which goes on to sell 25 million copies.

1957     Helps to found the peace movement SANE, the National Committee for a Sane Nuclear Policy. Marks the beginning of 11 years of political activism. Begins six-year empirical study of the social character of the villagers of Chiconcuac in Mexico.

1959     Death of his mother.

1960     Active engagement with the American Socialist Party, speaking on its behalf to mass audiences at Yale and Chicago Universities.

1961     Publication of *May Man Prevail?*, an analysis of U.S. foreign policy, and *Marx's Concept of Man*, bringing Marx's early philosophical writings to an English-speaking readership for the first time.

1964     Publication of *The Heart of Man*.

1965     Edits an anthology, *Socialist Humanism*, bringing in contributions from leading theorists from throughout the world and making an important contribution to the development of the New Left.

1966     Draws huge audiences to lectures for peace. In a three-week lecture tour of California in May he speaks to an audience of 60,000 people. In December, prior to speaking at an anti-Vietnam War rally at Madison Square Gardens, has his first heart attack.

1968     Supports and writes speeches for Eugene McCarthy's campaign to win the Democratic nomination for President. Publication of *The Revolution of Hope*.

1969     Begins to spend summers in Ticino, Switzerland.

1973     Publication of *The Anatomy of Human Destructiveness*.

1974     Leaves Mexico and retires to Ticino.

1976    Publication of *To Have or To Be?*, a summary of his social and political thought.
1977    Second heart attack. He is feted as a visionary figure by young radical movements in Germany and Italy.
1978    Third heart attack.
1980    March 18, dies following fourth heart attack.

# CHAPTER ONE

# INTRODUCTION: THE QUEST

The vision of the achievement of human solidarity is a recurring theme in the work of Erich Fromm, psychoanalyst and social theorist (1900–1980). His explicit commitment to a radical humanism that talks boldly about human essence and human potential runs counter to the skepticism and relativism currently prevailing in the academic social sciences. Despite the immense popular appeal of books like *Escape From Freedom, The Sane Society,* and *The Art of Loving,* his work now receives relatively little attention from academic writers. In his specialized field of social psychology and psychoanalytical theory there has been some attempt to draw attention to his significance,[1] but in the wider field of social and political theory his name is rarely mentioned. As a political theorist I find this neglect unfortunate, for although Fromm could not be regarded as a political theorist in the narrow sense, his transdisciplinary approach has much to offer to students of politics and society today. His ethically driven communitarianism based on a strong, normative theory of human essence is a bold and refreshing antidote to postmodernist relativism. This book aims to retrieve Fromm's valuable contribution to social and political thought and also to claim its continued relevance by relating his radical humanist approach to current thinking on feminism, work, consumerism, democracy, and globalization.

The concept of solidarity has been infused with both pragmatic and moral dimensions since its earliest use by English and French socialists in the 1840s. It referred to the collective resistance of workers to their exploitation and exclusion from political life, but it also expressed a conviction that such collective action contained within it the germ of a more just society. This ethical component, more often than not infused with a strong religious element, held out the promise that the solidarity of working people would lead eventually to human solidarity, a realization of the monotheistic ideal of the brotherhood of man.[2] This broader vision of human solidarity, in which the peoples of the world develop a sense of reciprocal sympathy and strive for the creation of social structures which promote it, is central to the normative goal of Fromm's radical humanism. He grounds it philosophically in a strong normative conception of human nature, informed by his long experience as a psychoanalyst. The origins of his normative position are to be found in his immersion in Orthodox Jewish scholarship during his upbringing in Frankfurt-am-Main, where he was born in 1900.[3] In an autobiographical sketch, he records his exhilaration at reading the Old Testament, particularly the prophetic writings of Isaiah,

Amos, and Hosea.[4] It was not their dire warnings that attracted him but their promise of universal peace and harmony between nations. As a Jewish boy in a Christian
environment, he felt himself to be an outsider, even though he went to a "mixed"
school, but he felt uncomfortable with the clannishness of both gentiles and Jews.
When the First World War broke out, the teenage Fromm was appalled by the
narrow-minded hatred and irrational nationalist fervor that he witnessed.[5] Driven by
the need to understand how the carnage could have happened, he turned to sociology and psychology.

Although he declared himself an atheist at the age of 26, Fromm never repudi-
ated the ethical significance of religion. He maintained that a nontheistic form of
religious thinking could help in the development of a truly critical consciousness and
contribute to an ethical reawakening, without which the prospects for social progress
were distinctly slight. This enduring conviction of the universal importance of the
religious impulse owed much to the critical-interpretative pedagogy of his rabbinical
teachers, particularly the socialist Salman Rabinkow, who exerted a profound
influence on Fromm's development during his student years in Heidelberg from
1919 to 1925. In addition, Fromm acknowledged his debt to the Kantian socialist
Hermann Cohen, who pioneered the use of the Old Testament to demonstrate the
symbolic roots of the human struggle for freedom and justice and whose major work,
*Religion of Reason*, was published in the year Fromm started his university studies.[6]
For Fromm, the Bible provides an ancient provenance for the quest for human
solidarity, expressed in terms of the "messianic time" or "the end of days". Biblical
quotations often find their way into his writings, as, for example, this prophesy
of Isaiah:

> Then the eyes of the blind shall be opened
> And the ears of the deaf shall be unstopped.
> Then the lame shall leap like a deer,
> And the tongue of the dumb shall shout aloud;
> For waters shall burst forth in the desert,
> Streams in the wilderness. (Isaiah 35:5–6)

and also Micah's famous prophesy of universal peace:

> Thus He will judge among the many peoples,
> And arbitrate for the multitude of nations,
> However distant;
> And they shall beat their swords into plowshares
> And their spears into pruning hooks.
> Nation shall not take up
> Swords against nation;
> They shall never again know war. (Micah 4:3)

He consistently associates his ethical commitment to communitarian socialism with
religious thinking, so much so that in his later years he planned to write a theoretical work on the role of religion and on Marxist socialism as a "secular though spiritual phenomenon."[7] The interpretation of Marx's thought as a form of secular

Messianism is controversial, as indeed is the Messianic streak in Fromm's own social theory, and the issue of his Messianic impulse will be considered later. At this point, however, it is important to understand the links, which Fromm draws between religious thinking and the normative commitment to human solidarity.

The three elements of religious thinking identified by Fromm are wonder, the ultimate concern, and the attitude of oneness.[8] Wonder refers to a marveling in the mysteries of life, the puzzling problems of our existence and our relatedness to the world. Fromm quotes Socrates as saying that wonder is the beginning of wisdom and adds that this is equally true for religious experience. Ultimate concern, a formulation borrowed from the theologian Paul Tillich, denotes concern with the meaning of life and human self-realization. Oneness is an attitude of oneness within oneself, with all others, and with all life. For Fromm there is nothing irrational in such thinking, for, on the contrary, the development of such thought involves a constant reexamination of assumptions, and it does not require a belief in God as an external demiurge. Buddhism, for example, which fascinated Fromm, expresses all the three elements without having recourse to a God figure. The concern for oneness is the element which is closest to the secular term "solidarity," which is found throughout his writings as the ultimate ideal of feeling and acting, a prerequisite for the full mental well-being of the individual as well as for the fulfillment of a peaceful and productive world. Human solidarity is Fromm's ultimate concern:

> Only when man succeeds in developing his reason and love further than he has done so far, only when he can build a world based on human solidarity and justice, only when he can feel rooted in the experience of universal brotherliness, will he have found a new, human form of rootedness, will he have transformed his world into a truly human home.[9]

This imperative is asserted by Fromm on the basis of a dialectical view of modernity. On the one hand, scientific and technical developments point to the real possibility of abundance, a day when "the table will be set for all who want to eat," and when the human race will form a unified community with no need to live as separate entities.[10] On the other hand, modernity discourages our natural sociality and restricts it to the public sphere. In the private sphere, the individual is moved by egotistical interest rather than solidarity and love for humanity, and although such feelings may be reflected secondarily in private acts of philanthropy or kindness, they are not part of the basic structure of our social relations.[11] As a social psychologist, Fromm spent his life investigating this dialectic. *Why* did the various social classes react to the challenge of modernity in the way they did, *why* was the promise of freedom and democracy thwarted by war, oppression, and exploitation, and *how* might it be possible for the cause of human solidarity to be advanced in an alienated world?

Before moving on to the specific areas in which Fromm explored his ultimate concern, some clarification of his normative goal is needed. He often talks in terms of what mankind needs to do if it were to achieve the change of direction necessary for human life to flourish. His analyses and prescriptions are unequivocally universalistic in nature, and, furthermore, based on an explicit theory of what human nature is *and* ought to be. Such universalism and essentialism is now routinely denounced for masking totalitarian designs, for presenting the one right way for people to follow, and for denying the richness of human plurality and the right to choose for oneself. However, as Terry Eagleton has recently argued, essentialism does not mean uniformity, and much recent anti-essentialism is largely the product of philosophical amateurism and ignorance.[12] Fromm's overriding concern is for the realization of human freedom, and he saw no contradiction between the uniqueness of the self and the realization of solidarity. Equality of esteem is necessary if solidarity is to emerge, but the thesis that we are all born equal means only that we share the same human qualities, the same basic fate, and the same claim on freedom and happiness. Only in a condition of solidarity will we escape relations of domination or submission, but it is imperative to grasp that the concept of equality does not mean uniformity but instead requires difference.[13] Difference, for Fromm, becomes something to celebrate only when it does not involve relations of superiority or inferiority. Only on the basis of equality and solidarity can the social conditions be created which will develop the positive side of the peculiarities of persons, sexes, and national groups. The resulting accentuation of difference makes for a "richer and broader human culture."[14]

Appeals to human solidarity on the basis of our shared qualities and potentials are treated with deep skepticism in the social sciences, and this has been expressed recently in Margaret Canovan's recent dismissal of the invocation of common humanity as "the grandest but flimsiest of contemporary imagined communities."[15] As a generalization, this may have some force, but I would argue that Fromm is unique among social scientists of the late twentieth century in offering a thoroughly worked-out and well-defended view of human essence as a philosophical grounding for an appeal for solidarity. The goal of human solidarity evokes a condition in which the vast majority of human beings have become conscious of our shared fate and are able to create social structures which enable them all to develop peacefully and harmoniously their uniquely human qualities of reason, productiveness, and love. This conception borrows from a rich philosophical heritage; the centrality of reason reflects the influence of Aristotle and Spinoza, the emphasis on productiveness reflects the influence of Marx, while the importance of love comes primarily from his own engagement with psychoanalysis. After completing his training in Berlin in 1930 he engaged in clinical practice and training until late in life, and he was quite clear that the insights gained from this work were vital in the development of his social psychology and his ethics. "There is not a single theoretical conclusion about man's psyche," he once claimed, "which is not based on a critical observation of human behaviour carried out in the course of this psychoanalytical work."[16] As a psychoanalyst, he was able to develop a scientific understanding of the range of neuroses, which, in his view, developed when the natural growth of our positive potentials was blocked.[17]

Fromm was well aware that his normative position might be dismissed as a "dreaming" form of utopianism, and he met the issue head-on in his final major work, *To Have or To Be?* Here he describes himself as an "awake" utopian pursuing the ideal of a "united new humankind living in solidarity and peace, free from economic determination and from war and class struggle."[18] He is distinctly sober about the prospects for the realization of this ideal, placing the odds at no better than 2 percent, but insisted nevertheless that this long shot must be pursued. It is, in his view, a matter of life or death for humanity as a whole, and if there is any chance at all, it needs to be worked for by people who are hard-headed realists who have shed all illusions and fully appreciate the difficulties.[19] He points out that we have for the most part fulfilled the technical utopias, which once seemed fanciful, but that what we need now is an entirely new type of science to move us closer to the fulfillment of a humanistic utopia, a "humanistic science of man as the basis for the applied science and art of social reconstruction."[20] He appeals for renewed energy in trying to further the goal of human solidarity, arguing that just as we cannot build a submarine by reading Jules Verne, we cannot construct a humanistic society by reading the Prophets. He calls for the emergence of many "designs, models, studies and experiments" that "begin to bridge the gap between what is necessary and what is possible."[21]

As the ultimate concern, human solidarity is given a rich normative rhetoric in Fromm's work, which presents a startling contrast with most modern social science and may be one reason for the neglect of his contribution by the academic world in recent years. In *The Sane Society* the language is often apocalyptic in tone, appealing for the creation of a society which conforms with human needs, one in which "man relates to man lovingly, in which he is rooted in bonds of brotherliness and solidarity, rather than in the ties of blood and soil."[22] In *To Have or To Be?* he speaks of solidarity on the basis of an ideal or a conviction as the highest kind of human behavior, and the realization of solidarity as the crucial factor in the health of a society.[23] In modern society, acts of solidarity are deemed exceptional, as the pursuit of short-term self-interest is structurally embedded in the way we live. Yet, despite the incisiveness that Fromm displayed in exposing the alienating character of modern market societies he remained convinced that the resources existed within humankind to build a qualitatively better world, and it is this reconstructive potential that I want to emphasize in this book.

## Three Paths

The word "quest" has connotations of myths and legends through which groups develop a symbolic consciousness of searching for truth or justice. I consider it appropriate to apply it to Fromm's work because there is a consistency of purpose in his long career and a conviction of the need for an explicitly ethical confrontation with modernity. In most quests, the object of the search is elusive, and ultimately its supreme importance is transcended by the lessons learned in the process of seeking. The journey becomes more important than the destination, and finding the thing "out there" becomes less important than finding oneself. There is a parallel here with Fromm's conviction that we need to move away from the "having mode" and closer to the "being mode" if we are to achieve happiness and human solidarity.[24] The being mode, in which human solidarity is preponderant, is something to be striven for but it does not imply finality. Fromm recognizes the human essence as an existential dilemma between being in nature and constantly needing to transcend it, so that any idea of a "final state" of human happiness is rendered chimerical. This emphasis on transcendence resonates with Charles Pasternak's argument that "questing" is the essence of humanity,[25] but Fromm's conception has rather more substance than that. He insists that human flourishing can become a reality only when the concern for the welfare of all humanity prevails over competing priorities for power and profit. This concern really exists in our daily experiences, in acts of consideration and kindness, and it is something that needs to be extricated, articulated, and politicized. It is possible to read Fromm's life and work as a series of stages in this quest, distinguishable not chronologically but rather in terms of related perspectives. The first is his social psychology, which involves a continuing dialogue with Freud and which, on the whole, produces a bleak analysis of the prevalence of authoritarianism and conformism in modernity. The second is his humanistic ethics, which comes into confluence with his social psychology in *Man for Himself* (1947), and which opens a vista on the possibility of achieving human solidarity. Finally, there is the political dimension, in its broadest sense, in which Fromm seeks to identify ideas and movements capable of challenging the alienated reality, which he depicts so vividly in *The Sane Society* (1955).

*Social Psychology*

Fromm began his interest in psychoanalysis after completing his doctorate at the University of Heidelberg in 1922 with a dissertation on the sociology of three German Jewish communities. Under the influence of Frieda Reichmann (1889–1957), who became his wife in 1926, Fromm immersed himself in Freudian psychoanalysis. In 1929 he returned to Frankfurt as cofounder of the South German Institute for Psychoanalysis, and the speech he delivered at its opening reveals the high ambition of his research goals, centered on the proposed fusion of psychoanalysis, as pioneered by Freud, and sociology, which for him meant Marxist sociology. Fromm argues that psychoanalysis can bring to sociology insights into the human psychic apparatus, for this should be regarded as a causal factor in social development along with technical and economic factors. Sociology can bring to psychoanalysis its knowledge of the social context in which psychological development takes place, in particular the extent to which the family is a product of the social system and the ways in which socially conditioned changes in the family influence the psychic apparatus of the individual.[26] In the lecture he expresses his excitement at Freud's move toward social psychology in *The Future of an Illusion* (1927), in which Freud had addressed the issue of religious belief, an issue which was close to Fromm's own research interests at the time. Fromm closes his lecture by referring to Marx as the greatest sociologist of all and quoting a passage from *The Holy Family* in which Marx asserts that it is not "history" that does things but real human beings who make things happen and achieve historical change.[27] So, in this short lecture he points to the decisive influences of Marxian sociology and Freudian psychoanalysis, and also refers to his continuing fascination with the sociology of religious thought.

His first major attempt at applying a social–psychological interpretive method comes in *The Dogma of Christ* (1930). The point of the essay is to show that antagonism between social classes provided the material basis for the doctrinal argument over the nature of Christ. We look at the argument in more detail in chapter three, but it is apparent in this work that Fromm was still working within Freudian orthodoxy. He uses the Oedipus myth to explain the early Christian belief (Arianism) in the elevation of a man to God as an expression of the unconscious wish for the removal of the divine father.[28] In identifying with the crucified Christ, they atone for their death wishes against the father, and at the same time displace the father by identification with the suffering of Jesus.[29] But the radical message of the work is that despite the triumph of authoritarianism in the doctrinal defeat of Arianism, the egalitarian impulse continued to express itself. As Fromm comments, "the humanistic, democratic element was never subdued in Christian or in Jewish history," and the radical message was "God is not a symbol of power over man but of man's own powers."[30] *The Dogma of Christ* received a glowing review by Franz Borkenau in the first edition of the journal of the Institute for Social Research, the *Zeitschrift für Sozialforschung*, and, at the invitation of the Institute's Director, Max Horkheimer, Fromm became a member in 1930.

An empirical social–psychological study of the attitudes and traits of the German working class was Fromm's first project with the Frankfurt School. It involved a questionnaire with hundreds of questions about all aspects of social life, distributed to over 3,000 workers during 1929–1931 and eliciting 1,100 responses, which were followed up by in-depth interviews. From the range of responses to questions varying from attitudes to fashion and popular culture to economic and political issues, Fromm was able to describe a distribution of character types from "authoritarian" to "radical revolutionary" with "ambivalent" in between. The findings revealed that the left-wing conviction that the working class would resist fascism was misplaced, for only 15 percent of KPD or SPD members showed strong radical character traits, while 20 percent of them were authoritarian to a considerable extent.[31] The majority of workers were more passive than either the socialists or the communists would have liked to think, and were considered likely to acquiesce to an authoritarian regime. Although this was a remarkable work, it was never published under the auspices of the Institute, even though it was ready for publication in 1938. It had taken an enormous amount of work by Fromm and his team, coordinated by Hilde Weiss, with the bulk of the analysis and interpretation undertaken in New York, where Fromm had joined the other members of the Frankfurt School in exile from the Hitler regime in 1934. The decision not to publish, taken by Horkheimer, has never been definitively explained, but it may well have been rooted in Fromm's contrast between two main character types, the authoritarian and the radical revolutionary. In some respects this categorization itself mirrored the increasingly polarized situation in Germany and the weakness of liberal democracy there, as Horkheimer suggested later,[32] but it may have appeared contentious not to acknowledge a distinctive "liberal" character type when publishing in English for an American readership. In Fromm's view, the study was simply "too Marxist" for Horkheimer.[33] However, another Frankfurt School member, Herbert Marcuse, commented that within the Institute the feeling was that the results might be interpreted as supporting the argument that the German workers had always been fascist at heart.[34] The study should have provided a salutary lesson to socialist political activists who tended to impute revolutionary attitudes on the flimsiest of evidence. As it was its methodology helped to inspire the analysis of the authoritarian character type by a team led by Theodor Adorno immediately following the Second World War, despite the latter's animosity toward Fromm.[35] Fromm's achievement in applying psychoanalytical insights into the interpretation of a vast array of attitudinal data is not simply of historical interest but reveals a path of immense promise, which has largely been neglected by critical social science.[36]

Fromm's other social–psychological work included a major article in the first edition of the *Zeitschrift für Sozialforschung* on "The Method and Function of Social Psychology," which made a powerful impression on Horkheimer and helped to establish the School's commitment to fusing Freudian psychoanalysis with sociology.[37] He also played a leading role in the Institute's study of *Authority and the Family*, which was published in Paris in 1936.[38] Although there are reservations about Freud's method in these early writings, Fromm accepted the centrality of the libidinal drive in explaining psychological development and neuroses. However, this was difficult to reconcile with the Marxist emphasis on the conditioning force of social factors. By 1937, Fromm had become convinced that Freud's theory of drives was misconceived, much to the chagrin of Horkheimer and Adorno. In chapter four, it is argued that the reconsideration of sexual difference that he worked on in the early 1930s played an important part in reaching this decision. Following his separation from Frieda Fromm Reichmann in 1933 he began an intimate relationship with Karen Horney, a leading psychoanalyst who had raised objections to Freud's lack of understanding of women and its effect on his theory. Once in the United States, Horney, Fromm, and Harry Stack Sullivan separately developed their psychoanalytical theory with sufficient common ground to become known as the "culturalist" school, placing a far greater emphasis on social conditioning than was allowed by Freud's theoretical framework.

Fromm considered that Freud's insistence that the unconscious was "the seat of the instinctive sexual desires" was a conception that "hobbled" psychoanalytical thinking.[39] Such a radical revision of Freud prompted John Schaar to suggest that Fromm was a revisionist of Freud much as the Prince of Darkness was a revisionist of the Prince of Light.[40] However, Fromm assiduously paid respect to Freud for his historical breakthrough in recognizing the significance of the unconscious, the power of repression, and the possibility of some form of satisfaction.[41] Furthermore, he resented the simplistic impression that his own culturalism was diametrically opposed to Freud's biologism, for he regarded his own orientation as a "sociobiological one in which the development of personality is understood as the attempt of man . . . to survive by dynamic adaptation to the social structure into which he is born."[42] What he rejected rather was Freud's "mechanistic physiologism"[43] and its overemphasis on sexual energy:

> I have wholly accepted Freud's clinical description of the various character syndromes. The difference lies precisely in the different biological approaches . . . For Freud the energy with which the character traits are charged is libidinal—that is, sexual (in the broadest sense in which Freud used this term). But as I have used the term, *energy* is the desire of the living organism to survive, channelled into various paths that enable the individual to react adequately to this task.[44]

This "revision" enables Fromm to develop a social psychology much more compatible with Marxist materialism, and it armed Fromm with the confidence to write his sweeping social psychology of modernity, *Escape From Freedom*, with an appendix in which he outlines his own concept of social character with no reference whatsoever to libido theory.

By the time *Escape From Freedom* appeared in 1941[45] Fromm had become an American citizen and had started an academic career, which was to take him to the

New School for Social Research in New York, Bennington College in Vermont, and Yale University. In *Escape From Freedom*, he situates the role of social psychology as attempting to resolve the Marxian dialectical contradiction that history makes "man" while at the same time "man" makes history. As well as understanding how passions and anxieties are molded by the social process, social psychology shows how those energies in turn become productive forces capable of molding that social process.[46] Social character refers to that part of the character structure of individuals which is common to most members of a particular social group, developed in response to their conditions of life:

> The social character comprises only a selection of traits, the essential nucleus of the character structure of most members of a group which has developed as the result of the basic experiences and mode of life common to that group.[47]

Character is shaped by the dynamic adaptation of needs to social reality, and in its turn, character conditions the thinking, feeling, and acting of individuals. Despite his use of the word "determines," Fromm consistently stresses the dynamism of human nature whereby individuals and groups are able to resist the seduction of certain enslaving adaptations and open up the possibility of positive freedom through self-realization.[48] The concept of social character helps to explain the link between the material basis of society and the ideological superstructure. It is the "intermediary" between the socio-economic structure and the ideas and ideals prevalent in society. The economic basis conditions social character, which in turn conditions the ideas and ideals of a class or group, and which in turn helps to mould the social character and, reciprocally, creates the ideological preconditions which support the economic structure.[49]

Fromm elaborates the social character types in *Man For Himself*, and while he acknowledges that they closely follow those of Freud, he insists that they are based on fundamentally different premises. Fromm's are based on specific forms of a person's relatedness to the world, whereas Freud's are theorized in terms of various types of libido organization.[50] Michael Maccoby points out that Fromm's "receptive" character orientation is equivalent to Freud's oral and erotic types, the "hoarding character" is the equivalent of Freud's anal and obsessive types, the "unproductive exploitative" is like Freud's oral sadistic type, and the more-productive exploitative is like Freud's entrepreneurial narcissistic.[51] Fromm's productive character can be likened to Freud's genital type, but the latter was under-theorized and Fromm's work here has more to do with Spinoza than anybody else. The marketing orientation, specific to affluent societies in the twentieth century, is uniquely Fromm's, and, as we shall see in chapters two, five, and six, it is central to his analysis of alienation in affluent liberal democratic societies. Fromm was mindful of the need for theory to yield hypotheses for empirical work, and he collaborated with Maccoby in a large empirical project using his character types in the late 1950s and early 1960s, published as *Social Character in a Mexican Village*.[52]

There can be no doubt that Fromm's rejection of Freud's theory of instincts led to a breakdown of relations with the core members of the Frankfurt School, Horkheimer, Adorno, and Marcuse, and was the root cause of his departure.[53] He left the Institute with a severance payment in 1939.[54] Why was the rejection of

Freud's theory of instincts anathema to the core leaders of the Frankfurt School? Adorno was the first to express publicly his anger at the "revisionists" who had rejected Freud's theory of instincts in a paper delivered in Los Angeles in 1946, "Social Science and Sociological Tendencies in Psychoanalysis."[55] Nine years later Marcuse started a dispute with Fromm in the pages of the journal *Dissent*, the opening article also appearing as an epilogue to *Eros and Civilisation*.[56] We can gather from the bitterness of the tone of these attacks just how seriously the break with Freud was regarded. Marcuse, for example, accuses Fromm of advocating a therapy of adjustment whereby humanistic values provide a means to adjust to the stresses of life in an alienated reality, whereas Fromm wanted to expose the irrationality of that reality and encourage opposition to it. Marcuse also interprets Fromm's use of "productiveness" to mean successful purposive behavior under the performance principle, which is a complete distortion of what Fromm has to say in *Man for Himself*.[57] For Adorno and Marcuse, the centerality of the libidinal instinct meant that there was always a built-in biological resistance to the repressive role of society. It was a striving for liberation at the unconscious level. They felt strongly that if "culture" was held to be the determinant factor in social psychology, then that culture was so pervasively unfree that there was no possibility of developing an emancipatory consciousness. This was not simply a theoretical disagreement, for it carried the implication that Fromm had accommodated to liberalism, and barbed comments about each other litter their later work. Many years later Marcuse conceded "without reservation" that the disagreement with Fromm over his revision of Freud led to an underestimation of Fromm's contribution to Critical Theory's early period.[58]

*Humanistic Ethics*
The rejection of Freud's theory of instincts undoubtedly had a liberating effect on Fromm's work, but it also left a hiatus. He felt the need to develop a revised theory of drives and passions, a task which demanded that psychological theory be supplemented by ethical philosophy, hence the subtitle of one of his most important books, *Man For Himself: An Inquiry Into the Psychology of Ethics*. As chapter three examines Fromm's ethics in some detail, we will restrict ourselves here to its principal features. Fromm's approach is much in the spirit of Aristotle and Spinoza, with the emphasis on the proper purpose of human life as the fulfillment of our essential human potential. The task of ethics is to work out how the human essence can achieve its *telos* or purpose through the exercise of the virtues. Fromm is concerned with the kind of society in which well-being and integrity can be realized by all people, through the exercise of the potentials, which are innate to us as human beings. He explicitly criticizes all versions of what he terms authoritarian ethics, whether in the theological form in the idea of the unworthy sinner in Augustine, Luther, and Calvin, or even in the apparently more enlightened moral system of Kant, which, in his view, harbors a deep suspicion of human nature.[59] For Fromm, loving one's self and loving one's neighbor are natural, inherent attributes of being human, and love is the power by which we relate to the world and appropriate it, finding fulfillment and happiness only in "relatedness and solidarity" with our fellows.[60] This version of humanistic ethics is based on the principle that what is "good" for us is the affirmation of life through the unfolding of our powers, provided

that this empowerment is not at the expense of others, for this would be tantamount to "evil," which he equates with the crippling of our power.[61]

What is it that makes us essentially human? Like Aristotle and Marx, Fromm asks what distinguishes us from other animals. In his view, humans have a relatively weak instinctual equipment for survival compared with most other animals, but this is compensated by the development of specifically human qualities, and "self-awareness, reason, and imagination" disrupt the harmony that characterizes animal nature. The human being is at once part of nature and yet transcends the rest of nature; reason drives us to endless striving for new solutions to the problems, which ever-developing needs confront.[62] The human life is essentially one of "unavoidable disequilibrium," an existential dilemma in which we constantly confront new contradictions and strive to resolve them. The response can be progressive or regressive, and this is reflected in Fromm's typology of social character, which reflects the dynamic adaptation of needs to socioeconomic reality. It conditions the thinking, feeling, and acting of individuals, but the process is by no means wholly deterministic, and resistance and alternatives to the various nonproductive character orientations are always possible. The productive orientation constitutes the progressive response to the challenge of life, and the productive character serves as an ideal type. In recognizing that the only meaning to life is that which is given by humans through productive living, we open up the possibility of achieving happiness through the full realization of the faculties which are peculiarly human—reason, love, and productive work. Furthermore, only through the development of a feeling of solidarity with fellow human beings can we attain happiness.[63] This is the normative basis of his humanism.

Fromm's conception of the unavoidable disequilibrium of human nature sets him apart from Marx, who, in Fromm's view, never overcame the problem of holding to the idea that humanity has a general nature while at the same time insisting that human nature developed in accordance with historical structures.[64] Fromm insists that it makes sense to talk about essential human qualities only within the framework of a more general view of human essence, that singular form of life which is aware of itself:

> Man is confronted with the frightening conflict of being the prisoner of nature, yet being free in his thoughts; being a part of nature, and yet to be as it were a freak of nature: being neither here nor there. Human self-awareness has made man a stranger in the world, separate, lonely, and frightened.[65]

The working through of the contradiction leads either to the final goal of human solidarity or, if the regressive path is taken, "complete dehumanization which is the equivalent of madness."[66] The progressive solution involves the development of authentically human qualities toward the goal of human solidarity, a condition in which all human beings feel sympathy for each other and are determined to resolve problems peacefully through cooperation. Of those authentic human qualities, his identification of rationality and productiveness echoes the views of Aristotle and Marx, while "love" reflects the importance accorded to the nurturing process in character development and the significance of close relationships in securing esteem.

"Love" is therefore at the heart of our sociality, although Fromm is under no illusions about the difficulty of expressing it in inauspicious times, as he makes clear in *The Art of Loving*.[67]

*The Art of Loving* has been translated into 50 languages and has sold in excess of 25 million copies,[68] and although it may appear to be a peripheral text for those primarily interested in Fromm's social and political thought, this is not really the case. Fromm was clearly stung by the scorn that Marcuse expressed in the appendix to *Eros and Civilization* toward his embrace of love and productiveness. He felt the need to clarify the issue of the social context in which relationships strive to express love, and the third chapter, "Love and its Disintegration in Western Society," makes clear that the capitalist principle of making the market the regulator of all social relations is inimical to the development of loving relationships. In the conclusion to the book, he stresses that the ideal of brotherly love is unattainable in the existing social system, and that people capable of love under the present system are necessarily exceptions. Fromm argues that radical changes in our social structure are necessary "if love is to become a social and not a highly individualistic marginal phenomenon."[69] In *The Art of Loving*, the humanism outlined in earlier works is illustrated in detailed discussions of our most significant relations in daily life. It is a masterclass in practical virtue ethics, with a stress on reciprocity and interconnectedness which Fromm later links with Zen Buddhism.[70] Its social significance lies in its elucidation of a practical humanistic ethics, which has long been neglected by the Western rationalist tradition.

In *To Have or To Be?*, Fromm argues that the capitalist ideology of unlimited production, absolute freedom, and unrestricted happiness amounts to a new religion of Progress, "The Great Promise," based on the psychological premises that radical hedonism and egotism will lead to harmony and peace. The promise, of course, can never be met, for it is premised on *not* delivering general satisfaction but on constantly encouraging acquisitiveness. The individual in this situation can never be satisfied because new needs are generated by the external stimuli of the market, so that there is no end to the wishes of the consumer.[71] The escalation of consumer wishes is not conducive to personal development, since the logic of the need to accumulate also encourages a constant fear of losing what we have gained.[72] Fromm's analysis of the "having mode" reads very much like a sociopsychological extension of Marx's commodity fetishism; at one point he claims that it "transforms everybody and everything into something dead and subject to another's power."[73] For Marx, alienation in the accumulation process permeates the entirety of social relations in capitalist society, and Fromm reveals how thoroughly this is transmitted in the practices of modern daily life. There is a tendency for the will of individuals to be broken by "a complicated process of indoctrination, rewards, punishments, and fitting ideology," but the process is not felt to be oppressive because most people remain convinced that they are following their own will.[74] The pressures to conform and compete are increasingly hard to resist. It is not simply the case that greed and envy are so strong because of their inherent intensity, argues Fromm, but because of the way they are enmeshed in our social relations, producing an urgency to be "a wolf with the wolves."[75] Fromm is concerned with the impact of an ultracompetitive social structure on the psyche of individuals, and, on the basis of his view of human nature, contrasts it with an image of an authentic life, the "being mode," which evinces a feeling of solidarity and caring.[76] Although he accepts that the having mode is socially dominant, he argues that only a small minority are governed entirely by it, and that there are still aspects of most people's lives in which they are genuinely touched by non-instrumental feelings for their fellow human beings. What distinguishes Fromm from his erstwhile colleagues in the Frankfurt School is that his critical analysis of the human plight is counterbalanced by a sense of hope developed from observing that despite the enormous structural pressures to pursue narrow self-interest most people have retained and developed "such qualities of dignity, courage, decency, and kindness as we find them throughout history and in countless individuals today."[77]

Fromm's conception of religion plays a vital role in his ethics. He argues that the need for a system of orientation and an object of devotion is deeply rooted in the conditions of human existence. If it is not manifested in conscious adherence to a particular religion, its various elements such as ancestor worship, totemism, or fetishism still figure largely in secular guise. The point for Fromm is, therefore, not whether we favor religion or not, but whether we favor a religion which furthers the power of human development or paralyzes it.[78] The churches have, in his view, consistently capitulated before secular power even when that power has violated its spiritual ideal. Adherence to an authoritarian religion is tantamount to surrender to a power transcending humanity, and involves unquestioning obedience, a submission to authority which enables the individual to escape isolation, but at the cost of her or his independence and integrity. Calvin's jeremiads on our unworthiness as miserable sinners are cited to exemplify the destructive nature of this self-hatred.[79] Humanistic religion, in contrast, emphasizes the power of human potential and the possibility of self-realization, and the prevailing mood is one of joy rather than misery. He cites as examples of humanistic religions early Buddhism, Taoism, the teachings of Isaiah, Jesus, Socrates, Spinoza, certain trends in Judaism and Christianity, and the cult of Reason in the French Revolution.[80] For Fromm, in humanistic religion God is the symbol of what humanity potentially can be, whereas in authoritarian religion God's perfection serves to highlight our own powerlessness.[81]

*Politics*

In the closing chapter of *Escape From Freedom* Fromm commits himself to democratic socialism as a way of resolving the problems he has identified, but there is little elaboration about what that entails. He makes a broad appeal for a rational economic system to serve the purposes of the people and for the extension of the principle of government of the people, by the people, and for the people from the formal political sphere to the economic one, but he does not discuss the political means to achieve those goals.[82] Such consideration was clearly beyond the scope of a book that was already sweeping in its endeavor, but Fromm was well aware of the need to engage with the question of political transformation and was critical of his former colleagues in the Frankfurt School for failing to do so. When Fromm deals with the issue of political alternatives in *The Sane Society* his dilemma as a democratic socialist becomes clear, for he is uncompromisingly hostile to Soviet communism and deeply skeptical of social democracy. He regards Lenin's decision to disband the Constituent Assembly in Russia following the October Revolution as symptomatic of a lack of faith in the ability of the working class to emancipate society. The danger of this dismissive attitude toward democracy had been pointed out at the time from a revolutionary *and* democratic perspective by Rosa Luxemburg, but, writes Fromm, when she and Gustav Landauer were murdered in the German counterrevolution of 1919 "the humanistic tradition of faith in man was meant to be killed with them."[83] Fromm considered that from the time of the Bolshevik suppression of the Kronstadt rebellion in 1921 there was no chance of any progressive development in Russia, and in the Stalin terror the last remnants of the original socialist intention disappeared. What took its place was ruthless exploitation and political terror.[84] For Fromm, regimes based on the Soviet model were not socialist at all, and their historical record had compromised even the words "socialism" and "communism."[85] However, the social democratic alternative held no appeal for Fromm, who regarded it as a highly bureaucratic movement which had lost its radical zeal and acquiesced to the inevitability of capitalism, concentrating instead on incremental materialistic progress. Allegations that Fromm's own work amounted to an accommodation with liberal capitalism came first from Marcuse and later other adherents of Marxism, but they show no understanding whatsoever of the radical nature of his vision. Even at the height of the Cold War Fromm wrote admiringly of Trotsky and considered that Marx, Engels, Lenin, and Trotsky represented "a flowering of Western humanity."[86] He was a revolutionary democratic socialist, "revolutionary" not in the sense that he supported insurrections to capture state power, but rather in his conviction that only with a radical change of direction could we create a social system worthy of our truly human needs and aspirations.

In terms of his own interventions in the social and political issues of his day, Fromm's deeply political phase dates from the late 1950s through to 1968. However, in 1948 he helped to organize a letter to the New York Times by leading Jewish American intellectuals, including Einstein and Martin Buber, protesting about the terrorism and "unbridled nationalism" of many Jews who were setting up the state of Israel and antagonizing the majority of the Arab population of Palestine.[87] He moved to Mexico City in 1950, largely in search of a kinder climate for his ailing second wife, Henny Gurland, who died in 1952,[88] and from then until 1968 he split his time between Mexico and the United States. He introduced the teaching of psychoanalysis in Mexico, setting up the Mexican Psychoanalytical Society in 1956, and opening the Mexican Psychoanalytical Institute in 1963 before becoming Emeritus Professor at the National Autonomous University in 1965. He remained a Mexican resident until 1974, then retired to Switzerland with his third wife Annis, living there for the remaining six years of his life. However, it was in the United States that Fromm made most of his political interventions. He was a founder member of the National Committee for a Sane Nuclear Policy, popularly known as SANE, through which he campaigned for détente between the superpowers and the negotiated disarmament of their nuclear arsenals. Indeed, he supported the idea that one power should move first on disarmament to break the logic of escalation, the initiative eventually taken by Mikhail Gorbachev in 1986. At the height of the Cold War, in the late 1950s and early 1960s, Fromm set his stall against reckless supporters of an aggressive foreign policy such as Hermann Kahn, who argued that if American losses in a nuclear conflict could be restricted to 85 million then the country could recover quickly in economic terms and the survivors could lead normal and happy lives.[89] In these years, Fromm engaged in numerous lecture tours on political themes, reaching massive audiences and establishing himself as a leading left-wing public intellectual, gathering a fat file at the FBI as a result of his efforts.[90] He joined the Socialist Party of America in the mid-1950s and drafted a revised program for it in 1960, although he encountered a great deal of opposition from the "old" Left.[91]

Fromm was an influential figure in the emergence of a "New Left" that became prominent in the cause of civil rights and the campaign against the Vietnam War. SANE invited him to speak to a rally against the Vietnam War in 1966 at Madison Square Gardens, for which he wrote a moving speech concentrating on the mental damage done by war, not just to combatants but to those who read about it and saw the images on the television.[92] His interventions anticipated many of the concerns of the new social movements, such as women's emancipation (see chapter four), consumer rights (see chapter six), and justice for the less developed world (see chapter eight). Nevertheless, he was not averse to pitching his arguments to those in positions of political power. He had a lengthy correspondence with Adlai Stevenson, which began when Fromm urged him to continue in politics despite losing the 1952 Presidential election. They were still in contact up to the time of the Cuban missile in October 1962 crisis when Stevenson played a pivotal role as U.S. Ambassador to the United Nations. He later had contact with William Fulbright, Chairman of the Senate Foreign Relations Committee. His final major campaign was when he acted as advisor and occasional speechwriter in the 1968 U.S. Presidential campaign of the radical Democrat Eugene McCarthy, but when Richard Nixon won the Presidential election Fromm effectively withdrew from political activism.

As for his written contributions, the publication of *The Sane Society* in 1955 marked his determination to clarify the social preconditions for emancipation and the immense obstacles that stood in the way. This political turn also saw him produce his major criticism of American foreign policy in *May Man Prevail?* in 1961, followed by a plea for democratic renewal in *The Revolution of Hope*, which appeared in 1968 just as the McCarthy campaign was generating immense radical enthusiasm.[93] He also played a major role in bringing the work of the early Marx to the attention of the English-speaking world with the publication of *Marx's Concept of Man* in 1961.[94] This comprised Tom Bottomore's translation of Marx's *Economic and Philosophical Manuscripts* and a long essay by Fromm that presented the humanism of the Young Marx and his alienation thesis as central to his entire work. As Stephen Erich Bronner has commented, "Fromm gave the humanitarian, idealist, and romantic proponents of the New Left a Marx they could love."[95] He also devoted a great deal of energy into persuading 35 leading socialists from around the world to contribute to his 1965 edited collection, *Socialist Humanism*, which helped to promote something of a renaissance in democratic socialist theory.[96]

*The Sane Society* is the central text of Fromm's social and political thought, and will figure prominently in the chapters to follow. In the foreword to the book Fromm claims that he is trying to show that life in twentieth century democratic societies constitutes in many ways another escape from freedom, and that the analysis of this escape centers on the concept of alienation.[97] The analysis is preceded by a lengthy recapitulation of his humanistic psychoanalytical approach to understanding the human situation. He traces the characterological changes that have developed with capitalism and the various social and political developments which have provided the institutional bonds of the alienated condition. His discussion of "Roads to Sanity" contains a trenchant criticism of what he considers to be the failed promise of both social democracy and soviet socialism, but he argues, without illusion, for a form of democratic communitarian socialism as the only path to social salvation. A reader approaching this text for the first time today will find it barely credible that it is now half a century old, for its concern with a lack of rational social direction, the overwhelming domination of corporate economic interests, and the anonymity and helplessness of the atomized individual in a post-spiritual world is as relevant today as it was in 1955. He warns that we are in danger of making a reality of Aldous Huxley's dystopia of the Brave New World,[98] but this warning is an invitation to resist. He invites the reader to strive for the sane society, "in which man relates to man lovingly, in which he is rooted in bonds of brotherliness and solidarity, rather than in ties of blood and soil; a society which gives him the possibility of transcending nature by creating rather than destroying it, in which everyone gains a sense of self by experiencing himself as the subject of his powers rather than by conformity, in which a system of orientation and devotion exists without man's needing to distort reality and to worship idols."[99] *The Revolution of Hope* is a reiteration of the central themes of *The Sane Society*, with less emphasis on the evolution of modern alienation and more detailed suggestions as to how it could be overcome, and this too will be discussed at some length in the chapters to follow.

## Chapter Plan

Chapters two and three outline the theoretical foundations of Fromm's thought. Chapter two considers Fromm's arguments about the ambiguity of freedom, which he brought to public attention with the publication of *Escape From Freedom*. He argued that the progressive development of freedom from external coercion in social, political, and economic life had not been accompanied by the positive freedom of self-development and self-realization. Instead our response to the dislocations of modernity involved retreating to the embrace of authoritarianism, destructiveness, or automaton conformity. Fromm uses his concept of social character in order to analyze how various social groups have reacted to the threats posed to them by the progress of modernity. Even when the extremes of authoritarianism and destructiveness have been overcome and affluent democratic societies emerge, the realization of freedom remains elusive. In "affluent alienation," the marketing character predominates, as people feel impelled to adjust their "selves" to whatever is expected to achieve "success" in the market society, surrendering independence in the process. The resulting conformity permits the unfettered development of the productive forces, but at a dangerous psychological and social cost. Whereas chapter two focuses on the negation of the promise of freedom, chapter three focuses on Fromm's ethical response to the alarm sounded in *Escape From Freedom*. His radical humanism takes the form of a character ethics that reaches back to Aristotle, Spinoza, and the young Marx, but in Fromm's case it is strengthened by his psychoanalytical knowledge. The development of an ethics that relies on a normative view of what it is to be human and what constitutes human flourishing provides a foundation for identifying the radical potential of various movements and ideas in everyday life and the political sphere. Fromm's ethics are also infused by a form of non-theistic religious Messianism, for he regards the religious impulse as an essential expression of a striving to make sense of life. Naturally this is a controversial view that will be examined in some detail.

The next four chapters examine Fromm's handling of specific aspects of social and political life, and in each chapter his contribution will be compared with the work of contemporary social and political theorists. Chapter four concentrates on Fromm's long-standing fascination with the characterological impact of sexual difference. The chief influence here is the nineteenth-century Swiss anthropologist J. J. Bachofen, whose work on *The Mother Right* inspired Fromm to develop a trenchant critique of patriarchy. Although most second-wave feminism rejected the idea of innate biological differences on the grounds that such ideas in the past had been used to subjugate women, Fromm is convinced that this difference could provide the basis for an emancipatory revolution in social relations. There are similarities of an unlikely sort here between Fromm's work and that of the French psychoanalyst and philosopher Luce Irigaray. Her work on sexual difference offers a complete contrast in style to Fromm's, but there are some fascinating points of comparison that point the way forward to a gendered radical humanism.

Chapter five deals with the world of work, covering Fromm's analysis of the alienating aspects of most modern forms of work, but also dealing with his suggestions for progressive alternatives. He was a keen advocate of workers' participation in the decisionmaking processes of their enterprise, greater popular involvement in humanistic planning, and a revitalization of the trades unions. Crucially he sought to transform the context in which work was conducted by introducing a guaranteed income scheme, which would give all citizens an unconditional basic income unrelated to any work they might perform. This would lift the threat of absolute poverty and place the onus on employers to make their work attractive. Fromm's philosophical view of work as a basic expression of what it is to be human, however alienated it might be in reality, contrasts sharply the view of André Gorz, who argues for liberation *from* work rather than liberation *in* work. However, it is argued here that in his recent book, *Reclaiming Work*, Gorz has moved closer to a Frommian perspective on the need to humanize the work experience, and that this provides some interesting ideas for the politicization of work.

Chapter six deals with the social effects of consumption. Fromm was greatly concerned with the danger involved in modern mass consumption, which, he argued, had become transformed into an insidious means of drawing the buyers toward conformity and greed to the detriment of their mental and physical health. This has become a major concern in contemporary sociology, and a comparison is drawn here between Fromm's dialectical approach and the more fatalistic perspective of Zygmunt Bauman.

Chapter seven focuses on political democracy, which Fromm regarded as alarmingly weak in modern liberal democracies. He consistently sought to supplement representative democratic institutions with more participatory forums, and although his concrete suggestions for reform are somewhat naïve, the issue which he is trying to address, that of a failing public life, is very much an issue for our time. Here I draw a comparison with radical suggestions for democratic reform made by Roberto Unger in his exhilarating book *Democracy Realized*.

Chapter eight deals with Fromm's anticipation of the "One World," the process we now commonly known as "globalization." It draws on Fromm's conviction that all forms of "tribalism," including nationalism and religious fundamentalism, must be overcome if there is to be any real hope of us moving closer to the ideal of human solidarity. Accordingly, the Frommian view is incompatible with modern theories of liberal nationalism, and the contradictions between these positions will be examined here. But even if Fromm's cosmopolitan ideal is desirable, how can this principled stance be articulated politically, and what sort of "real possibility" can it address? What I propose here is a defense of Fromm's appeal for the development of a new ethic of radical humanism, not as an abstraction but as a real tendency developing, albeit it unevenly and unsystematically, in disparate movements throughout the globe. In particular it is articulated by those social movements that have already embraced the idea that another world is possible.

The conclusion will reassert the validity of Fromm's radical humanism and show that without a normative view of human nature recent attempts to theorize solidarity are inadequate. Fromm's conception of human nature is neither so "thick" that it threatens to impose an authoritarian vision, nor so "thin" that it cannot provide guidance in discerning what is progressive or not in the quest for solidarity. Furthermore, in pointing to the need to challenge the status quo at a range of levels, from everyday life to global governance, Fromm's work opens up the scope of what we think of as "political" and can serve as a starting point for theorizing the concept of solidarity.

# CHAPTER TWO
## FREEDOM LOST

The drive for freedom is inherent in human nature, and although it can be corrupted and suppressed, it tends to reassert itself again and again; this is the message conveyed by Fromm in the foreword to *Escape From Freedom* written in 1965.[1] A few years later, in a television interview, he pronounced himself "terribly hopeful about the future of mankind," provided that we could avoid nuclear destruction.[2] In that particular formulation, the extremes of Fromm's position are displayed, and the tension is palpable between the somber conclusions of his social analysis and the upbeat nature of his normative theory. Is this symptomatic of a fallible utopianism? Utopians have often been criticized for providing fantastic visions of a better world precisely because they see no way forward from a social reality which appalls them, and Fromm urged his readers to be wary of those "dreaming" utopians who put on the mask of optimism in order to hide their unconscious despair.[3] He considered it imperative that we should be able to identify the ideas and social forces that hold out the real possibility for radical change, even in an inauspicious social context. What we have in Fromm is a genuine dialectic of human freedom in modernity in which he sees the individual becoming more independent, self-reliant, and critical, but at the same time more isolated, alone, and afraid. Individual liberation, for Fromm, was inextricably linked with social liberation, and the history of modernity was a prolonged dialectic of advances in social, political, and economic freedom dragged back by the reactive development of authoritarian or conformist values and behavior. Methodologically, Fromm considered it was essential that in order to understand the problem of freedom it was necessary to see both sides of the process without losing track of one side while following the other.[4] Nevertheless, by his own admission the emphasis in *Escape From Freedom* is on freedom as a burden and a danger, and as this "frames" his life's work this chapter concentrates largely on his social psychological critique of modernity.[5]

Fromm's concept of social character will be outlined in the next section, for it forms the theoretical framework of the historical analysis in *Escape From Freedom* and establishes the distinctiveness of his method from that of Freud. This will then be followed by a discussion of Fromm's studies on authoritarianism, paying particular attention to his analyses of the psychological impact of the Reformation and the psychology of Nazism. The section on destructiveness deals with Fromm's repudiation of arguments that destructiveness is a natural and ultimately irresistible urge in human beings. This is followed by a section dealing with his theory of affluent alienation in developed liberal societies, which is based on his category of the marketing character.

## Social Character

In the appendix to *Escape From Freedom*, Fromm outlines his key concept of social character, which he developed in the course of his rejection of the Freudian theory of biological drives. From his earliest work on religion, he had been concerned with how different social groups respond to changes in socioeconomic developments. For as long as he remained within the Freudian fold his attempts at classifying character types were infused with a conceptual language which explained character traits in terms of libidinally concentrated responses to erogenous zones (cathexis), so that we find repeated references to categories such as "oral" and "anal" types.[6] For example, in his 1932 article "The Method and Function of an Analytic Social Psychology" he claims that the fruitfulness of a psychoanalytic social psychology will rest on the significance of the libidinal forces in the social process.[7] For a Marxist this presents real problems, since the physiological basis of Freud's theory and the crucial importance attached to sexuality and early childhood appears to overdetermine social and cultural factors. As we saw in chapter one, Fromm's original answer to this problem is that the influences on the child come mainly from the family and the family unit is conditioned by its social and class background.[8] Yet, even in his early work Fromm expressed doubts about aspects of Freud's insights, such as the absolutization of the Oedipus complex, the relationship between nature and sublimation, and the late introduction of the death instinct.[9] By 1937, he had become convinced that psychological development could be explained without recourse to the libido at all.

For Fromm, the social character is the selection of traits that together form the essential nucleus of the character structure of individuals, which is common to most members of a group, developed in response to common life experiences. It is the specific form in which human energy is shaped by the "dynamic adaptation" of human needs to the socioeconomic structure.[10] He argues that thinking is not an exclusively intellectual process, and that it is bound up with the entire character structure. Doctrines, ideals, or even individual concepts have an "emotional matrix" rooted in the character structure of the individual, and the fact that ideas have an emotional matrix is regarded as the key to understanding the spirit of a culture.[11] The social character develops as an adaptation to changes in socioeconomic structure, and in turn, it influences the formation of ideas, doctrines, and even individual concepts. Reciprocally, the ideological superstructure then reinforces particular social characters that are functional for the further development of the socioeconomic structure. The social character operates as an internalization of external necessities and Fromm sees it as the harnessing of human energy for the tasks of a given economic and social system.[12]

Fromm conceives the social character acting as an intermediary between the economic basis of society and the ideological superstructure, although in his initial formulations he avoids such explicitly Marxist language. Analyzing the social character provides a means to look beyond the superficial indicators of political

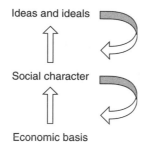

Ideas and ideals

Social character

Economic basis

**Figure 2.1.** The social character as intermediary between economic base and ideological superstructure.[13]

consciousness such as voting behavior or party membership. Even when operating from a very broad conception of an authoritarian character type in his empirical study of German workers immediately prior to the rise of Hitler, he was able to show a major discrepancy between their apparent radicalism, as denoted by party affiliation, and their conservative character. Their response to the economic crisis was politically left-wing but this superficial radicalism lacked cultural and emotional depth.[14] Fromm's approach represents a pioneer attempt to understand the rationalizations through which ideological control is maintained. The role of social character as intermediary between economic base and ideological superstructure is illustrated in figure 2.1.

The ideas and ideals of social groups cannot be simply "read off" from economic factors, for a whole emotional matrix intervenes and may reveal contradictions between, on the one hand, surface claims and affiliations, and, on the other, deep-seated dispositions. There is certainly a primary determination at work here, and the reciprocal flow whereby ideas influence the social character as well as the economic structure should be considered either as a consolidation of the total effect or else as unintended consequences. The latter could be extremely important, of course, in offering alternate directions and thus avoiding a determination so strong that no effective opposition is imaginable.

The concept of social character operates within the framework of historical materialism but adds a missing factor, the social psychological mediations that had been neglected by orthodox Marxism. Fromm's adherence to the framework of historical materialism is made clear in a revealing footnote in *Beyond the Chains of Illusion* in which, having praised the "masterful" work of the radical American social scientist C. Wright Mills in analyzing the power of entrenched elites in *The Power Elite*, then criticizes him for remaining at the level of description. In *The Marxists*, Wright Mills argues that economic factors are no more valid than military or political factors in explaining power, but Fromm insists that the power of such elites is best explained "precisely from the standpoint of the Marxian model."[15] However, he specifically distances himself from crude Marxist attempts to explain cultural phenomena by reducing them to *subjective* economic interests. For example, Fromm does not account for the success of Protestantism solely in terms of the appropriateness of its ideas to the economic needs of the bourgeoisie. The success of such ideas is not the product of conscious manipulation but rather of rationalization. Equally, his own approach rejects Freud's "psychologistic" determinism, particularly with regard to the death instinct, which leaves little hope for progress toward the ideal of human solidarity. Nor does his focus on the social psychology of ideas, doctrines, and concepts lead him to mistake them for prime causes in social change. He rejects Max Weber's "idealistic" approach, which implied that protestant ideas were the decisive factor in the development of capitalism, despite Weber's carefully worded caveats.[16]

It is important to note that Fromm did not give a detailed account of specific character orientations until *Man For Himself*, six years after the publication of *Escape From Freedom*. Those categories were not available to him when describing the psychological reactions of various social classes to profound socioeconomic change and the ideological movements which accompanied them. Instead, we have a generalized notion of the authoritarian character analyzed in terms of sadistic and masochistic perversions. However, the nonproductive orientations specified in *Man For Himself* relate to individuals rather than groups, and Fromm insists in his methodological appendix to *Escape From Freedom* that "the social character necessarily is less specific than the individual character."[17] Furthermore, in individuals who are primarily productive characters, their personalities will be blended with nonproductive orientations in such a way that they will manifest the positive aspects of those nonproductive orientations. So for example, a person displaying elements of the exploitative character would display arrogance insofar as the nonproductive orientations prevailed, but this would be manifested as self-confidence in a predominantly productive character.[18] It would be impossible to apply such discrimination to entire social classes.

This conception of social character opens up the ideological dimension of power in a way that had hitherto eluded Marxist theory. It could be applied theoretically, as Fromm does in his analysis of the Reformation and the rise to power of the Nazis, or empirically, as he does in his large-scale survey of the German working class and, 20 years later, in his study of the social character of Mexican villagers. The "social character" approach demanded that greater attention be paid to the deep-seated attitudes of social groups. At the time when the German study was being conducted many communist and socialist leaders underestimated the Nazi threat and considered that even if the Nazis came to power their failure was assured and would be but a prelude to a victory for the Left. They simply could not imagine that the mighty organizations of the working class could be swept away with minimal resistance. Fromm's empirical studies revealed the extent to which exploited groups adapt to their situation and imbibe the values that are suitable for the maintenance of the existing power structure. This development takes place over time, perhaps centuries, and requires more sensitivity from those seeking radical social change. As Fromm and Maccoby comment in the conclusion to their Mexican study, "the failure to understand this characterologically conditioned lag is one of the factors which Marxist theory overlooked, and...this led to the overoptimistic view that changed conditions would *immediately* produce a changed man."[19] However, the social character approach might also reveal contradictions between established values and the attitudes of oppressed groups.

## Authoritarianism

In his first major published work, *The Dogma of Christ*, Fromm analyzes the early theological disputes over the nature of Christ, relating the appeal of competing dogmas to different social classes in changing socioeconomic circumstances. He states that the aim of the investigation is to determine the extent to which changes in religious ideas express the psychic change of the people involved, and the extent to which these changes are determined by their conditions of life.[20] We see here the three elements outlined in the figure 2.1 from top to bottom, that is to say he is examining the ideas in a doctrinal dispute, relating them to the feelings of particular social classes in the light of their position to the economic changes of the time. In doing this he moves beyond the more abstract and generalized social–psychological accounts of the significance of religion, particularly the work of Theodor Reik, who thought about the development of Christian ideas in terms of the feelings of an undifferentiated "mass," a "unified subject," rather than understanding dogmatic disputes as reflections of conflicting class interests.[21] And although at this time Fromm was relatively uncritical of Freud, in suggesting that religion serves different social classes in different ways he goes further than the latter's generalization of the narcotic function of religion for all people as argued in *The Future of an Illusion* (1927).[22] In fact, Fromm did not share Freud's wholly negative interpretation of the psychological function of religious thought, but he accepted that certain forms of religious thinking were authoritarian in character. In *The Dogma of Christ*, he argues that the triumph of the theological viewpoint that Christ was God incarnate rather than a man adopted by God was of crucial symbolic significance in establishing an authoritarian Church closely tied to an authoritarian empire. More importantly, following Saint Augustine, Christian theology encourages the disposition that we are unworthy sinners entirely dependent on God's grace.

In *Escape From Freedom*, Fromm turns his attention to early modernity and the Reformation and considers the teachings of Luther and Calvin as exaggerations of those elements of submissiveness and authoritarianism that had long been a feature of Augustinian Christianity. He acknowledges that the new Protestant religions had a wide appeal to the urban middle class, the urban poor, and the peasants, because they gave expression to a new feeling of freedom and independence while at the same time responding to the sense of powerlessness and anxiety felt by those groups.[23] So, there is a theoretical affirmation of freedom as Luther and Calvin hand responsibility to the individual to find his or her way to God rather than submitting to the power of a corrupt Church, but this is contradicted by their emphasis on the fundamental evilness and powerlessness of humanity.[24] According to Fromm, Luther insists that we should humiliate ourselves and deny our will and pride if we are to be fit to receive God's grace, and this renunciation of free will has profound psychological consequences in terms of submissiveness and deference. There is also an aggressive certainty in Luther's view of faith in God, but for Fromm this reflects not a positive affirmation of life but, on the contrary, the need to conquer unbearable doubt, rooted in isolation and a negative attitude to life.[25] The certainty of faith was grounded in unqualified submission to God and acceptance of one's own worthlessness; life becomes a means to purposes outside ourselves. Although Luther would have hated the idea that life should become means for economic ends, his own theology developed just such a submission to the forces of economic productivity and the accumulation of capital.[26] The ideas of Luther meant different things to different social classes. The middle classes, endangered by the collapse of the feudal order (e.g., the erosion of the guilds system), gave expression to their helplessness and doubt and found a solution in submission to a loving God. The poor, however, were excited by the attack against the authority of the Church and this prompted them into rebellion, the Peasants' Revolt led by Thomas Müntzer, which was crushed at the battle of Frankenhausen. Not only did Luther preach obedience to all Princes, even evil ones, but also he denounced the "poisonous, hurtful and devilish" rebels and recommended that they be killed as mad dogs.[27]

Fromm viewed Calvin's theology as exhibiting the same desolate spirit as Luther's. Although Calvin opposed the authority of the Church and many of its doctrines Fromm considers that self-humiliation and the destruction of human pride are the guiding themes in his thought.[28] According to Fromm, Calvin warns against pursuing virtue for its own sake, for that would lead to nothing but vanity. Like Luther, he denies that good works can lead to salvation, and Fromm cites him as saying that no work of a pious man ever existed that God would not consider damnable.[29] Calvinism appealed to the small property owners of the conservative urban middle class who felt threatened by intensified competition and sought consolation in a doctrine that taught them that through complete submission they could find a new security.

What is distinctive in Calvin's thought is the significance accorded to the doctrine of predestination. God predestines some for salvation through grace and others for eternal damnation, and the verdict cannot be altered by a virtuous life. Fromm comments that Calvin's God, in spite of all attempts to preserve the ideas of love and justice, has all the features of a tyrant.[30] Two important psychological tensions are inherent in the doctrine of predestination, which have strong conservative implications; indeed Fromm asserts that they found a vigorous revival in Nazi ideology. First, it denies in principle the equality of mankind, since there are two kinds of people, the saved and the damned. In so doing it sweeps away the possibility of human solidarity, for it denies the equality of our fate—growing, learning, loving, suffering, and dying—on which rests the strongest basis for human solidarity.[31] The second tension lies in the contrast between the radical doubt that we can never know whether we are saved or damned and the absolute certainty of the duty to submit and, in practice, in the certainty that the "right" religious community represented those who had been saved. Righteous living was a sign that they were the chosen ones. One of the consequences of this deep anxiety was a busyness, a frantic activity frequently displayed by those under severe pressure. This compulsive effort was initially meant to be moral effort, but in practice, it translated into an emphasis on hard work and economic success. Fromm comments that this "inner compulsion was more effective in harnessing all energies to work than any outer compulsion can ever be."[32] Not only is this commitment to a virtuous life of unceasing effort well attuned to the needs of developing capitalism, but the resort to ceaseless activity as an unconscious device to avoid self-awareness and social awareness endures in the modern alienated character.[33]

Needless to say, Lutheran or Calvinist readers of Fromm's text would be dismayed by Fromm's interpretation of ideas and movements which are often regarded as a break from the tyranny, superstition, and corruption of the Catholic Church. Let us consider two related areas in which Fromm's thesis may be challenged. The first is that Fromm exaggerates the differences between the viewpoints of Luther and Calvin on the one hand and the Catholicism that they challenged on the other. Fromm accepts that medieval Catholicism had never argued that a person can get to heaven exclusively on the strength of his or her own virtues, but he argues that thinkers such as Aquinas, Bonaventure, Duns Scotus, Biel, and Ockham had emphasized that human nature innately strives for good, that human will is free to desire the good, and that human effort does contribute to salvation.[34] There can be no doubt that this theological strain existed, and that a connection can be drawn between it and the various ascetic movements, which renounced property and venerated the simple communistic holiness of the early Church. It is no accident that both Duns Scotus and William of Ockham were Franciscans. However, the "official" Church did everything in its power either to "canalize" the emotional energy of asceticism by supporting the Franciscan and Dominican orders, or, when that failed to contain the movements, declaring them heretical and crushing them.[35] The official view prevailed, for the 1000 years after Augustine, that we must accept our innate worthlessness. In *The Heart of Man* Fromm praises the humanistic Catholics such as Nicholas of Cusa, Ficino, Erasmus, and Thomas More, but he overestimates the extent to which they exalted human freedom. For example, he compliments Thomas More for speaking and dying for the principles of universalism and human solidarity,[36] but in his religious writings just before his death More refers to himself as a "vile and sinful wretch" who needs to humble and meeken himself before God.[37] However, what is apparent is that before the Reformation there was a greater scope for a variety of ideas to develop, at least in the Universities. Radical thinkers such as More and Erasmus were determined to stay within the Church despite their criticisms of its temporal failings, with Erasmus specifically defending free will against the authoritarianism of Luther.[38] The theology of Luther and Calvin amounts to a vigorous reassertion of the authoritarianism of Augustine, and it is this form of Christianity that reached the masses through the new medium of printing.

The other obvious criticism of Fromm's interpretation is that it misreads the theological positions of Luther and Calvin and, as a consequence, draws false conclusions about their social consequences. J. Stanley Glen's "Protestant Critique" of Fromm aims to undermine Fromm's treatment of the gospel of salvation by grace alone, and claims that Fromm misunderstands the doctrine of predestination. He argues that God's omnipotence does not reduce man to nothingness but rather liberates him because the omnipotence is expressed as forgiveness and not as force.[39] Such a formulation indeed reveals the renewed hope of the born-again Christian but for Fromm it would be a false conception of liberation—a self-deception—as long as it was based on our guilt feelings. Glen recognizes the attraction of Fromm's position, arguing that his form of spiritual atheism is more "dangerous" than the outright rejection of religion, because it is offering its own form of the gospel, a revolution-ary form.[40] It is quite true that Fromm ignores Luther's belief that despite the evil that exists it is still a good world, and also his various entreaties to set up communal systems of welfare and education, including education for girls.[41] However, Fromm admits that his interpretation is deliberately one-sided, as his concern is for the psychological consequences of their conception of humanity rather than their attack on existing authority.[42] On the central point of their emphasis on the fundamental evilness and powerlessness of humanity, his case is well supported and persuasive. Fromm's emphasis on the bleak and pervasive view of innate human worthlessness offers a social psychological foundation for the recurrence of authoritarian tendencies even as the liberal revolutions claimed greater social and political liberties.

The most frightening example of political authoritarianism that Fromm had to deal with, practically and intellectually, was Nazism. When he wrote his chapter on the "Psychology of Nazism" for *Escape From Freedom* Hitler and his party had been in power in Germany for seven years. All elements of opposition had been swept aside, including the largest labor movement in the world, and many intellectuals, artists, and Jews had elected to emigrate while they still had the opportunity. Fromm considered that neither one-sided economic explanations nor one-sided political explanations of Nazi power were sufficient to provide an adequate understanding of the phenomenon. Psychological factors must be taken into account, particularly to explain the "hold" that Nazism developed on widespread sections of the German people, although these factors themselves have to be understood as being molded by socioeconomic factors.[43] Fromm immediately differentiates between those who disliked Nazism but bowed to it without strong resistance, primarily the working class and the liberal and Catholic bourgeoisie, and those who enthusiastically embraced it, primarily the lower middle class.

In considering why working class resistance was so weak, Fromm drew on the empirical study of working class attitudes in 1929–1931, which he had conducted with a research team as his first project at the Frankfurt School. But before going into the special circumstances experienced by the German working class Fromm makes the important point that the class in general suffered from an "inner tiredness and resignation," which was shared by the working classes of other countries, including the democratic ones. Nevertheless, the German working class, in revolutionary mood immediately at the end of the First World War, had suffered from a series of defeats and the disappointment of all its hopes. The workers, despite retaining their affilia-tions to their trade unions and to either the Social Democrats or the Communists, "had given up any hope in the effectiveness of political action."[44] Like Wilhelm Reich before him, Fromm strove to understand the disjuncture between the psycho-logical structure of the workers and their declared ideological positions.[45] The deci-sive factor in securing the compliance of the class after Hitler's accession to power was nationalism, in that the Nazis identified themselves with the nation and opposition to them implied opposition to the nation. To stand against them was to choose isolation, and the fear of isolation, combined with a weakness of moral principles, led to an acquiescence to Nazi rule. Attacks on Germany served only to increase the loyalty of those who otherwise would not have been supporters of the Nazis. These dismal conclusions draw an idealistic response from Fromm, one that is central to his commitment to human solidarity and to which we return in chapter eight:

> This problem, however, cannot be solved basically by skillful propaganda but only by the victory in all countries of one fundamental truth: that ethical principles stand above the existence of the nation and that by adhering to these principles an individual belongs to the community of all those who share, who have shared, and who will share this belief.[46]

The role of nationalism as a central support for authoritarianism was consistently identified and condemned by Fromm, but in this case, he fails to mention the part which economic recovery played in consolidating nationalist sentiment. This omission is somewhat surprising, given his stated adherence to the orthodox Marxist heuristic priority accorded to economic factors. The fact that there were six million unemployed when the Nazis came to power in 1933 and full employment had been achieved within four years was of decisive importance in securing the acquiescence of the working class.[47]

Fromm identified the lower middle class—small shopkeepers, artisans, and white-collar workers—as ardent supporters of the Nazi ideology, particularly the younger generation, for whom it had a tremendous emotional appeal. He argues that the social character of the lower middle class is markedly different from that of the working class and also that of the upper middle class. He emphasizes love of the strong, hatred of the weak, pettiness, hostility, thriftiness (in feelings as well as money), and asceticism. This whole character structure was said to be typical of the class, even though some of these trends, such as respect for authority or thrift, were also found in most members of the working class, and many white-collar workers more closely resembled the character structure of the workers.[48] Fromm contrasts the position of the lower middle class before the war and after.[49] Before the war, there was sufficient stability and security for them to have a feeling of self-pride. The monarchy guaranteed order, there was a clear moral code in which religion was respected, and the lower middle class could feel a sense of superiority to the working class. The declaration of the republic enhanced the status of the working class, but for the lower middle class it was ruinous, particularly when the great inflation of 1923 destroyed their savings and undermined their faith in thrift and order. The economic recovery that followed might have gone some way to restore their positive sense of identity but this was blown away by the outset of the depression in 1929 and the swift onset of mass unemployment. Older members of the class were bitter and resentful but largely passive, but the younger members, in contrast, were ready for action. Denied the security enjoyed by their parents and angered by the lack of career prospects, they felt that their efforts in the war had been betrayed by the Weimar system. Fromm argues that resentment against the Versailles Treaty had its basis in the members of the lower middle class who projected their social inferiority onto national inferiority and yearned to rectify it by attacking those responsible within and without Germany. For Fromm, this projection of thwarted personal life chances on to betrayal of the nation was typical of Hitler's personal development.

Fromm offers two analyses of Hitler's personality. In *Escape From Freedom* he focuses on Hitler's autobiography *Mein Kampf* to reveal an extreme form of authoritarian character structure character manifested by the simultaneous presence of sadistic and masochistic drives. More than 30 years later Fromm performed a much fuller analysis of Hitler's character in *Anatomy of Human Destructiveness*, taking advantage of the literature that had become available since the war and also his discussions with Hitler's erstwhile associate Albert Speer. In this version, the emphasis shifts from Hitler's sadism to his "necrophilia," Fromm's term for the passionate attraction to death and decay.[50] This is manifested in such things as the rhetorical emphasis on disease and rottenness, and even in his facial expressions ("as if he were constantly smelling a bad odor").[51] Perhaps the most significant aspect of this fascinating account is Fromm's conclusion that Hitler was not a madman in the clinical sense that would apply to a severe psychotic or schizophrenic case, but that he was, in mental health terms, a very sick man. The conclusion is that there are many potential Hitlerian figures among us who do not have devil's horns but who could flourish in times of crisis if we are not fully aware of the enormity of their malignant aggression.[52]

In the earlier account in *Escape From Freedom* Fromm reveals the irrationalism inherent in the various devices used recurrently by Hitler to rationalize his lust for power. First, it is asserted that the domination of other peoples is for their own good or for the good of the culture of the world. Second, the pursuit of power is rooted in the laws of nature and he recognizes only these laws, so that he often speaks of being driven by God, Fate, History, or Nature; this rhetoric is rooted in crude social Darwinism and a simplistic reading of the philosophy of Nietzsche. Hitler's third device is blaming other states for pursuing the same sort of goals he himself was advocating for Germany; Nazi aggression is justified as legitimate defense against those who seek to dominate Germany.[53] Hitler's sadism is always expressed as a defense against the sadistic intentions of others. The masochistic side of Nazism is shown in Hitler's constant admonitions that the individual is nothing and the movement or nation everything, and Fromm quotes Hitler's demand that the individual must become "a dust particle of that order which forms and shapes the entire universe."[54]

In *The Heart of Man*, Fromm describes the widespread breakdown of rational judgment in the development of authoritarianism in terms of the pathology of group narcissism. He cites as examples the stance of the Nazis toward the Jews, and also that of poor whites toward black people in the southern states of the United States, and white South Africans toward other races in South Africa.[55] The satisfaction of the narcissistic self-image among these oppressing groups requires some confirmation in reality, and this is supplied simply by the evidence of their subjugation of the target group. As Fromm states, for a sadist the fact that he can kill a man proves that the killer is superior. In the absence of such a target group within the society, the narcissistically inflated group will be drawn to the possibility of military conquest. According to Fromm, if the narcissism of the group is wounded there will be a reaction of rage verging on insanity, so that insults against the group's version of God, or their leader or their national symbols will produce violent mass feelings of vengeance. The group normally requires a leader, and individuals with a strong narcissism are ideally suited. The half-insane leader is often most successful but is likely to fall victim to his own lack of objective judgment, but, as Fromm wryly observes, "there are always gifted half-psychotics at hand to satisfy the demands of a narcissistic mass."[56]

This analysis of the political psychology of authoritarianism is highly disturbing, because it indicates a universal phenomenon and therefore has implications far beyond the Nazi example, which might otherwise, with some justification, be treated as a unique and unrepeatable horror. Group narcissism can be expressed in religious terms, or in secular terms in the common forms of racism and nationalism. We shall return to this central problem in the conclusion to this book, but at this point, it is necessary to raise the question of the extent to which such authoritarianism is preventable. Clearly Fromm, very much in the spirit of Spinoza, considers that revealing the deeply irrational and malignant nature of authoritarianism will itself contribute to a more enlightened response to social development, but it is all too evident that in a highly competitive world authoritarian "solutions" are an easy option, fueled by irresponsible media and opportunistic politicians. Even in democracies, the lazy repetition of national superiority is so routinely served up that it raises no comment. Fromm has two responses. The first is a commitment to the idea of historical progress, which is in a dialectical tension with his sober analyses of the human condition throughout his career. The second is a refutation of the argument that there really is nothing that we can do to prevent the recurrence of destructiveness and authoritarianism because they are manifestations of our innate instincts.

Fromm's faith in humankind's progressive evolution shows itself toward the end of his discussion of the psychology of Nazism when he comes to the crucial question of its stability as an ideology. It is important to recall that at the time he was completing the manuscript of *Escape From Freedom* Nazi Germany had defeated France, and Britain alone opposed its hegemonic ambitions. It was only later that the Soviet Union and the United States entered the war. Although Fromm declares himself unable to make predictions he feels himself qualified to declare that in psychological terms Nazism cannot fulfill the emotional needs of the population. He argues that the fact of individuation cannot be reversed. The long historical process through which humankind frees itself from its primary bonds has been met by a profound fear of freedom, as expressed in the embrace of authoritarianism. But it had taken 400 years to develop the idea of the free individual following the breakdown of the medieval system, and short of complete regress to preindustrialism the quest for freedom will not be suppressed. Submission to an authoritarian system may gain a new security, but it is at the expense of the integrity of the self, and the authorities thwart and cripple the life of the individual even when the latter submits voluntarily. Authoritarianism functions like neurotic symptoms that emanate from unbearable psychological conditions and at the same time offer a solution that makes life possible. But such a solution does not lead to happiness or growth, for the conditions that gave rise to the problem remain unchanged: "the escape into symbiosis can alleviate the suffering for a time but it does not eliminate it."[57] Similarly, authoritarian systems cannot dispel the conditions that produce the thirst for freedom, and neither can they quench that thirst. This impulse for freedom is not, Fromm stresses, a metaphysical force explicable through natural law, but rather a result of the historical process of individuation and the growth of culture.[58]

## Destructiveness

The idea that human beings had a built-in instinct for destruction carries a profound threat for Fromm's radical humanism, and he combats it by rejecting, first, Freud's death instinct, and second, Konrad Lorenz's theory of instinctive aggression, which achieved immense popularity in the late 1960s and early 1970s. Freud had originally worked with a theory of two dominant instincts, sex and self-preservation, but in the 1920s he revised his theory of drives to create a new duality, between the biological drive to live (*Eros*) and the drive to die (*Todestrieb*). The death drive, when turned against external objects, is destructive, and when turned inward it is self-destructive.[59] In Freud's earlier version, destructive strivings are explained in terms of instinctual frustration, and Fromm comments that in this respect Freud is confirming Nietzsche's thesis that the blockage of freedom turns man's instincts back against himself.[60] For Fromm, the individual has an inherent drive for growth and integration, not because of some natural goodness but because in the nature of what it is to be human, the power to act creates a need to use this power and failure to use it results in dysfunction and unhappiness.[61] In Fromm's view, Freud adopted the theory of the death instinct in reaction to the senseless slaughter of the First World War, but it is based on abstract speculations, lacks convincing empirical evidence, and is inconsistent with animal behavior. He also argues that in order to achieve a neat, dialectical pairing of instincts (life versus death), Freud obscures the analysis of different forms of aggression.[62]

Fromm formulated his own theory of aggression largely in reaction to the widespread interest shown in Konrad Lorenz's *On Aggression* following its publication in 1966.[63] Lorenz argued that aggressiveness is an innate instinct shared by all animals, including humans, a built-in inner drive that seeks for release regardless of the adequacy of the outer stimulus. This instinct serves the interests of life, for even intraspecies aggression secures the survival of the fittest, but in the case of humankind, the aggression instinct has "gone wild." This argument is premised on the view that prolonged warfare dominated humankind's early development, despite the weight of anthological evidence pointing to the key importance of cooperative and adaptive skills in securing human survival. Fromm points out that widespread frequency of intraspecies destruction would not assist the development of humankind at all, for the higher loss of the aggressive individuals in wars would be a negative selection and lead to a diminution of the gene frequency.[64]

Fromm argues that it is vital to distinguish between two forms of aggression, defensive or benign aggression, which is in the service of the survival of the species, and malignant aggression, that cruelty and destructiveness which is specifically human and virtually unknown in other species. Most expressions of aggression belong to the former category, while the latter are less frequent, fostered by certain permanent conditions and mobilized by sudden traumatic events.[65] Fromm analyzes the various forms of malignant aggression and provides case studies to illustrate them, the significance being that these forms can be explained as responses to external stimuli rather than expressions of an instinctive drive. For Fromm, malignant aggression is always a secondary phenomenon, a manifestation of the thwarting of positive potential toward growth and integration; "destructiveness is the outcome of unlived life."[66]

The implications of accepting the Lorenz position are fatalistic. Fromm argues that Lorenz's book had become popular not because of the strengths of its arguments but because of the susceptibility of the readers. For people who are afraid and feel powerlessness, a theory that malignant aggression is natural helps to "soothe the fear of what is to happen and to rationalize the sense of impotence."[67] In effect the Lorenz thesis provides an alibi for those who are unwilling to face the daunting task of facing up to our responsibility for what happens in our world. If wars and acts of carnage are an inevitable expression of our dark nature, there is really nothing to be done to prevent them. Lorenz fuels this view by talking about the "naturalness" of militant enthusiasm through which men may enjoy the feeling of absolute right-eousness even while they commit atrocities. However much moral responsibility may gain control over the primeval drive, this militant enthusiasm is "an instinctive response with a phylogenetically determined releasing mechanism."[68] Fromm regards it as sheer bad science to claim that this is a universal human reaction with-out even trying to muster evidence for it, but it is typical of the widely prevailing view that we descend into destructiveness *because* of human nature. This erosion of human responsibility leads to an attitude of submission to stronger forces and a will-ingness to abandon rationality, which Fromm reveals in his concrete studies of authoritarianism.

## Alienation

In *Escape From Freedom*, Fromm comments that relations between individuals have lost their direct and human character and have assumed "a spirit of manipulation and instrumentality."[69] Following Hegel and Marx, he refers to an "alienation" in which relations between human beings assume the character of relations between things. The bulk of Marx's early writings had been published for the first time only in the late 1920s and early 1930s and the alienation thesis had a major impact on the theory of the early Frankfurt School. Herbert Marcuse published a brilliant review of the *Economic and Philosophical Manuscripts* in 1932 and an insightful application of the concept to modern technological society in 1941, but Fromm's book was the first to bring the contemporary relevance of the concept to the attention of a mass readership.[70] Marx's original emphasis had been on the centrality of alienation in the process of capitalist production, with workers deprived of control of the goods they produce, the process of their production, and ultimately, of their own human essence as creative beings. In the context of the mid-twentieth century the application of the alienation thesis required a considerable shift of emphasis from production to consumption, from grinding poverty to relative prosperity. Fromm comments that Marx never became aware of "that affluent alienation which can be as dehumanizing as impoverished alienation,"[71] and it is precisely this affluent alienation that is Fromm's central concern.

At one point in *Escape From Freedom* he argues that the right to express our thoughts means something "only if we are able to have thoughts of our own."[72] The rest of this chapter examines the controversial claim that, on a widespread scale, people are unable to feel, think, or act independently; they are, in short, suffering from a loss of self. Some of Fromm's detailed considerations of the process of alienation is dealt with in later chapters, particularly the one on consumerism, but it is essential to clarify the general position as originally set down in *Escape From Freedom*. He challenges the conventionally held belief that modern democracy has delivered true individualism, for the simple right to express our thoughts has meaning only if we are able to have thoughts of our own.[73] In modern society, argues Fromm, economic development produces atomization, and the isolated individuals seek to overcome their powerlessness either through the authoritarian path, or, within the liberal democracies, by conformity and passivity, surrendering themselves to the processes of production and consumption and becoming automatons. Fromm is convinced that through a variety of inculcatory processes in education and the media we are manipulated to the extent that "modern man lives under the illusion that he knows what he wants, while he actually wants what he is *supposed* to want."[74] He presents the idea that the apparently free individual in modern democratic society is manipulated into a condition of uncritical conformity. This is a controversial claim, since it involves the social scientist assuming responsibility for judging the authenticity of thought, feeling, and action. But Fromm argues that if we take the easy way out and adopt the view that all truth is relative we will never develop original thought. He complains that the "progressive" relativist thought of the mid-twentieth century already looked down on those seeking the truth as "backward," so we can imagine how he would have recoiled at the thorough relativism of much postmodern thought.[75] As a critical social psychologist, he considered it his vocation to use his skills to examine the issue and offer his conclusions, and he does so in support of the alienation thesis throughout his career.

Fromm regards the growing egotism and assertion of self-interest in modern capitalism not as an expression of the development of the autonomous self but rather as the loss of self. The "self" of self-interest in modern society is a socially constructed self, "essentially constituted by the role the individual is supposed to play," in effect the "subjective disguise for the objective social function." The modern self is only a segment of the total self, developed to the exclusion of all other parts of the total personality.[76] We are capable of producing with ever-greater technological prowess, but the rationality displayed in the mastery of nature is accompanied by the irrationality of the system of production in its social aspects, with widespread insecurity, atomization, and powerlessness flowing from the imperatives of economic competition. This weakening of the self has alarming psychological consequences for the individual, for it leads to a loss of genuine relatedness in which everybody and everything has become instrumentalized:

> He thinks, feels, and wills what he believes he is supposed to think, feel, and will; in this very process he loses his self upon which all genuine security of a free individual must be built.
> The loss of the self has increased the necessity to conform, for it results in a profound doubt of one's own identity. If I am nothing but what I believe I am supposed to be—who am I?[77]

Fromm cites Pirandello's view of modern man as the denial of identity except the one that is the reflex of what others expect—I am "as you desire me." This loss of identity makes it more imperative to individuals, but giving up spontaneity and individuality amounts to a thwarting of life, a deadening of the emotions, a deep unhappiness. We may struggle against this by asserting our individuality in trivial ways, such as customizing the products we buy or living vicariously through identifying with fictional screen heroes. However, these "last vestiges" of individuality mask a "profound feeling of powerlessness."[78]

Fromm's early attempts to describe the processes of alienation warn against the "hypnoid suggestion" of the advertising industry, a theme he was to return to time and again.[79] He criticizes the sound-bite approach to broadcasting important news issues, arguing that when news about the bombing of cities is interrupted by glib advertisements for wine or soap our ability to develop a structuralized picture of the world is being eroded.[80] This problem of "dumbing down" by a process of discouraging serious consideration was to grow more acute when television took over from radio as the main means of communication, and it remained an important theme in his later work. He also points to less technological manipulations, which have long been with us, such as the repression of emotions in order to adjust to the codes of the given social situation, a process that starts very early in life, and also to the tendency of educational methods to discourage original thinking by rote learning.[81] These insights are developed at much greater length in *The Sane Society*, by which time his stance is more pessimistic. Alienation is here considered to be all pervasive. The advance of consumer culture, particularly television, and the virulent anticommunism of the Cold War period, contributed to the gloomy conclusion that alienation is now "almost total," pervading the relationship of "man to his work, to the things he consumes, to the state, to his fellow man, and to himself." Despite creating a world of man-made things as it never existed before and a complicated social machine to administer it, this creation stands over and above him . . .

> He is owned by his own creation, and has lost ownership of himself. He has built a golden calf, and says "these are your gods who have brought you out of Egypt."[82]

This idea of alienation as a new form of idolatry is a device much favored by Fromm, who relished the biblical metaphor. At the end of *To Have or To Be?* he likens the deterioration of our vision of society to that of the Tower of Babel, which is about to collapse and bury everybody in its ruins.[83]

According to Fromm, alienation pervades our interpersonal relations. This alienation from each other (Marx's fourth aspect of alienation) is central to Fromm's concern as a humanist psychologist. Relations between people increasingly lose their direct and human character and assume instead "a spirit of manipulation and instrumentality" as the laws of the market impinge on all our social relationships.[84] Fromm talks about the sale of personality, a formulation that became crucial to the marketing character, which he identifies for the first time in *Man For Himself*. In the developed picture of character orientations Fromm characterizes the hoarding orientation as being dominant in the advanced industrial world of the nineteenth century, blended with the exploitative orientation. In the twentieth century, the passive orientation became prevalent, blended in with the marketing orientation.[85] The modern market, Fromm reminds us, is no longer a place for meeting people but is rather characterized by abstract and impersonal demand. The marketing character is rooted in experiencing oneself as a commodity and valuing oneself as exchange value.[86] Fromm argues that this market does not reward skills and human qualities such as decency and integrity so much as it favors an outgoing personality from the "right" sort of background. Skills and powers exist, but the use of them does not lead to self-realization for they are sold to others, developed for others, and valued by others. In productive individuals, a sense of identity would flow from the expression of their selves through their powers and their authentic aspirations, but in the marketing orientation the identity of the individuals is completely dependent on the opinion of others.[87]

The marketing orientation is explicitly linked to Marx's concept of alienation. Fromm draws heavily on the passage in Marx's *Economic and Philosophical Manuscripts* in which he contrasts being from having by stating "the less you *are* and the less you express your life the more you *have* and the greater is your alienated life."[88] The marketing character involves regarding oneself as a thing to be employed successfully on the market. The human being as a thinking and feeling being is replaced by the human being who is determined by the judgment of those on whom she is dependent. The need to exchange becomes a paramount drive and exchanging becomes an end in itself.[89] The individual who experiences his or her own life as a commodity on the personality market moves toward complete adaptation, losing a sense of "self" and authentic identity, and losing touch with deep emotions of any sort. There is a lack of caring, a lack of attachment that makes the marketing character indifferent to things. "The marketing character neither loves nor hates," writes Fromm, because the marketing character functions on the cerebral level and shuns feelings, functioning according to the logic of the "megamachine" without ever calling that logic into question.[90] This picture of social functioning should strike a chord with the modern reader, since the proliferation of competitive practices *within* work organizations in the decades since Fromm wrote about the marketing character requires people to make themselves "marketable" and proficient at advancing themselves in the "internal market." As he states in an article dating back to 1951, "each day is a new battle because each day you have to convince someone and you have to prove to yourself, that you are all right."[91]

But to which social class does the marketing character apply? In fact Fromm is referring primarily to what would be conventionally described as the middle classes, including white-collar workers and professionals. In *To Have or To Be?* he adds that in modern America it is the blue-collar working class which adheres to the old middle-class hoarding character and that this makes them less open to change than the more alienated middle-class. However, Fromm is not suggesting that the middle-class should be regarded as a new vanguard leading the way forward for social emancipation. Rather he points to a situation in which the old working class political agenda is not so clearly demarcated nor seen to be a threat to the interests of other classes. When virtually the entire population is dependent on the sale of their labor power, there is the possibility of an objective common interest in the idea of a new society from all those who are alienated and who are employed.[92] The ideals of this ideal new society, Fromm claims, can cross old party lines, although he accepts that the chances for radical change are slim unless there is some sort of ethical revolt to energize the new vision.

Although Fromm recognizes that ethical behavior is displayed in the concrete situations of many individuals, in *The Sane Society* he concludes pessimistically that society is marching toward barbarism.[93] However, it is essential to understand that Fromm was issuing warnings rather than surrendering to fatalism. Despite the apparent pervasiveness of the various blends of nonproductive orientations and the immense pressures that promote the marketing orientation in particular, he argues that very few people existed entirely in the "having" mode, that is, dominated by nonproductive orientations and with all sense of productiveness suppressed. The human qualities of reason, love, and creativity are not so easily destroyed. The progressive alternative is always present and Fromm attempts to identify the ideas and the movements capable of advancing toward the being mode. He recognized that a trenchant criticism of the way we lived required not only an analysis of specific social character types but also a character-based ethics, which sketched the lineaments of what a fully lived life might look like. In *Escape From Freedom* he suggests that a genuine ideal is one which has an aim, which "furthers the growth, freedom, and happiness of the self," in contrast to fictitious ideals with compulsive and irrational aims, which offer attractive experiences but which are actually harmful.[94] The self-realized person recognizes that there is only one meaning of life, and that is the act of living itself.[95] More specifically, the full affirmation of the uniqueness of the individual requires a commitment to equality, as relations of domination/submission are incompatible with the self-realization of individuals locked into such a pattern. Self-realization can be achieved only when human relationships are founded on solidarity.[96] These key elements of Fromm's radical humanism are analyzed in the next chapter.

## Progress?

Fromm had argued at the end of his chapter on Nazism in *Escape From Freedom* that the quest for freedom was part of the historical development of freedom and the growth of culture, and yet so much of his work, on both authoritarianism and alienation, appears to show an *intensification* of submissiveness, conformity, and social irrationality. How can these views be reconciled? Fromm, it seems to me, operates with a "long" view of historical progress, based on human evolution from prehistory to the present. As we see in chapter four he was fascinated by anthropology and in particular the creation myths that contain the guiding clues to our prehistorical social development. There is a clear pointer to his long view of historical development at the beginning of *The Anatomy of Human Destructiveness*, when he approvingly quotes Jan Smuts as saying "when I look at history, I am a pessimist . . . but when I look at prehistory, I am an optimist."[97] *Escape From Freedom* first appeared in the year that the Nazis initiated the holocaust,[98] but despite that horror, Fromm did not despair but instead developed a humanistic ethics with a strong emphasis on the positive potentials of human beings. This was not the forlorn hope of a despairing utopian, but an expression of faith in the possibility that mankind could learn from its mistakes. In analyzing authoritarianism and alienation, he sought rational explanations for phenomena that would otherwise be fatalistically accepted as manifestations of some incorrigible human lust for power or aggressive egotism. He maintained a firm conviction that antagonistic structures would always meet resistance, and devoted much energy to identifying the ideas and movements, which might move us closer to the goal of human solidarity.

# CHAPTER THREE
## HUMANISTIC ETHICS

Psychoanalysis, according to Fromm, can operate from two different conceptions of the aim of therapy, either that of "social adjustment" or "cure of the soul."[1] The first approach seeks primarily to address the symptoms of neurosis and to help the patient to act like the majority of people in his or her culture. For Fromm, as a radical critic of the prevailing culture, adjustment could only reduce the excessive suffering of the neurotic to the average levels inherent in conforming with an alienated reality. In contrast to this Fromm argues that it is necessary to operate from the standpoint of universal human norms, from which the therapist can help the patient to achieve optimal development of his or her potential and the realization of his or her authentic individuality.[2] Fromm is convinced that to know what is good for a person it is necessary to study our human nature. This requires the humanist psychoanalyst to specify those universal norms, and Fromm does this in *Man For Himself* (1947), which as we noted in chapter one, carries the subtitle *An Inquiry into the Psychology of Ethics*. Here he makes an important advance in his social theory by advocating a form of virtue or character ethics decades before it found a renewed interest in philosophical circles. In this book, his explication of the various character orientations gives new depth to his social psychology, and the original concept of the marketing character provides a means for understanding the process of affluent alienation, which is central to his later work. Above all, however, the affirmation of a humanistic ethics provides the normative foundation for all his later work. Fromm's ethics is grounded in the idea of the fulfillment of human potentials or, to use Aristotle's terminology, the pursuit of *eudemonia* or "flourishing." He argues "the virtuous or the vicious character, rather than single virtues or vices, is the true subject matter of ethical inquiry."[3] For Fromm, we have powers specific to us as human beings and our aim should be to affirm life as the unfolding of those potentialities.[4]

The stress on the good character or the right virtues to be pursued distinguishes virtue ethics from the "rules and principles" approach of both Kantian duty ethics (deontology) and utilitarianism, the two perspectives that dominated moral thinking for much of the nineteenth and twentieth centuries.[5] Unfortunately, Fromm's contribution has been unnoticed in the debates that have taken place about the return of virtue ethics, probably because he comes to the question of ethics as a psychoanalyst rather than an academic philosopher. In Alasdair MacIntyre's account of the limitations of Enlightenment moral theory, he argues that its attempts to justify morality was bound to fail because it had jettisoned the central element on which moral thinking up to that time had been based, namely, the idea of man as he could be if he realized his *telos*, in which *telos* is taken to mean "goal" or destiny.[6] In the Ancient Greek and medieval conceptions of morality the three key elements were untutored human nature, the idea of man as he could be if he realized his *telos*, and the moral precepts that would take you from one condition to the other. In Enlightenment moral thought, the abandonment of the idea of an essential human nature striving toward a *telos* leaves conventional moral philosophy the impossible task of deriving moral precepts from a view of "untutored" human nature.[7] More often than not, the moral precepts of Enlightenment philosophers are designed to override the "dangerous" inclinations of human nature. In this view what is natural to humanity is often seen as "an enemy within," something to be suppressed if good is to be achieved. Doing good involves renouncing our egotism, which is implicitly taken to be natural.

Fromm strongly criticizes this form of authoritarianism, expressed explicitly in the theology of Luther and Calvin but also implicitly in the moral system of Kant, for whom the pursuit of one's own happiness has no positive moral value and self-love is equated with selfishness.[8] Kant emphasizes our natural propensity for evil, which needs to be suppressed by the moral law to avoid us falling into chaos.[9] Fromm argues that the movement in modern thinking from Protestantism to Kantianism is the substitution of internalized authority for an external one.[10] This suspicion that dangerous human nature has to be kept in check by moral law is anathema to Fromm, for whom loving one's self and loving one's neighbor are inherent attributes of what it is to be human.[11] As he writes in *Man for Himself*, "not self-renunciation nor selfishness but self-love, not the negation of the individual but the affirmation of his truly human self, are the supreme values of humanistic ethics."[12] Self-love is the power by which we relate to and appropriate the world, and we find fulfillment and happiness only in "relatedness and solidarity" with our fellows.[13]

Although Fromm's ethics constitute a return to the tradition of *eudemonia* with a strong view of human essence and its *telos* or purpose, he believes that the insights developed by psychoanalysis enable us to speak with more confidence about human nature. That is not to say that the idea of unconscious motivation was unknown to Spinoza, for it was,[14] so much so that Fromm hails him as "the founder of modern psychology."[15] Nor does it imply that psychoanalysis has resolved the myriad problems of the human psyche. Fromm is not overcome by the scientistic inclination to certainty, and fully accepts that we have only a tentative picture of human nature, despite the progress made by Freud and his successors.[16] Nevertheless, advances have been made in the "science of man," and Fromm is prepared to take advantage of that knowledge to formulate a robust version of humanistic ethics.

The next section will look more closely at Fromm's humanistic ethics, and this will be followed by a discussion of the religious dimension of his ethical thought. The third section will anticipate a number of objections which might be raised to character ethics in general and Fromm's version in particular. Finally, the controversial question of the messianic nature of his social thought will be considered.

## Humanistic Ethics

Fromm rejects all forms of authoritarian ethics, by which he means those moral systems which rely on the authority of some norm-giver external to the subject, and in which the question of good or bad is related primarily to the external authority rather than the subject.[17] This applies to the various forms of theistic ethical systems, in which obedience is seen to be the main virtue and disobedience the main vice, a submissive outlook utterly at odds with a goal of self-realization. But what about the ethics of Kant and the ethical implications of Freud's science? Although Fromm credits Kant with showing respect for the idea of the integrity of the individual, he criticizes him for denying that the goal of happiness is a moral issue. As we have seen, Fromm considers that Kant's invocation of moral duty was a form of internalized authoritarianism, based on a profound mistrust of human nature, and Fromm links this outlook to Kant's submissive political position. Kant taught obedience to a head of state, even one abusing his power, on the grounds that "a state of right becomes possible only through submission to his universal legislative will."[18] In this respect, Kant echoes Luther's opposition to revolution under any circumstances.

As for Freud, his theory of characterological development implies the ethical superiority of the healthy, "genital" type,[19] although Freud does not elaborate on this. Fromm's own ethical goal of the "productive character" can be regarded as a nonsexual equivalent to the "genital type," but there are major differences between their ethical perspectives. In the first place, Freud is a relativist in the sense that he believed that psychoanalysis could help in the understanding of the motivation of value judgments but could not help to establish their validity. Second, Freud is authoritarian in the sense that conscience is seen as nothing but internalized authority, while the Oedipus complex is a secularized version of original sin whereby all men are deemed to have incestuous and murderous impulses.

The ethical positions that Fromm relates to most closely are those of Aristotle and Spinoza, and also that of the young Marx. Fromm approves of Aristotle's commitment to a deep knowledge of the appropriate object of study, so that the student of ethics must know about the soul of man just as a doctor must gain knowledge of the body. Happiness or flourishing is the result of activity, and Fromm praises Aristotle's avowal of the free, rational, and active person as the good and happy person to which we must aspire.[20] Fromm is attracted to the key role which Aristotle assigns to the concept of productiveness in his ethical system, in which the good person is one who "by his activity, under the guidance of his reason, brings to life the potentialities specific of man."[21] Fromm also approves Aristotle's rejection of the idea that the subjective experience of pleasure can be a criterion for the goodness of activity, favoring instead a view that the pleasure that follows from the highest development of our faculties affords the deepest subjective satisfaction.[22] However, Fromm considers that Aristotle's ethics suffers from his "static" psychology, which fails to grasp the conditions that might obstruct or promote the ethical goal for the individual and for society as a whole.[23]

Fromm regards Spinoza's *Ethics*, written in the 1660s, as a definite advance on Aristotle's, and the importance of Spinoza for Fromm's work is evident in the discussions in *Man For Himself* and later in *The Heart of Man*. According to Fromm,

Spinoza operates with a normative model of human nature, an ideal of the fully developed life that we should strive to fulfill. To be free is to be rational, and happiness accompanies the experience of improving our powers.[24] He maintains that everything is determined, by which he means that everything has a cause that can be discovered by rational individuals. In practice, most people are aware of their desires but not the motives behind them, and we need to penetrate this self-deception in order to become fully developed human beings.[25] It is possible for individuals to lead an ethical life provided they develop their distinctive human potentials and strive for harmony with others, not on the basis of fear of what might otherwise happen, but on grounds of justice, equity, and honorable dealing.[26] If we do not, the consequences are severe for individuals and the community.

Fromm admiringly quotes a passage in which Spinoza observes that a greedy person thinking only of money and possessions and an ambitious one only of fame is commonly thought of as annoying, but he argues that such behavior is much more serious and that in fact avarice, ambition, and lust are "species of madness."[27] This is very close to Fromm's own conclusions about the consequences of non-productive behavior, or living in the "having mode," as we shall see toward the end of this section. Spinoza's pantheism means that God is regarded not as the external cause of specific phenomena, but rather as the truth within all knowledge and right living. Many have seen it as a veiled atheism, although Santayana is perhaps closer to the mark when he describes it as "the intelligent affirmation of the Jewish belief in God."[28] It certainly chimes well with Fromm's conviction that the religious impulse carried within it a humanistic emancipatory significance. Fromm is clearly greatly impressed with Spinoza's emphasis on fellowship and care for the poor,[29] and above all on the liberating power of learning to live a good life through developing a critical awareness of our social conditioning. Convinced of the need for this self-awareness, Fromm maintained that an explicit ethical shift is a precondition for any movement toward the ideal of human solidarity.

Fromm mentions Marx only once in *Man for Himself*, citing a footnote in *Capital* which supports the need for a general view of human essence. In it, Marx criticizes the utilitarian philosophy of Jeremy Bentham because it lacks an objective criterion for judging what is good for human beings, commenting that in order to know what is good for a dog you must have a knowledge of the nature of dogs. Marx insists that what is needed is first, a view of human nature in general, and then, a view of human nature as modified in each historical epoch.[30] Fromm was among the first to appreciate the importance of Marx's philosophical humanism and to convey this interpretation of his work to a wide readership when *Marx's Concept of Man* was published in the United States in 1961.[31] The "mature" Marx insistently opposed ethical discourse of any description, adopting an antimoralism for tactical reasons, anxious as he was to present a scientific analysis of capitalist development and its inherent contradictions.[32] Nevertheless, there can be no doubt that within this science there is a powerful ethical commitment, which is explicit in the alienation thesis in his early unpublished writings and also in his treatment of commodity fetishism in *Capital*.[33]

Fromm insists that Marx's alienation thesis implies a view of what we are alienated from; in other words he maintained that Marx adhered to his early view that we are alienated from our "species being" and from each other as a result. Fromm comments that Marx had supplied "perhaps the most significant definition of the species characteristic of man" when he defined it as "free, conscious activity."[34] Fromm appreciates Marx's distinction between our physiological needs and our species-specific needs which are in continuous development and which require satisfaction if we are to lead a truly human life.[35] The frequent use of the word "dehumanization" in Marx's early writings reveals the extent to which he felt capitalism had stunted the development of the mass of individual working people even as the impressive products of industry showed the enormous potential of the species as a whole. Only when this potential can be expressed and experienced by all individuals rather than a privileged few, can we reach a stage in human history when "the free development of each is the condition for the free development of all."[36]

Although Fromm is highly appreciative of Marx's conception of the human essence as social creativity, he argues that Marx's focus on essential qualities such as productiveness and cooperation is not adequate for grasping the *essence* of what it is to be human. Marx, claims Fromm, did not solve the dilemma of affirming an essential human nature, with its implication of fixity, and squaring it with the view that human nature continually transforms itself through historic interaction.[37] Fromm proposes to resolve this dilemma by regarding the human essence not as a given quality or substance but as "a contradiction inherent in human existence."[38] This contradiction lies in our being simultaneously part of nature and yet transcending nature. As in the case of Aristotle and Marx, he begins his consideration of human essence by discussing the differences between human beings and other animals.[39] Unlike other animals, the instinctual apparatus of humans is very poorly developed, but this weakness is the basis for the development of the essential human qualities. The human being develops self-awareness, becoming aware of the past and the inevitability of death, of our own smallness and powerlessness, and also aware of others as friends, enemies, or strangers:

> Man is confronted with the frightening conflict of being the prisoner of nature, yet being free in his thoughts; being a part of nature, and yet to be as it were a freak of nature: being neither here nor there. Human self-awareness has made man a stranger in the world, separate, lonely, and frightened.[40]

Human self-awareness, reason, and imagination disrupt the oneness which other animals experience and turn us into an anomaly, both subject to the laws of nature yet transcending the rest of nature. Human existence is in a "state of constant and unavoidable disequilibrium," but this condition generates needs which transcend those of animal origin and result in an "imperative drive to restore a unity and equilibrium" between humanity and the rest of nature.

It is not simply the conflict within humans that denotes the human essence, but also the striving for a solution to that conflict. Devotion to an aim, argues Fromm, is an expression of "the need for completeness in the process of living," but although this has often been expressed in theistic religions, their insistence on an external demiurge encourages submissiveness and implies a fear of freedom. Fromm uses the phrase "frame of orientation and devotion" to denote the attempts to make sense of our existence and to seek a new harmony or oneness with ourselves and nonhuman nature. We can either advance toward a condition of freedom or regress to archaic tribalistic impulses. Freedom involves the achievement of happiness through the realization of the specifically human faculties of reason, love, and productive work, in a condition of human solidarity.[41]

The emphasis which Fromm places on love reflects the influence not only of his reading of the Prophets and his attachment to philosophical humanism, but also his clinical work in psychoanalysis, for it is here that he was able to see the damage caused by the withholding of love in childhood. He argues that love is a potential within us all, a character trait expressive of a loving person. It is not something suddenly "triggered" by our interaction with an intimate "other," but rather a capacity that is developed and expressed to all those with whom we come into contact. Erotic love, of course, is particular, not general, but it is likely to be deceptive if it is not infused with a more general, loving disposition.[42] Thus for Fromm, love is not an abstraction coming *after* the love of a specific person, but rather the premise of loving another person. He rejects the idea that we can love only a small number of specific people—the "not enough love to go round" thesis—as an expression of a basic inability to love at all.[43] Love is a natural capacity but like all arts it has to be learned and practiced. In ethical terms, it lends itself to a rather different interpretation of the Golden Rule than might be given by fairness ethics. "Do unto others as you would like them to do unto you" can be interpreted as no more than being fair in one's exchanges with others. As James Daly has argued, the version presented by Thomas Hobbes looks like a "deal" between mutually suspicious actors, rather than a universalization of a positive willing of good.[44] Fromm prefers another version, the injunction to love thy neighbor as thyself, so that one feels responsible for and "one" with her or him, as opposed to dealing with someone quite distant and separate. Naturally, he recognizes that in a commodity-greedy society it is difficult even for a nonconformist to express consistently a loving attitude, but he insists that we must struggle to realize this potential to love as a necessary aspect of the social struggle toward freedom.[45]

Although Fromm's discussion of the existential dichotomy of the human condition is couched at a higher level of abstraction than Marx's and is fleshed out with his psychoanalytic insights, there is a danger that their differences may be exaggerated. Daniel Burston, for example, suggests that Fromm's view implies that the condition of "homelessness" is an inescapable one, sounding a "sad and sober note," whereas the humanism of the young Marx amounts to "unbridled utopianism."[46] While it is true that Fromm speaks of the inevitably incomplete nature of the realization of the self as part of the "tragedy of the human situation,"[47] there is neither sadness nor sobriety here. When we experience a Shakespearian tragedy we are moved by human folly, learn from it, and take hope, in an emotional experience that is often intoxicating. This is what Fromm has in mind when he speaks about our difficulties in striving for positive freedom. He is committed to the positive resolution through productiveness of the existential dilemma of needing to be at one with others and at the same time needing to be unique and individual. It is necessarily always an unfinished project, both personally and socially, unlike those utopias that have portrayed final solutions to all our problems and which unwittingly deprive their fictional ideal of all dynamism.

According to Fromm, there will always be new problems in negotiating the complex interrelations between people and between humanity and nature, even if the general social condition dominated by exploitation is replaced by one of equality of respect. But clearly the abolition of exploitation and oppression would provide a fundamentally nonantagonistic framework for the working out of the dilemmas of human development. The ideal-type of the productive character is one who is always looking for new challenges, but one can be satisfied with the apparent unending nature of this striving if it is conducted with self-knowledge in a context of human solidarity. Nor is it correct to imply that Marx's vision of communist society is an end of history in which all problems have been resolved and all individuals have become fully developed. The vision of the "realm of freedom" expressed in the third volume of *Capital* makes it clear that while the realm of freedom strictly speaking excludes the realm of necessity, where we are obliged to work, it can flourish only on the basis of the rational organization of that realm of necessity.[48] Working out that rational organization necessarily involves argument, but it is clear from Marx's remark that the passing of capitalism will mark the end of the prehistory of humankind and that only then will real human history commence.[49] Both Fromm and Marx recognize that self-realization is active and therefore argumentative, but while argument implies disagreement, it also connotes negotiation, learning, and respect. The harmony they seek does not involve people singing the same tune, but, as in music, is constantly in development, restless for new forms to satisfy our aural inquisitiveness.

What are the attributes of a productive character? In *Escape From Freedom*, Fromm places the emphasis firmly on spontaneity, the autonomous expression of our emotional and intellectual potentials, of which love is the foremost component. Spontaneity is the expression of positive freedom and through it we are able to realize our true selves, overcoming the fear of being alone without sacrificing the integrity of the self.[50] However, although he points out that young children often display spontaneity, the overall impression is given of the artist as the great exemplar of spontaneity, or even some philosophers or scientists.[51] There is a tendency to think of the self-aware and self-critical development of potential in terms of the high achievements of modern society, giving the impression that productiveness must be the reserve of a gifted elite. The more extensive discussion of the productive character in *Man For Himself* reiterates the importance of the independent, rational realization of our potentials, in a general "mode of relatedness" in all realms of human experience.[52] He emphasizes that the full use of our powers refers to power *to* rather than power *over*, quoting Spinoza to the effect that domination is coupled with death and potency with life.[53] This warning against power *over* raises the issue of the difficulties faced by those in elite positions in achieving the sort of "total personality" productiveness that he advocates. There is, too, more emphasis here on love, in which he specifies the major elements of productive love as care and responsibility for others, respect for the other's uniqueness, and knowledge of the other gained through genuine desire to reach out.[54] In his discussion of productive thinking, he points to the importance of supplementing intelligence with reason that possesses depth, an ability to relate oneself to things, and to go beyond surface appearances to discover hidden essences and relations.[55] A picture is formed in which the productive character has to achieve a considerable distance from the requirements for success in an alienated society. The loving and wise individual who realizes the supreme importance of human relationships and the profound unhappiness of domination requires no special qualifications or superior skills. Through productiveness, we resolve the paradox of human existence by simultaneously expressing our oneness with others *and* our uniqueness.[56]

Fromm adopts an alternative formula in *The Heart of Man*, in which the non-productive orientations are rolled together in the concept of the necrophilous orientation (love of death) and the productive character is regarded as belonging to the biophilous orientation (love of life). Burston is correct to state that the change of language does not involve conceptual innovation, and that it indicates a move back toward Freudian life and death promoting forces, which is carried on into *The Anatomy of Human Destructiveness*.[57] Another change occurs in *To Have or To Be?* when Fromm talks about the ideal condition of the humanistic "being mode" in contrast to the instrumentalist "having mode." The terminology has the advantage of being applicable to both the individual and to society as a whole, and provides a helpful amplification of the original position set down here. The being mode is a situation in which our activities are productive in the sense of being consciously directed toward the enrichment of human existence, as opposed to the having mode in which activity is directed to acquiring wealth and power over others.[58] Although he accepts that the having mode is socially dominant, he argues that only a small minority are governed entirely by it. There are still aspects of most people's lives in which they are genuinely touched by non-instrumental feelings for their fellow human beings.[59]

One of the problems in establishing pictures of the productive individual and the being mode is that psychoanalysis has traditionally focused on neuroses rather than well-being. The extent of the difficulty of putting flesh on the skeleton of the productive character is underlined by Fromm's collaborator Michael Maccoby, who comments that when they did their study of peasants in a Mexican village in the 1980s they did not find a single productive character.[60] The problem is made more complex by the theoretical move from the consideration of the mental health of the individual to that of society.[61] Fromm is not able to point to any modern society that provides the conditions for the development of the productive character, although in his most overtly political books, *The Sane Society*, *The Revolution of Hope*, and *To Have or To Be?* he makes it clear that only some form of non-bureaucratic, radically democratic socialist society could provide the framework for the being mode to flourish.[62]

Despite these difficulties in visualizing the ideal of the productive character in the context of modern market society, a clear picture of the emancipated individual in the free society does emerge from Fromm's work, with the emphasis on a productive disposition and social relations infused with solidarity and love. Perhaps his clearest summary of the nature of the being mode is presented in *To Have or To Be?*, in which he claims that its prerequisites are "independence, freedom, and the presence of critical reason".[63] Its fundamental characteristic is described as being active, not in the sense of being busy but in terms of "inner activity, the productive use of our human powers." He speaks of giving expression to one's faculties, talents, to the wealth of human gifts with which we are all, in varying degrees, endowed. It means, he continues, "to renew oneself, to grow, to flow out, to love, to transcend the prison of one's isolated ego, to be interested, to 'list' [listen], to give." He goes on to list the qualities of the character structure of the "new," emancipated person, with the emphasis on the need to take full responsibility for our lives, to develop love and respect for life, to reduce greed and hate, and to exercise our imagination in the struggle to remove intolerable circumstances.[64]

It is not really surprising that there are few examples of wholly productive characters, since Fromm's analysis of the formation of social character in modernity reveals the predominance of various non-productive orientations, reflecting the alienation inherent in the socioeconomic structure. The marketing orientation in particular is portrayed as a pervasive form of alienation, in which even personal qualities and relationships are regarded as possessions, consolidating the negative power of the having mode. However, it is important to reiterate that in Fromm's analysis, the non-productive orientations are blended with the productive orientation in most people, and that non-productive orientations have positive and negative aspects, which vary according to the level of productiveness in the total character structure.[65] In identifying the ideal "virtuous" character, Fromm does no more than present a possibility to be striven for, rooted in propensities identifiable in most human beings. As Che Guevara once remarked, "the skeleton of our complete freedom is formed, but it lacks the protein substance and the draperies."[66]

Maccoby is right to be skeptical of Fromm's suggestion that the artist represents the model of a productive character,[67] as the radical artist in an alienated society is likely to need an abnormal degree of self-absorption to "take on" the world. In other words, the creativity of the artist may well be accompanied by a negation of some of the ethical qualities outlined above, such as caring for others in our everyday life. In fact, Fromm concedes that although the real artist is the most convincing representative of productiveness, it is not necessary to have such creative gifts in order to live productively.[68] Most occupations are not conducive to the development and expression of a productive character, but there may be scope in the world of work for such expression. However, it may be more meaningful to think of the productive character as manifested in those individuals who make creative use of their free time in activities which involve self-expression, learning, and non-instrumental social interaction. In these cases, the skills involved may not be advanced but the dedication is great and its social impact highly appreciated. A deep-seated consciousness that it is relations between people that are of paramount importance rather than the pursuit of power, wealth, and status is not so uncommon, despite everything.

## Ethics and Religiosity

At this point, it is appropriate to consider the relationship between Fromm's ethics and his understanding of the significance of religion. In the previous chapter we mentioned Fromm's "long view" of historical development, and he was fascinated by what he perceived to be the struggle between authoritarian and humanistic ethics in the history of religious thought. He defines religion as that which provides a common frame of orientation and an object of devotion,[69] and he distinguishes between authoritarian religion, in which the emphasis is on submission to an all-powerful deity, and humanistic religion, in which the emphasis is on the empowerment of men and women. Humanistic religion need not contain a notion of an external God, as, for example, in Buddhism,[70] and would be averse to any hierarchical Church authority. Fromm explicitly hopes for the emergence of a religious-like reverence for humanity, for what makes us truly human, our capacity to love and create. He considers faith to be a character trait without which we would be doomed to relativism and uncertainty,[71] and he is deeply interested in those religious expressions of faith in which the faith is directed not toward an external demiurge but rather toward the possibility that humanity can create universal peace and social harmony.

There are two principal reasons why Fromm considers the study of religion to be important for revolutionary social theory. First, many of the ethical tenets of religious thought are clearly at odds with the social practices of life in capitalist societies, and implicitly express a yearning for spiritual satisfaction, which could be met only through some sort of social revolution. Second, the identification of libertarian tendencies in the history of religious thought, particularly among the oppressed classes, shows an enduring urge for human freedom as self-determination which even societies in a condition of affluent alienation may find difficult to suppress. The first point is considered in the short book *Psychoanalysis and Religion*, published in 1950 as a continuation of the arguments contained in *Man For Himself.*[72] Toward the beginning of *Psychoanalysis and Religion* Fromm poses a rhetorical question:

> But will our children hear a voice telling them where to go [to find fulfilment] and what to live for? Somehow they feel, as all human beings do, that life must have a meaning—but what is it? Do they find it in the contradictions, double talk, and cynical resignation they encounter at every turn? They long for happiness, for truth, for justice, for love, for an object of devotion; are we able to satisfy their longing?[73]

Fromm comments that not only do we not know the answer to life's meaning but that we have even forgotten to ask the question. One response to this moral vacuum is the return to established religion, but this may be primarily because of the need for the security of a church and the safeness of an allegiance. Where there is no sense of devotion or spiritual concern Fromm considers such a turn to religion as simply another example of "the failure of nerve."[74] However, he argues that the need for a system of orientation and an object of devotion is deeply rooted in the conditions of human existence. If it is not manifested in conscious adherence to a particular religion, its various elements such as ancestor worship, totemism, or fetishism still figure largely in secular guise. The point for Fromm is, therefore, not whether we favor religion or not, but whether we favor a religion which furthers the power of human development or paralyzes it.[75] The churches have, in his view, consistently capitulated before secular power even when that power has violated its spiritual ideal. Adherence to an authoritarian religion is tantamount to surrender to a power transcending humanity, and involves unquestioning obedience, a submission to authority that enables the individual to escape isolation, but at the cost of her or his independence and integrity. Calvin's jeremiads on our unworthiness as miserable sinners are cited to exemplify the destructive nature of this self-hatred.[76]

Humanistic religion, in contrast, emphasizes the power of human potential and the possibility of self-realization, and the prevailing mood is one of joy rather than misery. His examples of humanistic religions are early Buddhism, Taoism, the teachings of Isaiah, Jesus, Socrates, Spinoza, certain trends in Judaism and Christianity, and the cult of Reason in the French Revolution.[77] For Fromm, in humanistic religion, God is the symbol of what humanity potentially can be, whereas in authoritarian religion, God's perfection serves to highlight our own powerlessness.[78] Fromm anticipates an objection on this issue of dependence. Why criticize religion for its emphasis on dependence when we really *are* dependent on forces beyond our control? Fromm accepts the premise of the argument but not the inference derived from it. Recognition of our dependence should not lead to worshiping the forces on which we depend, for indulging in our dependence is a form of masochism and self-humiliation.[79] Humanistic religious experience, on the other hand, enjoys a wonderment at the complexity of our life in the world, an ultimate concern with self-realization, and what Fromm calls an "attitude of oneness" with one's self, with others, and with nature.[80] He also emphasizes the importance of the semantic aspect of religious experience, the symbolic language which causes us to reflect on those things that are of deep spiritual concern to us. This symbolic language is inescapable, for we all experience it in dreams, though discussion of it is largely suppressed in modern rationalistic societies.[81]

Toward the end of *Psychoanalysis and Religion*, Fromm declares that the significance accorded to the question of whether or not we believe in the existence of God diverts us from asking more important questions. Many who profess to believe in God are clearly, in Fromm's view, idolaters who worship wealth, power, and prestige, while many atheists consistently adopt a caring attitude, which he regards as "profoundly religious." Fromm wants the discussion moved away from the existence of God and toward confronting modern forms of idolatry, which threaten our "most precious spiritual possessions."[82] However, whatever accord there might be between radical humanism and tolerant theistic religion on ethical matters, the gulf between them remains deeper than Fromm appears to realize.

Fromm's consideration of the message of human liberation in religious thought is expressed in his studies of the Old Testament and early Christianity, found in *You Shall Be As Gods* (1966) and *The Dogma of Christ* (1930). He provides a number of provocative illustrations of the humanistic "subtext" in passages of the Bible, which are normally construed as bearing an authoritarian message. The title of Fromm's *You Shall Be As Gods* is taken from the words of the serpent when tempting Eve to take the forbidden fruit, promising that Adam and Eve would not die if they ate it, but that their eyes would be opened and they would know good and evil.[83] As Fromm comments, the serpent was right—they do not fall dead, their eyes are opened, and they are able to distinguish between good and evil.[84] God had created man and woman in his own image, and the text of Genesis indicates God's fear that they could assume his power, hence his decision to expel them from the Garden of Eden. This story of the authoritarian God in fact undermines his claim to omnipotence and reveals the immense potential of humanity. Another example of a story of the authoritarian God whose authority is found to be lacking is the Great Flood. This is ordered by God because he was so displeased with his creations that he decided to destroy them all. Again, this reveals a God with human failings, and indeed God repents his decision and saves Noah, his family, and the animals. The story becomes even more interesting because after the flood God enters a covenant with Noah and his descendents, symbolized by the rainbow, promising not to destroy the earth by flood. This covenant is regarded as a progressive step toward a more mature view of the relationship between God and humanity, and, in Fromm's view, "prepares the way to the concept of the complete freedom of man, even freedom from God."[85] For all the reminders of the weaknesses of human beings in the Bible, there is always the insistence that they can be overcome, and that, through making the right choices, humanity can be blessed.[86]

The positive vision of what humanity can achieve through the enlightened exercise of its own powers is most strongly expressed in the prophetic writings of the Old Testament, particularly in the two Isaiahs and Hosea and their attachment to the idea of the messianic time. This is not brought about by an act of grace, nor is it brought about by an innate drive within man toward perfection. Rather it is brought about by the resolution of concrete problems of conflict and suffering; it is the time when humanity becomes "fully born."[87] Fromm concludes *You Shall Be As Gods* by stating that a "new humanism" of great strength and vitality is needed for the spirit and hopes of the Prophets to prevail, and for humanity to save itself from the idolatry of modern alienation and the threat of mass extermination.[88]

In *The Dogma of Christ*, Fromm argues that the early Christians were primarily poor, egalitarian, and opposed to all authority. Theologically, they adhered to the adoptionist doctrine of the nature of Jesus, that is to say, that he was a man who was not from the beginning the Son of God but was chosen by a distinct act of God's will. He was man chosen by God and elevated by Him first to the status of messiah and then to Son of God.[89] What is the significance of this? Fromm reads it first as a manifestation of the old myth of the rebellion of the son against the authoritarian father, for they were putting a man at God's side and making him a co-regent with God. For Fromm, the early Christian belief in the elevation of a man to God was an expression of the unconscious wish for the removal of the divine Father.[90] In identifying with the crucified Christ, they atoned for their death wishes against the father, and at the same time displaced the father by identification with the suffering of Jesus.[91] The early Christians were the oppressed, consciously in opposition to secular authority and unconsciously in opposition to paternal theistic authority, and this produced a radical egalitarianism. This is expressed in texts such as Luke 6:20 in which the poor are blessed and promised the Kingdom of God while it is "woe to you that are rich, for you have received your consolation." The Epistle of James, from the middle of the second century, is even more aggressive toward the rich, who are invited to "weep and howl for the miseries that are coming upon you."[92]

This phase of Christianity prevailed for little more than three centuries, during which the "Church" was unheard of as such, reference being made only to "churches." When Christianity became adopted as the official religion of the Roman Empire the elites of Church and Empire felt the need to build a strong hierarchical organization buttressed by ideological purity and discipline. The theological expression of this is the belief that Jesus was always God—the doctrine of Athenasius—which was adopted as official dogma at the Nicene Council in 325. It says everything about the "political" nature of this decision that the event was personally presided over by the Emperor Constantine. The old view that Christ was a man adopted by

God—the doctrine of Arios—was deemed heretical, although the Arian view contin-ued to command wide allegiance.[93] That was not the end of the struggle between authoritarian and humanistic versions of Christianity. A century later, Pelagius ques-tioned the doctrine of original sin and argued that people would find heaven as a result of their own moral efforts, and although Augustine and others fought success-fully against the Pelagian "heresy," it recurred in modified forms up to and beyond the Reformation.[94] As Fromm comments, "the humanistic, democratic element was never subdued in Christian or in Jewish history," and the radical message was "God is not a symbol of power over man but of man's own powers."[95]

Fromm clarified his views on messianism, atheistic religiosity, and its relationship to Marx's philosophy toward the end of his life in a manuscript originally intended to form a second volume of *To Have or To Be?*[96] He distinguishes between two kinds of messianism, on the one hand the catastrophic or apocalyptic strain, in which the savior would come at a time of mankind's utmost corruption,[97] and, on the other, prophetic-messianism, in which a new spiritual world is established as a result of humanity's progress to full self-realization. Fromm sees the libertarian thread running through religious thought as culminating in "atheistic religiosity," in which the unconscious striving for universal peace and harmony is no longer anthropo-morphized in an external God but philosophically and politically expressed as real possibility. The ethical thrust of the dichotomy between having and being is an appeal for a value shift away from the adulation of material acquisition toward concern for our fellow human beings. He argues that the distinction between "having" and "being" is central to the work of both Meister Eckhart, a thirteenth century Dominican mystic, and Karl Marx. According to Fromm, "Marx's was in the deepest sense a non-theistic religious system, concerned with the salvation of man, a reformulation in secular language of the ideals of prophetic messianism."[98]

Fromm engages in a perceptive discussion of Marx's famous characterization of religion as the "sigh of the oppressed creature, the heart of a heartless world...the spirit of spiritless conditions...the opium of the people."[99] Marx commends the reli-gious criticism of his day, led by Strauss and Feuerbach, for stripping away illusions and opening up the way for a liberating, spiritual humanism. This criticism does not simply strip the religious flowers from the chains that contain us, leaving just the bare chains, but rather breaks the chains and plucks the "the living flower" of a life of plenitude, peace, and human solidarity. Marx talks of religion as an illusory sun, which revolves around man as long as man does not revolve around himself. However, Fromm emphasizes that Marx does not intend to elevate humans into Gods, for this would lead to the kind of idolization of man adopted in modern industrialism, in which nature is treated with contempt. Marx's reference to the heartless and spiritless world implies a vision of a "heartful" and spiritual world, and his occasional references to communist society give a clear picture of the self-realizing human being, dwelling in the realm of freedom and constantly developing his/her creative and social potential.

It is this vision of the emancipated individual living in a society free from exploitation and oppression that Fromm develops in his humanistic ethics in the concept of the productive character. He views the Hegelian–Marxian concept of alienation as a secular equivalent of the biblical warnings against idolatry,[100] and he points out that this conception is not confined to the young Marx. The passages on the fetishism of commodities in *Capital* resonates with the theme of exposing "false Gods" in a manner just as powerful as his early writings.[101] He ends the manuscript on Eckhart and Marx by endorsing Ernst Bloch's assertion of the atheistic character of true Christianity, noting that at Nero's court the Christians were called *atheio*, and sharing Bloch's hope for a new fusion of revolution and religion such as occurred in the German Peasants' Revolt in the early sixteenth century.[102]

## Objections

Fromm's ethical approach operates with a strong conception of human essence and a commitment to its realization or fulfillment in human existence. This essentialism, with its naturalistic overtones and its teleology, is anathema to modern analytical philosophy, and it is important at this stage to anticipate some objections and attempt to answer them from a Frommian standpoint. The first objection, which applies to any form of essentialist ethics, is that of the "naturalistic fallacy." This objection, originating in G. E. Moore's *Principia Ethica*, holds that it is illegitimate to derive a moral "ought" from a factual "is," and its influence was so great in twentieth-century academic philosophy that it marginalized consideration of the sort of essentialist ethics common to Aristotle and Aquinas, which had held sway for more than 2000 years in the West. The misunderstanding arises from what is meant by the "fact" of what constitutes our human essence. Quite clearly, in the case of Aristotle, the view that we are essentially rational requires that this rationality ought to be actualized; the "fact" of what we are is permeated by the value of what we ought to be. As MacIntyre comments, in Aristotle's philosophy human beings have a nature in which they have certain aims and goals, "such that they move by nature towards a specific *telos*."[103] Aristotle expresses his ethics in functional terms, likening the relationship of man "living well" to a harpist playing the harp well,[104] and this is explicitly endorsed by Fromm. As Philip Kain has argued, the human essence is not just factually given but constituted by social and cultural activity, and as values and needs play a part in constituting that culture, our essence is formed by these values and needs. Values are therefore embedded in our essence so that when we derive morality from a view of the human essence, we are not deducing moral conclusions from non-moral premises.[105] Although Kain makes this argument to explain the essentialism of the young Marx, it also applies to Fromm.

A second possible objection might be raised as to why Fromm's view of what constitutes the fully lived or truly human life should be regarded as more valid than any other. Fromm insists that his normative principles are "objectively valid," rejecting the view that objectively valid statements can be made only about facts and not about values.[106] He points to the arts and also to applied sciences such as medicine and engineering, in which it is common to construct objectively valid norms by which to judge the success of a project, and in which failure to comply with them is penalized by poor results. In his own sphere, he insists that living is an art and that humanistic ethics is "the applied science of the art of living based upon the theoretical science of man."[107] Fromm accepts the limitations of this conceptualization, for despite a wealth of data from anthropology and psychology we have only a very tentative picture of human nature.[108] Nevertheless he insists that "objectively valid" does not mean absolute, and that all scientific progress is based on provisional truths.[109] Fromm repeatedly stresses the empirical and scientific nature of his psychology, based on his psychoanalytic practice and his large-scale empirical studies. In the course of discussing the early development of his interest in social psychology, Fromm emphasizes the critical importance of his observation of human behavior in his psychoanalytical work,[110] and it provides him with the professional confidence to say that failure to develop a productive character leads to dysfunction and unhappiness for the individual, and, when it happens on a widespread scale, to a "socially patterned defect."[111] For Fromm, capitalism does bad things to our mental health and it needs to be challenged at an explicitly ethical level. His approach echoes ancient Greek conceptions of ethics, but the idea of essentialist ethics has been revived in recent years. In a recent defense of a naturalistic version of virtue ethics Rosalind Hursthouse comments that if we argue that what is good for us as humans is to do what we can rightly see we have reason to do, then we quickly recognize that most humans do not live up to this goal. They are, in effect, "defective human beings," and, she adds, that is the judgment we should expect a plausible ethical naturalism to yield.[112]

A third potentially serious objection to his ethics centers on his faith in the capacity of collective humanity to realize its full potential through love, reason, and creativity in a general condition of human solidarity.[113] Why, it may be asked, should we consider only this positive potential, when humanity has all too often demonstrated its potential for wholesale destructiveness? Why conceive human nature in such positive terms?[114] It is important to note here that Fromm does not operate from the premise that humans are naturally good or bad. We are, rather, faced with an existential dilemma that we can respond to in progressive or regressive ways; hence the subtitle of *The Heart of Man* is *Its Genius for Good and Evil*. What he wants to dispel is the idea that nothing could be done to enhance the progressive responses or marginalize the regressive ones. Fromm was well aware of the danger to his humanistic thesis posed by views that emphasized destructiveness or aggression as ineluctable aspects of human nature. He rejected Freud's adoption of the death instinct, seeing it as a reflection of the collapse of liberal optimism in the face of the horror of the First World War.[115] For Fromm, destructiveness is essentially a "secondary potentiality," and although it possesses all the power and intensity of any passion, it is merely an alternative to creativeness, something that arises when the will to create cannot be satisfied.[116] In this respect, Fromm shares Marx's view of the historical progress of freedom while being under no illusion about the difficulty of advancing toward an emancipated society from a distinctly unpromising *status quo*.[117]

As we saw in chapter two, in *The Anatomy of Human Destructiveness* Fromm refutes the arguments of those instinctivists who view aggression *per se* to be natural and inevitable, arguing instead that "malignant aggression" is essentially a manifestation of the breakdown of creativeness.[118] Potentially serious destructive tendencies such as greed and envy are certainly strong, not, however, because of their inherent intensity but because of the difficulty of resisting the pressures to behave in a ruthless and inconsiderate manner.[119] In other words, it is the social requirements of the accumulation system, with its ultra-competitiveness and indifference to human suffering, which produces destructive behavior, and a non-alienated social system would nullify it. For Fromm, the anthropological evidence points to a preponderance of cooperation and sharing among prehistoric humans, with large-scale destructiveness following on from the development of civilization and the role of power.[120] Society could not have survived and developed if the destructive urges were a fundamental part of our human nature. The war of each against all would have led to extinction a long time ago.

A fourth objection to Fromm's humanistic ethics applies to all forms of essentialism, and, that is, that essentialist approaches necessarily favor particular, historically conditioned images of the ideal that will inevitability lead to privileging, partiality, and exclusivity. In other words, however libertarian are the intentions of an essentialist theorist, the outcome is likely to be authoritarian. If we read the utopias of the past, we invariably see various social arrangements which would be anathema to the vast majority of us today. For example, Thomas More, deeply attached to the virtue of chastity, prescribed the death penalty for repeat adulterers in *Utopia*, clearly opting for social stability and individual restraint over the gratification of the passions. Seyla Benhabib views the Marxian commitment to the reappropriation of the human essence as implicitly collectivist and authoritarian, and therefore opposed to "the meaning of human plurality."[121] Iris Marion Young has argued that any definition of human nature is dangerous "because it threatens to devalue or exclude some acceptable individual desires, cultural characteristics, or ways of life."[122] The problem here is the word "acceptable," for if this means acceptable to a tolerant Western liberal, then a conception of human nature is clearly already at work, normally expressed in the language of a demand for the recognition of certain rights. If not, it could mean acceptable to a majority of people within a particular culture, but this sort of relativism means that we have to forego any judgment on cultural practices which may cause offence to sections of that community. The minority within that community who seek assistance in their struggle against certain cultural practices will look in vain for support from Western liberals adhering to this form of radical relativism.

Paradoxically, Young acknowledges that all normative theory relies on a conception of human nature, but she wants to avoid the difficulties which that implies by focusing instead on processes wherein group differences can be accommodated and oppression resisted. This evasion leaves us without a criterion by which to judge the effect on human welfare of certain cultural practices. A commitment to the idea of a common nature does not infer the erasure of difference, and in Fromm's case the qualities to be developed in the productive being requires difference and the development of our unique traits and attributes.[123] In Fromm's view, we share the core of human qualities with all members of the species; each individual is a unique entity who can realize his or her human potentiality only in the process of realizing his or her individuality or self.[124] This self-realization cannot be gained by thinking that our self-interest lies in the acquisition of money, prestige, and power, which become both incentives to act and ends in themselves. Rather it is life itself that must become the end, and humanistic ethics serves as a guide toward that goal.[125]

However, it must be conceded that Fromm's interpretation of what is natural can lead to problems. The danger of sexual "naturalism" is expressed most unfortunately in his treatment of sexual orientation and the significance he gives to the polar attraction of the sexes in his discussion of love. Fromm clearly considers the rejection of this attraction to be unnatural, and describes homosexuality as a "sexual disturbance" in *The Heart of Man* and a "deviation" in *The Art of Loving*.[126] In the latter he asserts that because the homosexual cannot achieve the "polarized union" of heterosexual relations, he or she will suffer from "the pain of never-resolved separateness," a "failure," he adds, which is shared by heterosexuals who cannot love. Here Fromm falls into the error of the sort of biologism that he had previously found unacceptable in Freud. One would have expected his "relational" perspective to explain psychological problems among homosexuals in terms of the cultural climate of aggressive homophobia rather than in some notion of biological destiny. The error is important because it reveals the possibility of importing particular prejudices into apparently benign universal categories. However, this refusal to accept natural attraction as "natural" is a mistake, which should not deter us from recognizing the centrality of love to human nature, or the value of the general approach of specifying the qualities required for human flourishing.

A final objection surrounds the anthropocentrism of Fromm's ethics and the implications this may have for human relations with non-human nature, and, more specifically, its privileging of the species *vis-à-vis* other animals (speciesism). Certainly, Aristotle would be considered guilty of speciesism, having a dismissive view of animals, but it does not follow that every form of humanism based on the distinction between humans and other animals necessarily involves a dismissive or exploitative view of other animals, or nonhuman nature in general.[127] Such a view would constitute a "narrow" form of anthropocentrism, a crude instrumentalism in which non-human nature is seen as of value only as a resource for humans. A broader form of anthropocentrism, however, could extend the commitment to human flourishing to non-human nature, on the understanding that humans would do their own nature a disservice if they did not treat non-human nature with respect. Fromm's approach is one of broad anthropocentrism, in which respect for the positive ideal of human nature is extended to respect for non-human nature. In order to understand what is good for humans we need to grasp essential human needs, and similarly in order to know what is good for non-human nature we must study the particular needs of plants and animals. When Fromm talks about the distinction between humans and animals he comments that the instinctive apparatus of humans was so inferior to that of other animals that compensation had to be found in the development of the brain; there is no implication here that this makes other animals inferior or unworthy of respect.[128] Indeed Fromm shows a sensitive appreciation of the desired relationship between human and non-human nature in a discussion of poetic attempts to grasp the wonder of nature in *To Have or To Be?* Here he compares poems by Tennyson, the seventeenth-century Japanese poet Basho, and Goethe, all dealing with the reaction to seeing a flower. Tennyson plucks it "root-and-all" in order to grasp what it tells us about life, unaware of the irony that he has ended the life of the flower. Basho celebrates its blooming by the simple device of an exclamation mark, while Goethe carefully extracts the flower from the ground to re-plant it in a more favorable position so that it can grow better. Tennyson's attitude reflects the impulse of nineteenth-century science, wanting to extract and dissect in order to advance knowledge, a form of possessiveness that Fromm condemns as belonging to the "having mode." Goethe, "the great lover of life," and Basho, on the other hand, display an attitude belonging to the "being mode," in which the human is at one with the world.[129] Fromm's radical humanism views life as a whole in terms of enhanced relatedness, learning, understanding, and respecting life in all its rich variety.

## Messianism

As we have seen, Fromm is an admirer of the messianic tradition and his radical humanism is often couched in a rhetoric of redemption or salvation. But does this messianic urge detract from the analytical strengths of his social psychology? This is the view of his former collaborator Michael Maccoby, who comments that Fromm's "prophetic" impulse underestimates the need for individuals to adapt to a society before attempting to transform it, thereby hindering the development of feasible strategies for making the world a better place.[130] Maccoby is undoubtedly correct when he states that at his most prophetic, Fromm's mission was to contribute to bringing about "a messianic age of peace and human solidarity,"[131] but he has strong misgivings about Fromm's view of human nature and about what we can expect people to achieve. It is also clear that he resists Fromm's conviction that there is an urgent need to achieve ethical and political transformation. Nevertheless, the ontological and political differences between them do not make the problematic nature of the messianic impulse disappear. If Fromm's messianism unwittingly leads him away from a politics of self-realization toward one of mystical deliverance then clearly he is undermining his own project.

For the most part Fromm avoids falling into the trap of the "dreaming" utopians whose rhetoric masks a deep despair. However, there is one isolated instance when Fromm's messianism appears to reflect a loss of faith in the real possibility of social transformation along radical humanist lines. This occurs toward the end of *The Sane Society* in a passage in which he speculates that it is not too far-fetched to believe that within the next 500 years a new humanistic religion will develop, which will appeal to the "spirit of reverence toward life and the solidarity of man." Commenting that religions are not simply invented, he fantasizes that it will develop when a new "great teacher" emerges, as they have appeared in previous centuries.[132] There is a danger inherent in any approach that encourages us to hope for a new savior, for the emphasis on redemptive vision tends to dissever real struggles against exploitation and oppression from the concrete goal of a more humane democratic society. The image of the new messiah promotes a feeling of waiting rather than acting, of being led rather than leading. Rather like the theatrical device of a *deus ex machina* intervening to save a seemingly hopeless situation, the implication is that the situation really *is* hopeless. In *To Have or To Be?*, he rejects such a view as belonging to the "dreaming" utopian who puts on the mask of optimism in order to hide a real despair.[133] Any reliance on "rescue" by an external force contradicts the commitment to self-emancipation and self-realization, and in some respects offers a variation of the vanguardism, which he condemns in its Leninist form as lacking faith in "man."[134]

However, I do not consider that passage from *The Sane Society* to be typical of Fromm's whole endeavor, and in the remaining chapters of this book it becomes evident that in all the areas of social and political life in which he identified domination and manipulation he also looked for the ideas and movements which held out the real possibility of moving us in the direction of radical social change. As we have seen, in the discussion of prophetic messianism late in his life Fromm was at pains to argue that emancipation is not something that can be delivered *to* people. Freedom emanates only from self-emancipation, not by humans elevating themselves to God-like status over nature but by the realization of positive human potentials, which have developed over thousands of years. The suppression of those powers, particularly our emotional underdevelopment—"man's indifference to himself"—is, in his view, the principal ethical problem of our time. He concludes that it will not be resolved by the concentrated efforts of piecemeal reformers, no matter how ingenious, as long as the social framework within which they operate is not challenged and eventually transformed. For Fromm, the magnitude of the task requires an ethical revolution as a prerequisite for structural transformation.

# Chapter Four
## Toward a Gendered Humanism

From early in his career Fromm was a consistent critic of patriarchy and a supporter of women's emancipation, but his position is based on a controversial assumption that there are distinctively male and female psychic structures. He was fully aware that the attribution of natural character differences between men and women had been used historically by men to justify the exclusion of women from public life and their subjugation. However, despite this historical abuse Fromm was convinced that gendered character differences could be discerned, and that, in asserting the merits of the female psychic structure, the conservative power of patriarchy could be undermined. His outlook has interesting similarities with modern "maternalist" feminism, though, in particular Carol Gilligan's defense of a female ethics of care,[1] and also with the French theorists Luce Irigaray and Julia Kristeva.[2]

Fromm's interest in the idea of distinctive female and male psychic structures developed during his membership of the Institute for Social Research in the 1930s, and it continued to have a profound influence on the development of his mature social psychology. His principal source of inspiration was *Mother Right*, the work of the Swiss jurist and anthropologist Johann Jacob Bachofen (1815–1887), who argued that matriarchy—societies in which women were in positions of authority—preceded patriarchy as a stage in human development.[3] Fromm was not the first socialist to appropriate the positive evaluation of matriarchy made by Bachofen, as both August Bebel and Friedrich Engels had done so with considerable popular success.[4] However, Fromm's thesis that gender difference is reflected in psychic structures and that "matricentric" psychic structures are more amenable to socialism is theoretically bolder and potentially more controversial. I use the term "maternalism" to denote this positive attribution of female qualities arising from maternal functions. Modern anthropological research does not support the views postulated by Bachofen and Engels that a matriarchal stage in human development existed, at least in the sense of societies in which women dominated men, but there is plenty of evidence to support the existence of societies which practised lineage through the female line (matriliny) and in which women experienced parity of esteem.[5]

In order to explore this neglected aspect of Fromm's work, this chapter examines three pieces on matriarchy written by Fromm in his Frankfurt School years and assess their significance in the development of his social thought. His first contribution was a review of Robert Briffault's book *The Mothers* in the Institute's journal, the

*Zeitschrift für Sozialforschung*, in 1934,[6] followed in the next edition later that year by a full length article on "The Theory of Mother Right and its Relevance for Social Psychology," which focuses on the implications of Bachofen's work.[7] The third piece, "The Male Creation," was only recently discovered by Fromm's literary executor, Rainer Funk, but the presence of some sharp criticism of Freud indicates that it was probably written later than the other two.[8] In the first section, the central arguments of these pieces will be outlined, clarifying points where necessary with reference to some of his later papers. The second section will discuss the wider implications of these arguments for the evolution of Fromm's thought. In particular, it will be argued that the work was an important stage in Fromm's rejection of Freud's theory of instincts, which was to lead to his departure from the Frankfurt School in 1939 and his public disputation with Marcuse in 1955.[9] It will also be suggested that the work on maternalism was important in the development of his theory of human nature and the ethics that flowed from it. The third section compares Fromm's views with those of the psychoanalyst and philosopher Luce Irigaray, and the chapter concludes with a discussion of the controversial issues raised by the question of gendered character differences.

## Maternalism and Socialism

In the review of *The Mothers*, Fromm praises Briffault for developing the insights originally set down by the Swiss jurist and anthropologist Johann Jacob Bachofen (1815–1887) and the American anthropologist Lewis Henry Morgan (1818–1881) in the 1860s and 1870s. They had argued that not only did matriarchal societies precede patriarchies but that they contained elements of love and cooperation which were in many ways superior. He praises Briffault for arguing that the social instincts originate in the maternal instincts, but what is important is that his conception of "masculine" and "feminine" does not rely on unchanging natural difference but on the material ways in which men and women have interacted in the evolution of humankind:

> Masculine and feminine are for Briffault definitive psychological categories, but unlike the Romantics, he does not derive them from the "nature" of the two sexes but from the difference in the way they function in practical life. With this shift he rescues the issue of sexual difference from the darkness with which natural philosophy had cloaked it and examines it in the light of scientific research.[10]

The distinction that Fromm fastens onto here is vital, for he is well aware that the historical exclusion of women from public life had been justified on arbitrary naturalistic grounds. Men had used their notion of the innate nature of women to justify their unsuitability for a range of endeavors, which were considered to be the exclusive province of men. It is therefore not surprising that mainstream feminism has resisted all attempts to speak of specifically feminine qualities. However, Fromm does not consider that the dangers inherent in attributing gender-based orientations should prevent the investigation into the psychological differences which may have developed as a result of the different relationship that men and women have had to the process of reproduction over centuries. There is no implication that such differences are fixed, and, as we shall see, Fromm's ideal is that one day the social conditions can be created in which the two tendencies are united in a productive synthesis.

Fromm points to two crucial factors in the evolution of the maternal instinct, the unusually long period of gestation compared with other mammals and the protracted period of the immaturity of the human child. This necessitates many years of caring and is the source of maternal love, which Fromm regards as one of the most important sources of all societal evolution, and, furthermore, the source of love in general.[11] Fromm approves of Briffault's argument that the origin of social instincts in general is to be found in the maternal instinct. Briffault suggests that primitive human groups developed from families rather than herds, and that the family was based on maternal instincts, in contrast to the herd, which was based on the male sexual impulse and lacked stability. The merging of these families, formed by the bonding of the mother with her offspring, leads to the establishment of primitive societies centered on the mother. Although Fromm seems persuaded by the idea that matriarchies did constitute a distinctive stage in the evolution of all societies, he makes a distinction between a "gynecocratic" structure, in which women rule over men in a reversal of the roles under patriarchy, and a "matricentric" structure, which denotes a social order characterized by "the relatively great social and psychic influence of women."[12] Clearly it is the latter that interests him.

Fromm is critical of some of Briffault's conclusions, in particular his suggestion that women are innately conservative and unable to learn beyond the age of 25, and he comments that this "slip" shows how deeply rooted in the unconscious, even of a progressive author, are traditional, biologically based value-judgments.[13] The same could be said, of course, about Fromm's views on homosexuality. In general, however, Fromm is impressed by a work of historical materialism, which explains changes in sentiments and institutions on the basis of changes in economic conditions. He goes so far as to say that the book's major significance lies in "its recognition of the social determination of all sentiments, even those that appear to be the most natural,"[14] which implies that Fromm was already moving away from Freudian orthodoxy.

In "The Theory of Mother Right and its Relevance for Social Psychology," Fromm focuses on Bachofen's *Mother Right*, which was constructed largely from an impressively extensive study of myths, dramas, and symbols from the ancient world, supplemented by evidence from early commentators such as Herodotus, Aristotle, and Plutarch. Bachofen postulates two societal stages in which women were in a position of authority in society. The first was the primitive stage of humankind associated with the nomadic life and dependent on hunting and fishing. It was allegedly governed by the natural law of lust-driven promiscuous sex with no known relationship between sex and conception, and its crude justice was based on retaliation. Its symbolic Goddess figure was Aphrodite, and its vegetal symbolic was the swamp. However, even at this stage the humanizing factor of motherly love is at work, "the only light in the moral darkness, the only joy amid profound misery."[15] The second stage of matriarchy, the Demetrian stage, is portrayed as a stable society in which agriculture flourishes and the woman is accorded great respect because of her fertility; the mythology of the earth goddess prevails. "Mystery" is valued and the matriarchal societies are noted for their spiritual devotion. The maternal principle becomes the basis for "universal freedom and equality," and Bachofen conjures an image of peace-loving, cooperative, and caring societies in which the common good prevails.[16] Matriarchal peoples are distinguished by rectitude, piety, and culture, a necessary period in the education of mankind and the fulfillment of a natural law.[17] But this closeness to nature was also a weakness, and Bachofen considers the victory of the paternal principle to be progressive, bringing with it a "liberation of the spirit from the manifestations of nature" and the divinity of the mother gives way to the divinity of the father.[18] State-building and ordered justice can now develop, and the Roman empire embodies the victory of patriarchy as a progressive development. However, this conservative conclusion does not hide the radical nature of Bachofen's enthusiasm for the matriarchy, and his work undermines the idea of the eternal naturalness of male rule, which is enshrined in the Bible.

Fromm begins his article by noting that Bachofen's work had drawn appreciation from opposite sides of the political spectrum. In the late nineteenth century it had been admired by socialist writers such as Bebel, Marx, and Engels, but then in the 1920s it drew praise from conservative philosophers Klages and Bäumler. Whereas the socialists fastened onto the radical potential of his demolition of the assumption that patriarchy was the natural order of things, and also in his positive evaluation of many of the characteristics of matriarchy, the conservative admirers emphasized the importance that Bachofen had given to the power of religion and to the "exclusive rule of naturalist values based on the blood bond and earthly ties."[19] They also shared Bachofen's view that the supersession of matriarchy by patriarchy was a positive advance, and it did not occur to him that his findings could have radical implications for his own society. He remained a conservative who opposed democracy and the involvement of women in public life. Fromm acknowledges the danger that any theory propounding the universal significance of sex differences "would appeal very strongly to the champions of male, hierarchical class rule,"[20] but he insists that this should not deter socialists from pursuing the truths revealed in the work and the radical message contained therein. What is interesting here is the criticism which Fromm levels at the Enlightenment theorists who posited the fundamental sameness of the sexes—"souls have no sex"—and who demanded the emancipation of women on that basis. While this was obviously progressive, it took for granted that the ideal was emancipation within bourgeois society, without questioning whether human emancipation was possible at all within that framework:

> Emancipation did not mean, therefore, that she was free to develop her specific, as yet unknown, traits and potentialities; on the contrary, she was being emancipated in order to become a bourgeois man. The "human" emancipation of woman really meant her emancipation to become a bourgeois male.[21]

For Fromm, the goal of the emancipation of women ought not to be simply equality with men under existing social conditions but should strive for the revolutionary transformation of all human relations. As we shall see, Fromm stood by this position in his pronouncements on feminism several decades later.

Fromm concedes that there is a mystical side to Bachofen's work which does not lend itself to materialist analysis. He comments that one of Bachofen's most brilliant insights is to relate a given structure of the human psyche to a specific religion, but argues that Bachofen is wrong to derive the psychic structure from the religion, rather than the other way round.[22] Bachofen emphasizes the importance of naturalistic religion in matriarchies, focusing on the primacy of generative maternity, but considers that the progress to paternity involves a "liberation of the spirit from the manifestations of nature."[23] The difference stems from the more distant relationship of the male in procreation, and Bachofen cites the myths set down by Aeschylus and Euripides, which demonstrate the struggle between the old matriarchal order and the new patriarchal one. In Aeschylus's *Oresteia*, Orestes murders his mother Clytemnestra to avenge her killing of his father, and when he does this the ancient maternal goddesses, the Furies, are overthrown. They pursue Orestes for his crime, as for them his crime is inexpiable, but he is defended by the new gods of the victorious paternity, Apollo and Athena, who sprang from the head of Zeus rather than a natural birth process. As Bachofen comments, a new ethos is in preparation in which the divinity of the mother gives way to that of the father. For him, the Pelasgian culture, marked by the operation of unconscious law, derived from maternity, while Hellenism, with its individualism and its transcendence of nature, is inseparable from the patriarchal view.[24]

One of the things that attracted socialist theorists to Bachofen's thesis was the dialectical nature of his argument. Not only does he portray one sociospiritual structure arising in struggle against another, but vestiges of the older one are shown to reappear to challenge the new order. In this way he characterizes the spread of the cult of Dionysus, which revived the maternal principle against the paternalism of the Delphic Apollo, only to be eventually overcome by the Roman *imperium*. For Bachofen, this signified how hard it had been for men to overcome the inertia of material nature in order to achieve the "highest calling, the sublimation of earthly existence to the purity of the divine father principle."[25] In this conclusion, we can understand the attraction of these ideas for sections of the extreme right, but in the depiction of the struggles it is also possible to see how socialists could be enthused by the idea of the fragility of the patriarchal order, stripped of its claim to natural universality. For Fromm what was important was the idea of the enduring strength of the matricentric psychic structure, offering a still-powerful challenge to the extreme authoritarianism of the patricentric structure. The latter had reached its apotheosis in bourgeois-Protestant society, but as that society developed our productive capacity it had revived as real possibility the idea of abundance for all and human flourishing, the psychological conditions that would undermine that patricentric structure.[26]

The "discovery" of matriarchal societies, or, more accurately, matrilineal societies, opened up an imputed world of "matricentric" tendencies, which could be contrasted with patricentric psychic structures. Unlike Bachofen, Fromm was eager to relate these structures to modern institutions and movements. Fromm accepts Bachofen's view of matriarchal society as a democracy in which maternal love and compassion were the dominant moral principles, injury to others was the biggest sin, and private property did not yet exist.[27] In Fromm's view, the matricentric complex is grounded in the mother's unconditional love for her children, emanating not from any moral or social obligation but from the biological necessity of pregnancy and nurture. This fosters a propensity for unconditional love in the woman's emotional disposition. The matricentric complex, then, is characterized by a feeling of trust in the mother's unconditional love, far fewer guilt feelings, and a far weaker superego than in the patricentric complex, a greater capacity for pleasure and happiness, an ideal of motherly compassion, and love for the weak and others in need of help.[28] Fromm then comes to the rather startling conclusion that the working class is the fully fledged representative of new matricentric values and that the psychic basis of the Marxist social program is predominantly the matricentric complex. The argument is rather attenuated but Fromm suggests two things. First, the working class relates to its work not through an internal compunction such as the work ethic but from economic necessity, and in the process the workers develop cooperation and solidarity and are open to the idea of a more rational and less oppressive way of organizing production. Second, the Marxist program offers them that way, with the promise of sufficiency of goods for all and the unconditional right of happiness for each individual, residing in the harmonious unfolding of the personality. For Fromm these are the rational, scientific expressions of ideas that under earlier economic conditions could be expressed only in fantasy, namely, "Mother Earth gives all her children what they need, without regard for their merits."[29]

As for the patricentric complex, this is a psychic structure in which the relationship with the father is central. In the patriarchal family because the father is the source of authority the love is not unconditional, and the moral dictates issued by him contribute to the formation of conscience and a sense of duty. However, it also leads to a loss of psychic security and the development of guilt feelings because we are never able to fulfill the ideals imposed on us.[30] Fromm summarizes the patricentric individual and the patricentric society as manifesting a complex of traits, the predominant ones being "a strict superego, guilt feelings, docile love for paternal authority, desire and pleasure at dominating weaker people, acceptance of suffering as a punishment for one's own guilt, and a damaged capacity for happiness."[31] For Fromm the patricentric complex achieved its dominance in bourgeois-Protestant society, a theme he was to develop at length in his discussion of Luther and Calvin in *Escape From Freedom* (1941).[32] The emergence of a triumphant patriarchy produced a patricentric psychic structure in which the fulfillment of duty and the achievement of success become the major driving forces of life, with love and happiness relegated to a secondary role.[33] It is also important to note that Fromm argues that societal restrictions on sexual satisfaction contributes greatly to the development of guilt feelings, and that sexual liberation would "necessarily lead to intensified demands for satisfaction and happiness in other areas."[34]

Fromm's assertion of the superiority of the matricentric structure over the patricentric structure is reiterated in his third contribution to the consideration of male and female principles in psychic life, "The Male Creation." In it, he makes a bold assertion not simply of the superiority of woman in respect of her natural productiveness but also the recognition of that superiority in both the male and female unconscious:

> In the male unconscious there is still a recognition of woman's superiority and her natural productiveness; there is still envy of her power. And in the unconscious of woman there is pride in this power and a recognition that she is superior to man.[35]

We must assume that this controversial view was based on his own clinical observations, although he acknowledges his debt to George Groddeck, who countered Freud's concept of penis envy with one of "pregnancy envy," and Karen Horney, who had recently published papers on the distrust between men and women and had voiced doubts about Freud's theory of instincts.[36] Fromm supplements Bachofen's work by using his knowledge of early religion to show the different emphases on the man–woman relationship in the creation myths of the Babylonian religion (the *Emunah Elish*) and the Old Testament. He regards the latter as the "triumphal hymn of the victorious male religion, a song of victory commemorating the destruction of all traces of the matriarchy in religion and society."[37] Contrary to everything we know about nature, no woman is involved in the birth process of the world, which is ascribed to the will and word of a male God. In detail we see that God made man first, Adam, and that Eve was created from his rib. Furthermore, in the account of the fall of humankind we have an authoritarian God issuing prohibition about eating the forbidden fruit, and Eve succumbing to the temptation to eat it and seducing Adam to do likewise.[38]

The Babylonian myth is approximately 500 years older, and although it also reflects male power, it shows that power developing in the course of a struggle against maternal power. It portrays the rebellion of two sons against the mother goddess, Tiamat and her husband Apsu. Apsu is overcome but she resists mightily and compels a male god, Kingu, to lead her forces and act as her consort. Eventually her son Marduk is victorious against her, and he creates the heavens from her cleaved body and creates humanity from Kingu's blood, after which he sets free the male gods. Fromm describes the struggle between Tiamat and Marduk as a metaphor for the sex act, and despite the male victory, Tiamat is portrayed as a powerful figure commanding respect. According to Fromm, this creation myth confirms the view that the patriarchal society had been a relatively recent development, and that it had emerged in struggle from an epoch in which women had a much more significant role in society.[39]

It is clear from these papers that Fromm held to a distinction between patricentric and matricentric psychic structures but this leaves an important question—how significant are such differences compared with the array of familial and social conditioning factors, which affect all human beings? He clarifies this in a 1948 article, "Sex and Character," in which he argues that certain biological differences result in characterological differences, which are "blended" with those directly produced by social factors. However, the latter are much stronger and can either increase, eliminate, or reverse biologically rooted differences. He refers to the effect of characterological differences based on sexual difference as "coloring," a process that supplements the formative influence of social roles. Men and women are first of all human beings "sharing the same potentialities, the same desires, the same fears."[40] Although biologically rooted character differences are "insignificant" in comparison with socially rooted differences, Fromm nevertheless insists that they should not be entirely neglected.[41] For Fromm, genuine equality requires difference, and it is the authoritarian personality who is unable to grasp this, seeing difference only in terms of power over other human beings, either despising those with less power or revering those with more. In contrast, he calls for the creation of social conditions that will develop the positive side of the peculiarities of persons, sexes, and national groups. This diversity, he claims, would make for "a richer and broader human culture and a more integrated family structure."[42]

## Implications for Theoretical Development

In this section, I suggest that Fromm's maternalism in the 1930s was an important factor in his move away from Freud's theory of instincts and his simultaneous move toward a new conception of human nature and a humanistic ethics, which culminates in the publication of *Man For Himself* in 1947.[43] At the time of writing the three pieces on maternalism he was still operating within the framework of Freudian orthodoxy, but there are clear signs of the difficulties Fromm was having with some of the Freudian concepts. For example, in the article on Bachofen for the *Zeitschrift* although he approvingly cites Freud's Oedipus complex whereby the son sees the father as a rival, but in the process of wanting to replace him he also identifies with him; the son wants to be loved by the father and at the same time needs to rebel against him. However, Fromm adds the qualification that Freud overestimated the universality of the complex "because he lacked the necessary distance from his own society."[44] He is even more outspoken in the "Male Creation," for here he explicitly endorses Karen Horney's criticism of Freud's one-sided masculine standpoint; Fromm concludes that Freud was more of "a captive of the prejudices of his bourgeois-patriarchal society" than Bachofen.[45]

Perhaps the clearest indicator of this can be found in the way in which he uses Bachofen in a piece written in the late 1940s in which he pulls apart Freud's reading of the Oedipus myth.[46] Freud interprets Oedipus's incest with his mother and murder of his father as reflecting a primitive childhood wish within all males, the sexual impulse toward the mother and jealousy of the father. This Oedipus complex became for Freud the cause of psychopathological development and the kernel of neurosis. Fromm notes that Freud concentrates on only one of the three plays which Sophocles wrote featuring Oedipus, namely *Oedipus Rex*. In that play, Oedipus kills an old man in an argument without knowing he is his father, and then becomes King of Thebes and takes Jocasta for his wife, not knowing she is his mother. The play ends with Oedipus blinding himself, overcome with guilt as the truth is revealed, while Jocasta commits suicide. Fromm questions why, if the incestuous drive is paramount, Oedipus does not fall in love with Jocasta, but rather takes her as his Queen in accordance with convention rather than out of passion. He then proceeds to develop an alternative reading based on all three plays, including *Oedipus at Colonus*, and *Antigone*, in which he sees the myth not as a symbol of incestuous love and jealousy but rather as the rebellion of the son against the authority of the father in the context of the specifically patriarchal family.[47] Fromm draws explicitly on Bachofen's work on the struggle between matriarchy and patriarchy to show, in a meticulous analysis, that the central theme of the three plays taken as a whole is the struggle against authoritarian patriarchal rule. In *Oedipus at Colonus*, Oedipus explains that the marriage to Jocasta was not a love match, thus undermining the idea of an unconscious sexual urge.[48] In Fromm's reading, Jocasta's real crime in *Oedipus Rex* is not the incest, which was unknown to her, but the fact that at the beginning of the play she had been prepared to kill her son in order to save her husband, thus violating her duty as a mother, a heinous crime by matriarchal standards but not by patriarchal ones.[49] *Oedipus at Colonus* ends with the death of Oedipus, but here he is surrounded by two loving daughters and new friends, no longer tortured with guilt but with a conviction of right, "one who has found his home with the earth and the goddesses who rule there."[50]

According to Fromm's interpretation, the conflict between patriarchal and matriarchal principles becomes explicit in *Antigone,* in which Creon, the new tyrant of Thebes, refuses to allow the body of one of Oedipus's sons to be buried. This abrogation of "the laws of blood and of the solidarity of all human beings" is opposed totally by Oedipus's daughter Antigone, who represents the matriarchal principle. She knows her opposition will cause her death but she defies Creon and accepts her fate "faithful to the laws of heaven." She is supported by Creon's son Haemon, but her sister Ismene is afraid to act with her, and this, according to Fromm, symbolizes the female submission to patriarchal domination.[51] Antigone's death shames Creon, the symbol of patriarchal authority, and the play ends with Creon admitting his own moral bankruptcy. According to Fromm, Sophocles is presenting not only a memory of the ancient struggle between two value systems, but is making a political argument against the Sophists and in sympathy with the old pre-Olympian religion which emphasized the sanctity of human bonds. It is clear by the end of the third play that incest and jealousy of the father are not the central themes.[52]

By 1937, Fromm had rejected not only Freud's theory of instincts but the whole conception of humanity, which informed it. In the opening chapter of *Escape From Freedom* (1941), he complains that Freud views "man" as fundamentally antisocial and is captive to the traditional doctrine of the evilness of human nature, seeing cultural progress only through the suppression of natural drives.[53] However, this flight from Freud left a gap, for libidinal theory had hitherto provided the framework for understanding the problems of the unconscious and the goal of good mental health. The break with Freud's theory of instincts caused Fromm to reconsider the perennial philosophical question of human nature, of what it is to be human and what is required psychologically for human flourishing. His own humanistic ethics were set down in *Man for Himself* in 1947, and his consideration of human nature was heavily influenced by the maternalist conception of love. This is particularly evident in the final piece he wrote while still a member of the Frankfurt School, "Selfishness and Self Love," which was published in the journal *Psychiatry* in 1939. The article begins with the paradox that in modernity there is a moral and philosophic condemnation of selfishness coexisting with a principle that pursuing one's own interest will indirectly lead to the benefit of the whole society.[54] Fromm cites a number of thinkers who assert a negative view of human nature, from obvious cases such as Calvin and Hobbes to the not-so-obvious Kant. Love for oneself or striving for one's own happiness can never be a virtue in Kant's philosophy because it undermines morality, conceived of as doing one's duty. Acting morally is conceived as overcoming what is natural to us, a form of inner authoritarianism.[55] Fromm notes that there are other thinkers, in particular Stirner and Nietzsche, who share the view that love of self and love of others are incompatible but who opt for the former *against* the latter, and although he sees elements of an affirmative, noninstrumental love for others in some of Nietzsche's philosophy the different forms of love remain as an antinomy.[56]

Fromm recognizes the difficulty of developing a cool and critical analysis of the phenomenon of love, a word frequently misused and prostituted, but he considers it an obligation for the psychologist to try. Love for Fromm is an affirmation of life, growth, joy, and freedom, and flows from the positive condition of having experienced love in childhood and the negative condition of having escaped those factors that foster chronic hatred. Love is rooted in a basic sympathy, and the objects of love do not have the quality of exclusiveness. Love for humanity is not something abstract that develops after the love for a specific person, rather it is the premise of that love— love for one person implies love for humanity as such. It follows from this that the self, is, in principle, as much an object of our love as another person:

> The affirmation of my own life, happiness, growth, freedom is rooted in the presence of the basic readiness of and ability for such an affirmation. If an individual has this readiness, he has it also toward himself; if he can only love others, he cannot love at all.[57]

Fromm concludes that in modern democratic society the problem is not so much that there is too much selfishness but that there is too little self-love, too little affirmation for the individual self with all intellectual, emotional, and sensual potentialities.[58]

The article is an important step toward a more general consideration of what it is to be human, and the ethics associated with it. In *Man for Himself* he defines the human essence in terms of our inherent drive for growth and integration, a drive we must strive to fulfill or else lapse into dysfunction and unhappiness.[59] In later work he emphasizes that the human essence is found in the tension between being in nature and transcending nature, an existential dilemma that can be responded to in a progressive and productive way or in a regressive way. The progressive way involves the fulfillment of our unique potential for productiveness, reason, love, and solidarity.[60]

## Toward a Gendered Humanism

As Rainer Funk has pointed out, it is impossible to overestimate the importance of Bachofen's work for the development of Fromm's thought.[61] References to Bachofen recur in his later writings and he continues to argue that sexual difference has characterological implications. The importance for humankind of the mother figure is expressed emotionally by Fromm in a television interview with Oliver Hunkin for the British Broadcasting Corporation in 1968 in which he talks about the mother figure as "certainty, protection, the absolute; the ocean, the earth, the heaven (or the haven)."[62] In this respect there are similarities between Fromm's approach and that of the English psychoanalyst Donald Winnicott, whose work Fromm commends (along with others such as R. D. Laing) for its commitment to the rebirth and growth of an authentic self.[63] However, when it comes to the specification of the characterological differences appertaining to the sexes Fromm runs into significant problems of the sort that have been faced by maternalist feminists more recently, as we shall see in the final section. In *The Sane Society* (1956), he maintains his support for Bachofen's views on the positive aspects of matriarchy and contrasts them with Freud's negative view of the attachment to the mother figure. Fromm concurs with Bachofen's view that there are both positive and negative elements of the matriarchal structure and lists the positive elements as "affirmation of life, freedom, and equality," while the negative side is that the bond to nature blocks humankind from developing individuality and reason.[64] He also endorses Bachofen's findings on the patriarchal character, with the positive aspects cited as "reason, discipline, conscience and individualism" and the negative ones as "hierarchy, oppression, inequality, submission."[65] However, he adds the important qualification that, unlike Freud, he recognizes that there is maternal conscience based on love and forgiveness as well as the paternal conscience based on duty.[66] In view of this important qualification it is not surprising that in his next book, *The Art of Loving*, he drops "conscience" from the list of positive elements of the male character. Instead he defines the masculine character as having the positive qualities of "penetration, guidance, activity, discipline and adventurousness," and the feminine character as having the positive qualities of "productive receptiveness, protection, realism, endurance, motherliness." Fromm emphasizes that both sets of characteristics are blended in each individual, but with a preponderance appertaining to his or her gender.[67]

The formulation of such lists of qualities tends to "fix" character traits in preordained meanings and actually undermines the strength of Fromm's position. Bachofen's work had directed Fromm to consider the implications of the unconditional love of the mother, and this led him to place a strong value on love in his consideration of what it is to be human. However, when formulating his humanistic ethics in *Man for Himself* the "thick" conception of human essence is expressed without references to sexual difference.[68] Sexual difference is not considered to be significant when it comes to grasping the essence of human nature, but it *is* significant when it comes to the existential question of how we live together and how we may live together more harmoniously in the future. This was the position in the 1948 article on "Sex and Character" mentioned above, and it is an important step toward a humanism which recognizes the importance of gender difference. Unfortunately, the "listing" of qualities exaggerates the characterological impact of the differences and detracts from the subtlety of the term "coloring," which he had used in that article to indicate the supplementary nature of the gender-based character traits.

When he returned to the subject of the relevance of maternalism in 1970, Fromm reiterated the need to forge a new synthesis of the broad gender differences, calling for the replacement of the opposition between mercy and justice by a union of the two on a higher level.[69] Then in his last major work, *To Have or To Be?* (1976), he reiterates Bachofen's distinctions between, on the one hand, matriarchal unconditional love and its association with mercy, and on the other patriarchal conditional love and its association with justice. He wants to see a productive synthesis, although he acknowledges that this could not be fully reached in a patriarchal society:

> The deepest yearning of human beings seems to be a constellation in which the two poles (motherliness and fatherliness, female and male, mercy and justice, feeling and

thought, nature and intellect), are united in a synthesis, in which both sides of the polarity lose their antagonism and, instead, colour each other.[70]

Here again Fromm treads a dangerous path, for the idea that "thought" and "intellect" are predominantly male qualities does not follow logically from the view that the female psychic structure is more caring because of the experience of motherhood. While this is another illustration of the dangers of the crude specification of male and female qualities, it is nevertheless clear that Fromm shows enthusiastic support for the emancipatory potential of the women's movement. He regards the liberation of women from patriarchal domination as an essential feature of a new, truly humane world; it is a "fundamental factor in the humanization of society."[71] He considers that the 6000-years-old subjugation of half the human race has done immense damage to both sexes. He argues that as the exercise of power over those who are weaker is the essence of patriarchy, the feminist challenge is of enormous significance because it is a threat to the principle of power on which contemporary society lives. If the women's movement can identify itself as the representative of "antipower," then women will have a decisive influence in the battle for a new society. The argument here is similar to his critique of the liberal Enlightenment view of women's emancipation in the *Zeitschrift* article on Bachofen. Equality with men under existing social conditions produces only a limited emancipation; only when we accomplish a revolutionary transformation of human relations will we all be free.

## Fromm and Modern Feminism

The danger of exaggerating the character differences between men and women has been recognized by modern feminists who want to affirm the positive aspects of the distinctively female but who refuse to be drawn into such conventional categories which are already loaded with meanings inscribed in patriarchal society. This applies to the work of Carol Gilligan, whose "ethics of care" chimes well with Fromm's position,[72] and also to the French philosopher/psychoanalyst Luce Irigaray, who makes a powerful case for the unique subjectivity of women but has been wary, until recently, of "listing" gender differences. In the remainder of this chapter, I look at some of the similarities in the work of Irigaray and Fromm and some of the questions raised for radical humanism by her ethics of sexual difference. At first sight it may seem a strange comparison, for they inhabit different intellectual worlds and eras and there is no indication that Irigaray is aware of Fromm's work. Whereas Fromm has articulated a strong theory of human essence, Irigaray and her sympathizers would be unhappy with the connotations of certainty and determination carried by the term "essentialism." Also, whereas Fromm writes in an accessible style, consciously reaching out to a wide readership, Irigaray has been inclined to write in an allusive, elliptical style through which she seeks to convey a different, female way of thinking and arguing (*parler femme*). However, they both argue with great normative force, and there are fascinating similarities in the content of their work. In the first place, they both affirm characterological differences between men and women and the difficulty of expressing these differences without implying permanent predetermined qualities. Second, they both attach importance to Bachofen's revelation of feminine values in a prepatriarchal age and the implications that has for the critique of Freud's view of women. Third, they place a stress on love, and indeed the love of self as a prerequisite for a reconciliation of humanity. Finally, they both appreciate the potential importance of religious thought in the development of an emancipatory consciousness. Irigaray's invocation of a female divine suggests a symbolic force for women to grasp their uniqueness and power, while Fromm understood that certain developments in religious thought had reinforced patriarchy. I will argue that Irigaray has urged feminism to express itself as an "antipower" along the lines called for by Fromm in *To Have or To Be?*, especially in her more recent writings.

At the heart of Irigaray's project is the conviction that women's exploitation is based on sexual difference and that its solution will come only through sexual difference.[73] She rejects the strand within feminism that seeks to neutralize sexual difference, saying that this would amount to nothing other than a loss of human identity.[74] Instead she argues for the positive expression of the uniquely feminine, in the process exposing the essentially masculine nature of supposedly neutral language and culture. This requires a rewriting of the suppression of the historical identity of women, and in this respect she, like Fromm, recognizes the significance of Bachofen's contribution in uncovering the eras when "women reigned as women," not just in the narrow sense of matriarchy.[75] The political project, which becomes more important in her later works, calls for the adoption of laws in accordance with sexual difference, such as the banning of the commercial use of female bodies and images and the stipulation of equal representation on public bodies.[76] The question arises, what is the uniquely feminine? In her early work Irigaray uses various rhetorical strategies to address this question, particularly metaphor and allusion, often drawing links between emotional expression and the female body. She is reluctant to reduce the uniquely feminine to simple definition or lists of qualities, and, when we consider the difficulties that Fromm gets into with his lists, Irigaray's original position is understandable. Irigaray believes that women need to grasp their own uniqueness, and to discover and create their own identity, and she presents her own insights in order to light the way. Early in her career she argues that it is useless to "trap women in the exact definition of what they mean,"[77] and in response to the question "what is a women?" she asserts "what is?" is the metaphysical question "to which the feminine does not allow itself to submit."[78]

In recent writings, however, Irigaray has become more explicit about the differences between men and women. In one instance she states that is an error "to want to quantify or enumerate a difference which is of another nature than one which can be described, evaluated, counted," but she then goes on to enunciate four factors which determine a different "structuring of subjectivity." The first of these is being born from the same or different gender from one's own, that is to say the relationship between mother and son is importantly different than that between mother and daughter. The second is whether or not one can conceive a living being in one's own body, and the third is whether one procreates within oneself or outside oneself. Finally, she speaks of whether one can nourish another living being from one's own body or only through one's own labor. These factors create two identities, two ways of looking at the world, which cannot be reduced to one.[79] In fact, in the introduction to the same book Irigaray ventures further than merely outlining the biological factors which condition difference:

> Women privilege intersubjectivity, relationship with the other gender, the relationship of being-two, the physical and, particularly, natural environment, the present and future tenses. Men, in contrast, prefer the subject–object relation, the production of pieces of work rather than respect for the world as it already exists, the use of instruments, the relationship between one and an imprecisely defined multiple: people, others, nations, etc., the representation of the universe as made up of abstractions, the past tense.[80]

The reference to the relationship of being-two is a distinctively Iragarayan concept, alluding to the idea that woman's sexuality is plural ("at least two sex organs") and that the "She" is "indefinitely other in herself." Yet, in other respects, despite the difference in language, the ascriptions bear a similarity to those of Fromm. A more detailed discussion of sexual difference is contained in her discussion of "love of self" in *A Ethics of Sexual Difference*.[81] As we have seen the consideration of "self love" was an important step in the development of Fromm's ethics of self-realization, but in dealing with the question of human essence and its realization he did not consider the different forms of love of self, which the sexes might experience. Yet once importance is granted to the idea of maternal unconditional love, it follows that the female love of self ought to be different to the male love of self. For Irigaray, the male love of self often takes the form of nostalgia for the mother-womb entity, a longing for a return that can never be achieved, but the distance for this return can be conquered by what she calls "the transcendence of God" which is achieved through sexual potency. Male love of self is not self-evident but rather always achieved through exterior mediation. Love of the self for women, according to Irigaray, is more complex. The female does not have the same relation to exteriority as the male because she loves and loves herself through the children she gives birth to, and the experience and expression of self-love is central to that significance. In her sexuality she is expansive and unending, a "horizon" forever open.[82] However, Irigaray recognizes that a whole history separates woman from the love of herself, and she cites Freud as an example of the predominant male view that woman has to renounce her love of self in order to begin to love men. Overcoming this historical oppression requires a detachment from the traditional role in which women have been placed, the development of a love for the child she once was and still is—a shared "enveloping" between child and mother—and an openness which allows access to difference between mother and daughter and among women.[83] For Irigaray, self-intimacy for a woman can be established or reestablished only through the mother–daughter relationship. In order that love in general in our society might flourish it would be necessary first that the hierarchy of maternal and paternal functions must be overcome, second, there must a reassociation of love and eroticism, and finally, that women must be able to form themselves into a social group.[84]

In the chapter of love of self, Irigaray suggests that one of the steps that women can take toward the assertion of their identity is the creation of a female "divine." As this resonates with Fromm's conviction that the need to hold a "common system of orientation and an object of devotion" is deeply rooted in the condition of human existence[85] it is worth a brief consideration here.[86] Fromm's work on the Old and New Testaments pointed to both authoritarian and emancipatory elements, the latter ultimately asserting that we could, through our own actions, move closer to the divine state, that is, we can be as Gods. Irigaray recognizes that our historical relationship to the divinities has been crucial in the creation of our subjectivity, and the fact that God has always been male, has played a major part in the reproduction of patriarchy:

> Man is able to exist because God helps him to define his gender, helps him orient his finiteness by reference to infinity. The revival of religious feeling can in fact be interpreted as the rampart man raises in defense of his very maleness.[87]

Irigaray maintains that to posit a gender a God is necessary, as a guarantee of the infinite, and that as long as woman lacks a divine made in her own image she will be unable to establish her subjectivity or achieve a goal of her own.[88] Irigaray tends to set aside the question of who or what God is,[89] and as long as she is exposing how male subjectivities have been constructed or supported in historical–philosophical accounts of God this is not a major problem. In a more positive sense, the advocacy of a female divine is more problematic. In Fromm's non-theistic religiosity the object of devotion is humanity itself, but for Irigaray it appears impossible to recover female subjectivity without creating an external, infinite Goddess (or Goddesses[90]). In her rejection of Levinas's idea that we achieve an ethical relationship with "the other" only through seeing him through the face of God, she points out that such a move involves imposing my God on him or her, and prevents a dialogue between us. She concludes "passing through a God in order to respect the other does not appear to be the best way of recognizing either gender."[91] So, despite her occasional references to ideal-types relationships such as Mary, the mother of God, and her mother, Anne,[92] and Francis of Assisi and Catherine of Siena,[93] her appeal to the divine appears to be symbolic rather than theological in any orthodox sense of the term.

Finally, when we consider Irigaray's political turn in her later writings the similarity with Fromm is really quite strong, as both favor a gendered humanism in which difference is preserved in a new, more fruitful synthesis. As Fromm put it, the aim is to work toward a concept of polarity in the relationship between the two sexes in such a way that the very polarity is the basis of productive forces.[94] Even Irigaray's language begins to take on a humanistic tone similar to that of Fromm, especially when she calls for "an education in being, not having."[95] There are two senses in which her political work extends in directions that fit nicely with Fromm's radical humanism. First, her feminism without doubt constitutes an anti-power, even though she shows little direct concern for the economic. The transformation of relations she works for is unimaginable within the structures prevailing under late capitalism, and the fact that she has done much of her work within Italian postcommunist circles is an indication of where her sympathies lie. Second, however, she does not confine herself to general statements of principle but shows a willingness to involve herself with projects, which attempt to alter the agendas of European politics. This work includes collaboration with the Commission for Equal Opportunities for men and women in the region of Emilia-Romagna, and working on a Draft Code of Citizenship for the

European Union with Renzo Imbeni. In *Democracy Begins for Two*, she experiences the frustrations of failing to sway the key committees to move on issues such as violence against women, the right to control one's sexuality or maternity, the right to choose specific working hours, the custody of children in the event of separation, divorce, or intercultural marriages, and the "necessity of a sexed culture."[96] But the setbacks do not render the process futile, as progressive relationships are made in the process of struggle and the arguments—in this case over Citizenship in the European Union— are only just beginning. Toward the end of the first chapter of *Democracy Begins Between Two*, which is entitled "I Want Love, Not War," she claims that the universal is two, it is woman and it is man, and the universal is found in the crossroads between these two universals. She adds "at this crossroads, or in this cradle, which is both natural and cultural, humanity can be born or reborn."[97] Although she comes at the relationship between the sexes from the opposite end of the polarity than Fromm, their contributions point the way to a vibrant emancipatory project.

## The Problems and Promise of Difference

The difficulties that Fromm gets into when specifying male and female qualities recur in Irigaray's work. Because her entire work is concerned with difference and recovering the distinctively feminine, her reluctance to give a concise account of difference was immensely frustrating for some critics. Now that she has overcome her reticence, she instantly opens herself to the accusation of offering unsustainable stereotypes. Readers of both genders are likely to say "well I'm not like that," or else think of many examples of people whose characters contradict the ascriptions. If we take Irigaray's list literally, for example, we might question why there are women who have a passion for history or science, or whether the Buddha was a man at all. And, as Kate Soper has questioned, if the maternal function is central to difference, does it not imply that some women are "cast out from femininity" because they are not mothers nor intend to become so?[98] However, we may take the lists of male and female qualities in a less specific way, as generalizations reflecting thousands of years of a sexual division of labor, which has shaped successive social structures. The maternal function may be central in accounting for the origins of the division of labor which has given rise to the shaping of gender qualities, but that does not entail that all women need to directly experience motherhood to authenticate themselves. Indeed many women would argue that they could achieve autonomy only by foregoing motherhood. The argument from the maternalists is couched in more general terms, suggesting that women would be inclined to have (and value) more direct relationship to other subjects than would men. As we have seen, in Fromm's view this is "productive receptiveness," in Irigaray's it involves "privileging intersubjectivity," but I think it is important to bear in mind Fromm's emphasis that such inclinations are but a "coloring" of character traits which are shared by men and women. The significance of difference lies in the need for a transformation of values if there is to be genuine emancipation for women and for society as a whole, a transformation that must involve a critique of the values that have propelled patriarchy.

Nevertheless, there remains a serious concern that in insisting on sexual character differences from an anti-patriarchy position the maternalists inadvertently reproduce the stereotypes, which were used for centuries to deny basic rights to women. Soper argues that although the maternalists want to celebrate the distinctiveness of woman, in focusing on maternity or the body and claiming that female subjectivity must be expressed in a new, intuitive way, the old male prejudices about women are unwittingly reaffirmed—women are "natural" and "intuitive," men are rational and transcendent.[99] This argument, directed at the work of Irigaray, Kristeva, and Hélène Cixous, could also be applied to Fromm. There is, I think, a line of defense that the politics of difference can take. For thousands of years women, for the most part, were excluded from public affairs and consigned a subordinate role in the family. It would be surprising if the sexual division of labor over such a long period of time did not leave an impact on the character differences between men and women. The differences may be natural in origin, because of the maternal function, but they have been consolidated and rationalized over time. An ethics of care may be seen as distinctively feminine, but it does not mean that every woman displays it or that men cannot learn it. Conversely women can demonstrate that the positive qualities historically associated with men are easily mastered.

Fromm's critique of the patriarchy that sustained the oppression of women is impressive because it recognizes that the processes of power replicate certain characteristics of a male psychic structure. There is no suggestion here that the male and female "colorings" are fixed for all time. On the contrary, Fromm welcomes the possibility that dominant patriarchal structures will wither, and anticipates a time when positive qualities of both male and female structures are fused. In recent times we have taken some steps toward this, with many men developing much closer relationships with their children than was normal in the past, and many women pursuing careers that have historically been the preserve of men. But even in the most affluent and liberal countries in the world, it is still the case that many professions and positions of power are dominated by men, and women still play the major role in bringing up children. As Fromm recognized, equality between the sexes will be achieved only if feminism remains an "anti-power," and this means a constant criticism of life under the tyranny of the logic of capitalist accumulation, a logic which has no respect for persons, or nature of any sort.

# Chapter Five

# Work

In principle, work for Fromm is a key expression of our humanity. He argues that in productive activity we transform the world and realize our own nature as rational, creative beings. In his discussion of what constitutes an authentic "self" in *Escape From Freedom*, he extols the virtues of spontaneous activity and specifies our capacity to love and work as the two foremost components of this spontaneity. He refers to work as an act of creation, which binds us close to nature in distinction from work either as compulsive activity to escape from loneliness, which he characterizes as "busyness," or as a drive to dominate nature, which ends up enslaving us to technology.[1] Later, in *The Sane Society*, he comments that humans go beyond the animal realm when they work, and in the process they create themselves as social and independent beings. We separate ourselves from nature by molding it in our creations, but we reunite with nature, as "master and builder."[2] The ideal here is the work of the craftsman, the *faber* of *homo faber*, exemplified by the great Gothic constructions of the thirteenth and fourteenth centuries, in which there is no split between work and culture, and expression through work is truly self-expression. "Mastery" is used by Fromm to denote accomplishment rather than to imply "domination," as in mastering a difficult skill, although he is fully aware that since the development of capitalism there are few opportunities for people to experience the deep pleasure of practising such skills.[3]

The idea that work as a creative interaction with nature is central to what it is to be human has the teleological implication that self-realization should involve individual control over creative acts, yet the technical and social division of labor negates this possibility. The experience of work for the vast majority of people, even many highly remunerated workers, is such that they yearn to be released from their onerous burdens. Fromm insists that this reaction to work as it is presently organized does not constitute a rejection of the need to work as such. He argues that laziness is not normal but rather a symptom of "mental pathology." Boredom, for Fromm, is one of the worst forms of mental suffering, and most people would prefer to be active even without monetary reward.[4] It is natural, he argues, for children to display immense energy and inventiveness in such activities as play, learning things, and inventing stories, but they are also anxious to participate in the work of the family, such as carrying shopping, helping in the garden or cleaning the house. Fromm insists that all the evidence shows that we have a natural tendency to be active, and that the often-expressed desire to escape from work is a reflection of the fact that it is work under a system of "forced labor." If the entire system of production were transformed in such a way that coercion and threat were removed from the work obligation, only a minority of ill people would prefer to do nothing.[5] So, there is an inherent and deeply rooted desire in human beings "to express our faculties, to be active, to be related to others, to escape the prison cell of selfishness,"[6] but modern society does little to satisfy this desire, and indeed the organization of the productive system actively discourages it by imposing insecurity and anxiety on the workers.

In his extended analysis of human aggression, Fromm reasserts his argument that the human being is naturally a constructive and cooperative being, and that boredom sets in when the individual fails to respond productively to activating stimuli. Unfortunately, in a cybernetic society most people suffer from a milder form of pathology comprising insufficient inner productivity, which he labels the "pathology of normalcy."[7] This boredom is kept at bay by a range of unproductive activities, which fill time without in any way extending the scope and depth of the individual's life. Fromm relates this issue of the "escape from boredom" to the world of work, noting that complaints about the mindless repetitions involved in automated production are common among blue-collar workers. One response to this was the introduction of "job enrichment" practices such as increasing the variety of tasks performed and giving more responsibility about limited aspects of the process to the worker. Fromm was writing this in the early 1970s in anticipation of what was to become known as "postfordism," and although he comments that breaking down monotony seems to be a step in the right direction it is a very limited one "considering the whole spirit of our culture."[8] Nor is Fromm convinced by the argument that merely reducing working hours would enable people to develop their faculties and interests in the extra leisure time available. As we see in chapter six, he is convinced that leisure time itself is manipulated by the entertainment industry and is really as boring as work. Only a wholesale transformation whereby the economy is subordinated to human need would enable work to become a true expression of human creativity.[9]

It should be clear from the comments above that Fromm saw a stark contrast between the life-affirming potential of work and its reality as drudgery in capitalist society. However, Fromm was always interested in concrete advances toward a more satisfying experience of work and ideas for reform which could be operationalized within the existing property arrangements. This does not amount to an accommodation with capitalism, as Willmot and Knights have suggested,[10] but rather a support for intermediate improvements, which would empower workers and therefore curtail the power of corporate capital. His ideas for improving the work experience have to be seen as a step toward his long-term goal of communitarian socialism, not a self-deluding attempt to fashion some form of communitarian capitalism.

The next section deals with Fromm's analysis of the world of work as he saw it in the advanced industrial world of the mid-twentieth century, and this is followed by a discussion of the various ideas and innovations, which, in his view, held out the promise of radically improving the work experience for the majority of producers. A comparison will then be made between Fromm's approach and that of the influential French social theorist André Gorz, who appears to operate from diametrically opposed premises but who moves closer to a Frommian position in his most recent work.[11] The concluding section summarizes the significance of Fromm's writing on work for emancipatory social and political theory.

## The Reality of Work

In *Escape From Freedom*, Fromm relates how the clocks in Nuremberg had been chiming on the quarter hour since the sixteenth century, an indication of the revolution in the way that we began to think about the importance of time brought about by the early development of capitalism. The measurement of work by time became of great significance. Too many holidays were considered to be wasteful and resentment developed against the unproductive nature of institutions such as the Church. The old social system was destroyed and individuals were left alone to cope with the demands of the new social system, selling their products or their labor power in an increasingly competitive market system.[12]

In the modern period the need to work becomes an inner compulsion, far more effective than any external compulsion could be, but also leading to a particular form of hostility and resentment among the middle class. Members of the working class could express more-or-less openly their resentment of harsh working conditions and low pay, while the aristocrats too could display open aggressiveness as they tried to hold on to their social and political power. Those in the middle-class, however, were essentially conservative, seeking to stabilize society so that they could become more secure and gradually prosperous. Their hostility was strong, directed against inherited wealth and power, but it was not expressed overtly. However, Fromm argues that repression of hostility does not abolish it but merely removes it from conscious awareness. This pent-up hostility "increases up to a point where it pervades the whole personality, one's relationship to others and to oneself—but in a rationalized and disguised form."[13] This insight of Fromm's is made in relation to the historical development of the middle class in the early centuries of capitalism, but it also pertains to the ethos of modern employment relations. The repressed hostility is manifested as "a spirit of manipulation and instrumentality," which pervades human relationships. According to Fromm, the relationship between competitors is necessarily based on mutual indifference, and this applies to the relationship between employer and employee. The owner "employs" another human being in the same sense that he employs capital, and the relationship is such that both use each other as a means to an end. The same applies to the relationship between the businessperson and the customers, and, indeed to all personal relations in capitalist society in which humans sell themselves as commodities.[14] In this idea of the production of personality for sale, Fromm moves close to his conception of the marketing character, which he later articulates in *Man For Himself*.[15]

If work in the early stages of capitalist development was linked with a religious sense of duty, in twentieth century "fordist" production there is no sense in which the worker feels actively related to the product. Fromm defines work of this sort as "the performance of acts which cannot yet be performed by machines."[16] The operations of workers are measured through Tayloristic techniques to maximize their efficiency, but employers began to recognize, mid-way through the twentieth century, that improving the job satisfaction of workers was a means to improving productivity. One of the ways this may be achieved is through the application of the findings of industrial psychologists in what became known as human-relations management, including such devices as the provision of social facilities, the playing of music during production, or even painting the walls a color more amenable to sustained output. Fromm naturally scorns this blatant manipulation:

> One speaks of "human relations" and one means the most in-human elations, those between alienated automatons; one speaks of happiness and means the perfect routinization which has driven out the last doubt and all spontaneity.[17]

The importance of these remarks is that they emphasize the radical nature of Fromm's demands to humanize work. The fact that the concrete suggestions that we look at in the next section are intermediate measures based on what might be achieved even in an alienated context should not be interpreted as a sign of a naïve underestimation of the scope of the transformation required for work to become a positive experience.

"Human relations" approaches prospered at a time of relatively full employment precisely because every incentive was needed to maximize the productivity of labor at a time when the threat of the dole queue was not so great. All Fromm's contributions in this field came during this period, when capital *needed* to make work attractive. Many of the measures introduced to combat such problems as absenteeism and sabotage in times of full employment were quickly dropped with the return of mass employment in the late 1970s. The move back to fordist work practices has been accompanied by the replacement of workers by robots,[18] as well as the computerization of skilled and semiskilled work, in many cases deepening the alienation of the work experience.[19]

Fromm notes the immense changes in the structure of employment in the United States, from a situation at the beginning of the nineteenth century when approximately 80 percent were self-employed to the situation in the mid-twentieth when approximately 80 percent were employees.[20] This shift away from "independent" work is naturally accompanied by decreased work satisfaction as the workers become accessories to the organization and lose control over their activities. In the past, this loss could be mitigated by the development of specialized skills, but the continued mechanization of production involves a reduction of skilled work. Some skills are required by service and administrative workers, but flexibility and "pleasant personality" become more and more important. Even among the managerial or professional groups, there is often indifference to the products they produce or the services which they provide. Increasingly, the motivation for work is based on money, prestige, and power, while there is less emphasis on independence and skill. Fromm concludes, "dissatisfaction, apathy, boredom, lack of joy and happiness, a sense of futility and a vague feeling that life is meaningless, are the unavoidable results of this situation."[21] In fact the questionnaire findings cited by Fromm are less decisive, showing about 85 percent satisfaction from professionals and executives, 64 percent from white-collar workers, and 41 percent from factory workers. However, he justifiably cautions skepticism about such findings, stressing that they might well hide unconscious dissatisfaction, since people will have adjusted to their situation and would be unwilling to admit to themselves that they derive no satisfaction from what they do all day. Many may exhibit their underlying unhappiness with their work through sleeplessness, heavy drinking or other compulsive behavior. Fromm questions how many of the consciously satisfied professionals suffer from nervous tension and fatigue, ulcers, or stress-related high blood pressure.[22] The pressures that such executives face are even greater in the more "flexible" forms of work, which have developed in recent years, with far greater geographical mobility and unpredictable hours eroding the executive's "free" time, as Richard Sennett has described in his recent book *The Corrosion of Character*. The drive necessary for success in the workplace is infused with anxiety and dissatisfaction at the pressures, risks, and occasional failures of flexible working.[23]

Fromm's concept of the marketing character is central to his social psychology, for it marks the biggest development in the social character in the core countries in the world economy in the late twentieth century. Among the middle class, the authoritarian-obsessive hoarding character that began to develop in the sixteenth century and prevailed until the late nineteenth century, becomes blended and then replaced by the marketing character.[24] The marketing character experiences himself or herself as a commodity and considers his or her value not as use value but as exchange value, to use Marx's terminology. The living being becomes a commodity on the "personality market" and success depends on how well they present themselves in terms of disposition and social contacts. Skill and ability are still important, but not sufficient in themselves, and indeed, they are subordinated to the need to project one's saleability.[25] The hierarchical and authoritarian nature of the vast majority of corporate enterprises leads to recruitment and promotion of the same types of people who are deemed suitable to "fit in" with the existing organizational culture. In the absence of democratic processes within the workplace, managerial elites display virtually unlimited power, a "power without control by those submitted to it."[26] In this situation, managements create their own organizational culture and rewards accrue to those who revel in it rather than to those who display a sensitivity to the impact of change on the workforce. "Only in exceptional cases," comments Fromm, "is success predominantly the result of skill and of certain other human qualities like honesty, decency, and integrity."[27]

Fromm goes so far as to suggest that the marketing character avoids "old fashioned" emotions like love and hate, repressing all feelings that interfere with successful functioning according to the logic of the "megamachine" of which they are part. The marketing characters, lacking a deep attachment to themselves and to others, do not care deeply for the social and political problems around them.[28] It might be objected that, now that there is a new emphasis on teamwork in working practices the impersonality of hierarchical "control" systems should disappear. However, the new teamwork succeeds in bringing responsibility for senior management decisions down to each member of the team, so that the imperatives of the management are internalized by the employers. For all the rhetorical emphasis on listening and interaction, the boundaries to honest relations are clear. Sennett notes the lack of depth and hidden coercion behind the teamwork strategy:

> The good team player doesn't whine. Fictions of teamwork, because of their very superficiality of content and focus on the immediate moment, their avoidance of resistance and deflection of confrontation, are thus useful in the exercise of domination.[29]

If work relations were to encompass deeper shared commitments involving trust and loyalty it would require something quite unacceptable to employers, namely, far more time to discuss goals and processes. The compression of time in the execution of tasks is vital for senior management to preserve flexibility and their power to manipulate their "human resources." The pressures of accelerated competition are spread to the workers and the managers often wield power without responsibility.

As well as emotional retardation, Fromm associates the marketing character with the tendency to think only about the functionality of things rather than acquire a deeper understanding of the products with which they deal. He cites evidence from Michael Maccoby's extensive study of American executives to support both points. Maccoby found very few of his 250 top executives to have a strong scientific interest in their work or to place great value in close emotional ties.[30] This data is old but the conclusions are surely not outdated. A more recent example of the preparedness of senior executives to operate in complete ignorance of the scientific content of their products was provided in a radio program concerning the introduction of the new technology of digital broadcasting into Britain. In a forum of 100 executives from the leading firms in the market, the presenter decided to begin by asking someone to give a succinct explanation of the new technology. The first five replies evaded the question and focused instead on the exciting potential application of the technology. The incredulous presenter repeatedly asked for a technical outline and found only one executive able to offer it. What it shows about the pervasiveness of the marketing character is the willingness of the others to expose their ignorance as long as their name and their company were mentioned. The marketing character cares only about the marketability of herself or himself through the marketability of the product; nothing else counts. Interestingly, the ignorance in this case also extended to ignorance of how a new market might develop, and in vastly overestimating demand the service providers suffered substantial financial losses.

Despite the fact that enormous changes have taken place in the structure of the workforce and the nature of work since his death, Fromm's insights are still relevant. Indeed, he anticipates the change of direction capitalism might take in his discussion of the possibility of the emergence of "supercapitalism" in *The Sane Society*. He highlights the work of James Lincoln, head of Lincoln Electric, one of the originators of profit-sharing. In his book *Incentive Management*, he argues that industrialists make a grave error in offering no incentives for their workers to develop themselves or take an interest in their work, for this will hold back productivity or encourage industrial disputes.[31] His solution is based on the assumption "selfishness is the driving force that makes the human race what it is," and involves all individual workers being rewarded with bonuses and penalized according to their contribution to the success of the enterprise. As the bonuses he suggests amount to at least 20 percent of total income, the workers would have a real financial stake in the success of the enterprise.

Fromm comments that the system is not as new as it pretends to be, as it is a glorified form of the piece-work system and all decisions about evaluation and rates of bonus remain firmly in the hand of an autocratic management. But he sees that it is a logical step for corporations to take, as the dissatisfaction of the worker may be overcome "by making him feel that he too is a capitalist, and an active participant in the system."[32] Fromm's assessment of the attractiveness of such schemes for managements has been amply confirmed in practice, although most bonus schemes and performance-related pay packages are not so ambitious except at the highest level. Among the effects of such schemes are the erosion of solidarity among the workforce, for workers competing for incentives will not only maximize their own achievements but may be tempted to devalue the contributions of their fellow workers. The overall culture of the corporation can be enforced through highly subjective appraisal systems. "Success" will fall to the most developed marketing characters, and resistance is rendered very difficult in a system in which, as Fromm says, there is "public pressure to be a wolf with the wolves."[33]

### The Humanization of Work

In setting down the essential elements of a "sane society," Fromm begins with the requirement that people are treated not as a means to another's end but as ends in themselves, "always and without exception."[34] The creative human being is at the center of society and all economic and political activities ought to be in the service of the aim of unfolding the human powers of all citizens. The society would be structured in such a way as to provide no material incentives, as qualities such as greed, exploitativeness, possessiveness, and opportunism will have been condemned as being antisocial. Finally, he specifies the centrality of human solidarity and the importance of productive work:

> A sane society...is one which furthers human solidarity and not only permits, but stimulates, its members to relate themselves to each other lovingly; a sane society furthers the productive activity of everybody in his work, stimulates the unfolding of reason and enables man to give expression to his inner needs in collectives and rituals.[35]

But is this possible in relation to the world of work? Fromm considers two arguments that dissolve the problem of humanizing work. The first is that necessary labor will diminish naturally as a result of automation, and that we need to adjust to doing a much smaller amount of repetitive work and re-focus our lives on our leisure time. Fromm is rightly skeptical that the advance of automated production *will* bring a radical reduction of working time to all workers, but even if it does he suggests that we would still be requiring workers to perform tasks that offer no satisfaction, and discouraging them from developing a more positive attitude to the creative nature of work. He also makes the point that even if automation produced a radical reduction in work time it would take several generations to achieve, and when one considers that advanced capitalist production is not confined to North America and Europe but is spreading to the whole world, it is clear that the problem of excessive working time will be with us for a very long time.[36]

The second argument he deals with is that it is simply impossible to humanize work, given the nature of modern production methods and the context of a highly competitive market. Fromm is unwilling to concede this, and is particularly resistant to the idea that participation in decision-making in work is intrinsically inefficient. His arguments for workers' participation will be considered separately below, but let us note here that he considers this issue of the quality of the work experience as a political one as much as a technical one. There are clearly structural constraints on the humanization of the work process, which would have to be tackled by a political change of direction. In *The Sane Society* he talks in terms of the continued relevance of the goal of communitarian socialism in creating a society in which every working person would be an active and responsible participant, "where work would be attractive and meaningful, where capital would not employ labour, but labour would employ capital."[37] In a different social and economic culture, work which is currently poorly rewarded and carries no prestige, such as waiting at table, could be rewarding because of the social interaction and the knowledge required in advising people. He also contrasts the tasks of a check-out worker at a till with that of the Mexican peasant who sells his goods in the market. Both are engaged in a sales process, but for the former there is little meaningful human contact whereas for the latter the social aspect of market day is as important as a successful return. In a talk on humanistic planning presented in 1968 to the Institute of Management Science in California, Fromm makes it clear that optimum efficiency may be humanly and socially detrimental and that therefore we must prepared to make hard choices between our real ends—"either the maximal unfolding of man or the maximal growth of production and consumption." Fromm has no doubts that it is possible to build an industrial society centered on the full development of human potential, but concedes that this would mean "a radical change in our social structure, in our overall goals, in the priorities of production and in our methods of managing."[38]

Let us now turn to the various suggestions he makes to advance the humanization of work, which, taken together, offer us a picture of a "Frommian" approach to the politics of work. The first concerns his comments on humanistic planning, which clarifies the framework in which the more specific suggestions are made. The second is his support for a Guaranteed Income, and while this is not directly related to employment it has enormous implications for relations between employers and workers. The third area is his promotion of workers' participation schemes, not only in *The Sane Society* but also in a draft manifesto which he wrote for the American Socialist Party in 1960. Finally, there are his ideas on the role of trade unions, which he considered to have immense potential.

*Humanistic Planning*

As we saw in chapter three, Fromm operates with a humanistic ethics that posits human welfare as the sole criterion for social progress and provides a normative framework to guide our choices. Humanistic planning would have to reconcile economic efficiency with what is good for us as rational, loving, and productive beings. The material basis for this has already been reached, for our scientific and technical achievements enable us to visualize the day "when the table will be set for all who want to eat, a day when the human race will form a unified community and no longer live as separate entities."[39] The task is to devise ways of planning the productive system which would move us in the direction of human solidarity. One of the obvious problems is the persistence of national divisions in a competitive world-system. Governments are obliged to work within the framework of global economic competitiveness, and therefore suggestions for human-centered planning and management must conform to the criterion of economic efficiency.

In *The Revolution of Hope*, Fromm insists that the impending significance of computerization poses a vital choice for social planning. Computers should become "a functional part in a life-oriented social system" but they could all too easily become a "cancer which begins to play havoc and eventually kills the system." Computers could assist planning based on optimal human development or they could serve merely to maximize production.[40] Fromm was writing at a time when there was general agreement that good planning was essential for economic success, so it is perhaps understandable that he should envisage a future in which computers could assist in social planning. In the years since his death the emphasis has swung dramatically to market solutions, and computerization has been directed largely toward cost-cutting. Nevertheless, it has also made available information to masses of groups and individuals who are thereby able to participate in the debates about the social consequences of economic and administrative decisions. This is the sort of public involvement that Fromm considered necessary.

The way to adjust planning to humanistic values, according to Fromm, is through more active participation in political decision-making, and by finding ways in which government planning is controlled by those who are going to be directly affected by the plan.[41] Aware that government planning has historically been associated with remote and insensitive bureaucracy, he sees the introduction of more participatory forms of democracy as the only solution. This was a standard view of left-wing socialists at the time. Where planning was highly developed in democratic societies, the key decisions were usually arrived at through three-way negotiations between the political elites and those representing capital and labor. Interests not adequately covered by these elites could effectively be ignored in this system of social-democratic corporatism, which flourished in Sweden and Austria.[42] Only through broadening the consultation processes could this problem be overcome. Decentralization might help, but Fromm does not discuss this. He rejects the arguments that planning should be taken out of the hands of the public bodies and left instead to the private sector. The priority of making profits militated against the projection of humanistic aims, as did the complete absence of democracy within corporations. Fromm suggests instead that corporate planning be subject to controls from government, semi-public agencies, and the public who are going to be affected by the decisions.[43] There was an element of this thinking contained in the Labour Government's introduction of Planning Agreements in 1975, although the scheme was never implemented. Nationalization *per se* did not provide a guarantee that humanistic values would prevail, and he cites the Soviet system as a case in point.[44] The British experience of 1945–1951 is perhaps a more relevant example, for the industries that were nationalized did not adopt schemes for workers' participation and were not coordinated into an overarching national state plan.[45]

Fromm recognized that planning, whether at the level of the state or major enterprise, required bureaucracy. He distinguishes between the "humanistic bureaucratic" and the "alienated bureaucratic" method, but his aversion to the negative connotations attached to the word "bureaucracy" prompts him to refer to "humanistic management."[46] The principal aim has to be a "two way street" of decision-making and response in the planning process so that decisions are transparent, justified, and carry with them consensual support. Fromm dismisses the objection that this process of negotiation is incompatible with the effectiveness required, and points to the consequences of *not* adopting more participatory forms, such as passivity and lack of self-confidence.[47] He supplies no examples of what "agreed planning" might look like, but one example from Sweden in the mid-1980s provides a useful illustration of the feasibility of such a model. "Renewal Funds" were provided by a 10 percent tax on a firm's profits and were available to be used for research and training, but the money could not be spent unless there was negotiated agreement between management and unions, an initiative that gave more meaningful participation in decision-making to the unions than the more common form of seats on the board.[48]

One suggestion that Fromm made for the Manifesto of the American Socialist Party was for an economic commission to assess the overall needs of the economy and formulate a strategy for economic and social development.[49] The commission would consist of representatives of industry, commerce, trade unions, economists, and consumer representatives. This idea for a representative "think-tank" could be extended to other policy areas, and their reports should be widely disseminated as part of a process of civic education. He also suggests the development of publicly owned "yardstick" enterprises to compete with the private sector to force it to raise its standards, and he mentions the fields of broadcasting and film as likely candidates. This idea was popular in some quarters of the British Labour Party in the early 1970s and figured in the Party's 1973 economic program,[50] but like so many left-wing ideas of the period it foundered on the rocks of the international crisis of capitalism.

*Guaranteed Income*
The modern idea of providing all citizens with a basic income unrelated to any work performed was first articulated by Bertrand Russell in 1918 in *Roads to Freedom*, although, as Philippe Van Parijs points out, Tom Paine advocated something similar in 1796 as a compensation for the loss of our collective right to land ownership, which followed from the introduction of private property.[51] Although Fromm uses the term "universal subsistence guarantee," in recent years it has become better known as "basic income." The three main features of basic income are that it is paid to individuals rather than to households, that it is paid irrespective of income from other sources, and that it carries with it no requirement of past or present work performance or the willingness to accept the offer of a job.[52] For Fromm, the attraction of the scheme lies in the fact that it abolishes one of the main obstacles to freedom, the economic threat of impoverishment that forces people to accept working conditions that they would otherwise not accept.[53] Genuine freedom of contract is possible only when both parties are free to accept or reject it. Not only would a guaranteed income constitute the beginning of a real freedom of contract, but it would also "enhance tremendously the sphere of freedom in interpersonal relationships between person and person in daily life."[54] The guaranteed income would mean that people freely choose to work and employers would have to recognize that their workers are genuinely free to leave them. Employers would have to compete to make their work environments more attractive than their rivals, potentially transforming the working environment and putting an end to "no union" despotism. Workers would no longer have to suffer the ignominy of being treated with no respect by bosses.

Those who wished to change occupations in mid-life would be able to engage in the necessary retraining or education. It would have a wider social impact, enabling people to leave social arrangements they felt trapped in through economic necessity to become free to develop their independence.

Fromm deals with two objections to such a scheme. The first is that it would deprive people of the incentive to work. He argues that this is based on the fallacy of the inherent laziness of human nature, and that very few people would choose to do nothing rather than to work. He posits a relatively low guaranteed income, suggesting that the choice to live entirely on that single resource would be deliberately to choose a very frugal way of life. Fromm builds in another safeguard, to limit the income to a period of perhaps two years to avoid fostering a "neurotic attitude" which refuses any kind of social obligation.[55] This danger of developing a dependency culture would be mitigated by the need to make work more attractive. Fromm assumes that once the coercive aspect has been removed from the labor contract there would be not only better working conditions but also a higher level of worker participation in decision-making.

The second objection is to the costs of such a scheme. Fromm's first response is that the extra cost would involve only a marginal increase in the existing welfare budget. While it is true that there would be a considerable saving in the costs of administering the expenditure, it is not clear that the overall increase would be marginal. If the payment to individual recipients is at the level of the payment given to a household in receipt of maximum benefits under the old welfare regime, it is clear that the additional cost would be high. Fromm makes the point that the introduction of a guaranteed income would reduce costs indirectly in areas such as health care and crime-fighting because these were the hidden costs of chronic poverty and boredom.[56] The scheme could be afforded out of public expenditure already available, but this would mean diverting some from the vast amounts of public money devoted to military purposes, and Fromm raises the question of whether there is a will to do so.[57] The obvious problem here is recisely the absence of such a will, either on the part of politicians and political movements or on the part of voters prepared to accept higher levels of taxation.

Fromm returns to the subject of the guaranteed income in the 1960s, when the idea began to be pushed as a real possibility for social policy in the United States. In "The Psychological Aspects of the Guaranteed Income," he not only re-states the arguments originally set down in *The Sane Society* but also comes up with some refinements and qualifications. He suggests that an important addition to the guaranteed income would be the free provision of basic goods such as bread, milk, and vegetables, and perhaps also transport, clothing, and housing.[58] Fromm also shows awareness that the guaranteed income might not bring the liberating results he desires if it were not adopted in conjunction with other changes. The first of these is a change in our habits of consumption. This is discussed at length in chapter six, but here it is important to note Fromm's point that for as long as society as a whole is driven to acquire and consume unlimited quantities of commodities of every description, then those on the minimum guaranteed income would feel "frustrated and worthless" while the others would remain servile in the workplace, fearful of losing their standard of living. Fromm insists that we would have to move over to a commitment to "optimal consumption," and the provision of free public goods and services would be part of such an endeavor.[59] The other conditions required to make a success of the guaranteed income principle are the development of a new spiritual attitude, which he terms humanism, and a renewal of democratic methods, which is discussed in chapter seven.[60] Although these prerequisites appear to be somewhat idealistic, they are, it could be argued, an unavoidable part of the answer to the problem of the steady decline in social capital.[61]

In *The Revolution of Hope*, he argues that while most people are averse to work as long as work amounts to forced labor, their attitudes would be entirely different if coercion and threat were removed. He accepts that a minority of people would prefer a life of study and contemplation, as they did in the Middle Ages, but says that any bureaucratic methods of insisting that someone make "good use" of his or her time would vitiate the whole principle.[62] He repeats his suggestion that the minimal requirements for a "dignified life" be provided not on a cash basis but as free goods and services in areas such as higher education and transportation.[63] In this way, whole areas of socioeconomic life could be decommodified. At that time, there was a strong movement in social democratic circles to extend free goods and services, particularly in transport and leisure services, but since then, of course, the trend has been reversed and the market has been introduced to many sectors which were previously in public provision.

It may seem surprising now that the idea of guaranteed income received active consideration in the United States. A version of it proposed by the Nixon administration in 1972 was narrowly defeated in Congress and another version became part of the program of the unsuccessful Democratic candidate for the Presidency in that year, George McGovern.[64] In 1968 a group of 1200 mainstream economists, led by Paul Samuelson, James Tobin, and J. K. Galbraith, called for a national system of income guarantee, but another advocate of something apparently similar, Milton Friedman, refused to lend his support.[65] The fact that Friedman, a right-wing advocate of radical free-market policies, was associated with the idea of a "negative income tax," gives an indication of why the idea had become a real possibility. Friedman saw it as a substitute for the welfare state, a device whereby unemployment simply ceased to be a problem, and he opposed the proposal by the other economists because it was too generous.[66] A right-wing version would involve the commodification of services such as health and education, and this is one of the reasons why the proposal was popular. As Fromm and Gorz have pointed out, the broad idea itself is not in itself a guarantee of freedom; it becomes progressive in the way outlined above only when combined with other humanistic measures.[67]

The theoretical difficulties of assessing the social impact of basic income are complex, as we shall see when examining Gorz's recent change of position. In the 1980s he supported basic income only if it were tied to the obligation to work, for without the right to work it could simply be used as a smokescreen to hide the issue of poverty and social exclusion. More recently, in *Reclaiming Work*, he has abandoned the link with obligatory work and called for a basic income without conditions.[68] The problem lies in the extent to which a basic income scheme promotes freedom for all individuals and solidarity in society. As Brian Barry has pointed out, if the basic income was low there would be the danger of the creation of a permanent underclass which would be anathema to egalitarians. But if it were high and uncon-ditional, it would seem unfair to those who chose to work hard.[69] However, Barry concedes that an ethical commitment to freedom is likely to provide the strongest foundation for such a scheme, and that is what Fromm's own commitment is based on. Realistically, the level of any such income would have to be lower than the mini-mum wage, as Fromm concedes, and would have to be related to a guaranteed right to work.

### Workers' Participation

As we have seen Fromm was dismissive of human relations management approaches, which sought to extract greater productivity from workers by the introduction of certain emollients to the work experience without conceding any power to the workers. Singing the company anthem should be seen for what it is; the manipulation of the servile. However, he was interested in the work that showed that productivity increased when workers were given a meaningful say in the organization of their work. In particular the famous work conducted by Elton Mayo at the Western Electric Company in Hawthorne, Chicago, in the 1940s illustrated the important difference between the technical and social aspects of work. Over five years various experimental changes in work practices were undertaken. Improvements in working conditions such as rest breaks and a slight reduction in work time brought with them increases in productivity, but the biggest surprise was that productivity continued to improve even when they returned to the initial position.[70] The strong indication was that the mere fact that the workers were consulted about the nature of the experi-ment improved their attitude toward the work, even though the technical aspects of the work remained monotonous. Fromm then cites similar studies that support the argument that participation that enhances the social experience of work helps to compensate for its technical unattractiveness.

Fromm was extremely enthusiastic about experimental forms of ownership and control. In *The Sane Society*, he mentions the Communities of Work which flour-ished in the immediate postwar period in France, Belgium, Switzerland, and Holland, and in particular the example of the Boimondau watch-case factory. Here the workers were brought together to discuss new, nonhierarchical ways of working, and the result was a fully fledged community in which decisions were arrived at democratically and in which reductions in the hours of work enabled them to engage in a wide range of educational, cultural, and recreational activities. There were 28 social sections. One of the important developments from Fromm's point of view was that the workers considered it necessary to formulate a code of ethics broad enough to encompass the views of people from immensely different backgrounds— Catholics, Protestants, atheists, socialists, and liberals.[71] The community published a monthly review, which included reports and lectures, passages quoting warnings by Thomas Aquinas against the power of money, and reviews of plays by Sartre. For Fromm this signified a group of people who had said "yes" to life, with a "maximum of consciousness."[72] He emphasizes that what attracted him to the Communities of Work was the demonstration that people from different ideological backgrounds could work and play together creatively and display economic efficiency.[73] Fromm did not envisage such experiments taking over control of production from major corporations, but they provided practical examples of alternative systems of work organization and some of their practices could be adopted on a wider scale.

The draft proposals for the manifesto of the American Socialist Party offer a more programmatic set of suggestions. He insists that humanistic socialism means the extension of the democratic process into the economic sphere so that control of economic activities is exercised by the participants, including manual and technical workers and administrators. For Fromm, the stress should be on control rather than ownership:

> Humanistic socialism is not primarily concerned with legal ownership, but with social control of the large and powerful industries. Irresponsible control by bureaucratic management representing the profit interest of capital must be replaced by administration acting on behalf of, and controlled by, those who produce and consume.[74]

The general aim should be the introduction of maximum decentralization compatible with the minimum of centralization necessary for efficient production and effective delivery of goods and services. So, unlike some anarchist conceptions of workers' control, it was acknowledged that the autonomy of the enterprise was restricted by central planning and the general subordination of production to democratically agreed social ends. The argument that ownership was not as significant an issue as control was controversial in left-wing circles at that time, for those who dropped their insistence on social ownership were suspected of surrendering to the argument that capitalism had withstood its crises and was now stable and irresistible. Yet, Fromm was merely pointing out that nationalization as such did not deliver socialism to society at large or transform the work experience of the public sector workers—the Soviet Union being the obvious case in point.

Fromm insists on distinguishing between final goals and intermediate goals, and this permits him to consider a range of schemes which might be limited in immediate impact but could light the way for more radical developments in the future. He calls for experiments in different forms of workers' participation and makes a concrete suggestion that 25 percent of the votes on the decision-making boards of large private corporations should be given to workers and employees, freely elected in each enterprise.[75] The traditional response to proposals for workers' participation from the Left in the 1960s and 1970s was to resist them as mere palliatives designed to seduce the workforce into joint responsibility for profit-making without conceding any real power. For example, when the Labour Government in Britain set up the Bullock Committee of Enquiry on Industrial Democracy in Britain in the mid-1970s the majority of trades unions who submitted observations were opposed to anything short of full workers' control.[76] However, Fromm saw advantages arising from workers' participation. The workers would gain experience in the range of concerns facing management, and bring a new perspective to the decision-making process. Many cheap or costless operational improvements could be identified. Workforce representatives would also be in a good position to advise on the likely impact of proposed changes on the workforce and so anticipate and avoid unintended consequences of the negative kind. Participation offers no major challenge to the logic of capitalist accumulation *per se*, but it is one way of achieving a modicum of respect for the workers. It chips away at the alienation of the worker from the product and the process of production and has much wider consequences than simply improving the work experience. Fromm argues that if people are passive in work they will be passive at leisure too, and he comments that work is such a fundamental part of human existence that "only when it ceases to be alienated can leisure time become more productive."[77]

### Trades Unions

Fromm argues in *Escape From Freedom* that the trades union movement is of the "utmost importance" in drawing the workers together and giving them a sense of power. It is a focus of resistance to the power of monopolistic capital.[78] Later in his career, when the new politics of new social movements appeared to be taking many of his concerns forward, he continued to insist that the trades unions had a creative role to play. He recognized their importance in challenging the power of capital at the point of production but he advocated a much wider role for them as well. In *The Sane Society*, he expresses a positive interest in Tannenbaum's suggestion that the unions could buy sufficient shares in an enterprise to eventually control its management.[79] This idea was later adopted by the Swedish labor economist Rudolf Meidner and was eventually introduced, in a somewhat diluted form, as the Wage Earner Funds in 1984. It was perhaps the most radical threat to the principle of the private ownership of corporations ever introduced in a democratic state, but it met with intense opposition from the owners and was withdrawn as the pressures of global competition began to bite.[80]

In his reaction to Tannebaum's initiative, Fromm emphasizes that not much will have changed if the enterprises continue to compete in the same way as under the old system. The workers must always look beyond their immediate "team" to take on the social viewpoint, including the concerns of consumers, environmentalists, poorer-paid workers and the unemployed. According to Fromm, "there is only one truly social orientation, namely the one of solidarity with mankind."[81] He advocates a strengthening of the influence of trades unions, not simply with regards to wage negotiation but also in dealing with problems of working conditions and practices. Issues such as equality of opportunity, respect for persons, flexible hours, child care arrangements, and so on, should be at the center of union activity. He also calls for the furthering of the democratization process within the trades unions.[82]

The return of mass unemployment in the late 1970s, combined with legislative restrictions in some countries, greatly weakened the conventional powers of the trades unions. However, part of the response by the union movement has been to devote more energy and resources to issues surrounding the experience of work, including health and safety issues and major human relations problems such as sexual harassment and bullying. The response of the trades union movement to globalization has run along the lines advocated by Fromm. In the United States, a renewal of grass-roots unionism culminated in the success of the "New Voice" movement in the AFL-CIO,[83] and the involvement of the unions in the radical protest that disrupted the meeting of the World Trade Organization in Seattle in December 1999.[84] This meeting of "old" and "new" social movements—the "Teamsters and Turtles" as it became known—resonates with the Frommian concern for an ethically driven humanistic internationalism. Although it would be foolish to exaggerate the strength of this new alliance, the revival of labor's internationalism is likely to play an important role in the global politics of this century.[85]

## Reclaiming Work

André Gorz is one of Europe's most influential theorists of work, and his "politics of time" puts the issue of the reduction of working hours in the forefront of emancipatory struggle. He shares with Fromm a commitment to the creation of a de-alienated society in which the diverse talents of humanity can flourish, and in which social goals are not dictated by the logic of capitalist accumulation.[86] More particularly, both support the introduction of a guaranteed income as an important step toward achieving a societal change of direction and both regard ownership of the means of production as a secondary rather than a primary concern. However, at least until the publication of *Reclaiming Work* in 1999, Gorz's views on the nature of work were based on radically different premises from those of Fromm, with important consequences for developing strategies to deal with the alienation of the work experience. The appearance of *Reclaiming Work*, however, signals a change in Gorz's position, which brings him closer to the perspective of Fromm. The title of the book was itself surprising, since for much of the previous three decades Gorz had vigorously opposed work as such, and the idea of "reclaiming" it seemed to be ruled out of court. In his 1994 book, *Capitalism, Socialism, Ecology,* Gorz devotes a chapter to refuting an attempt by Oskar Negt to re-state the old socialist argument that the experience of necessary work would have to be transformed along humanist lines if people were to become free. Gorz insists that we must reject the idea that work is the essential factor of socialization and development of the human faculties.[87] This is consistent with his emphasis on liberation *from* work rather than *through* work, first set down in *Farewell to the Working Class* (1980), with the clear implication that work, as heteronomously imposed, necessary work, is something that has to be reduced and limited in scope and influence. Before looking at the similarities between Fromm and the Gorz of *Reclaiming Work*, it is important to examine the theoretical differences between the two approaches and their implications for emancipatory strategy.

For Fromm, work is an element of our human essence which we need to engage with positively if we are to be free. Ideally, we must experience it as our contribution to our individual and social realization. It is therefore necessary to struggle to exert as much control as possible over the work experience, both directly, through social regulation, participation in decision-making processes and cooperative enterprises, and indirectly, through the basic guaranteed income. Gorz, on the other hand, seeks liberation *from* work, and treats the reverence paid to the centrality of work in human life as part of the problem, serving to bind people to the "economic reason" of capitalism. Fromm operates with an inclusive conception of work, denoting all transformative activity, whereas Gorz treats it more narrowly and associates it with the rise of capitalism. Gorz claims that the French word *travail* historically refers not to a productive or creative act "but the activity in so far as it entailed pain, annoyance, and fatigue." What defines work is not so much that it is paid activity but that it is done in the public domain and appears there as a "measurable, exchangeable, and interchangeable performance."[88] As such it is dictated by systemic needs, and takes place in the sphere of *heteronomy*. This is contrasted with "true work" as self-realization, which cannot be done "at work" but exists as free-time activity, which he calls "autonomous activity" or "work for oneself" in the sphere of *autonomy*.[89] For Gorz there is clearly no hope of achieving freedom within the world of work at presently constituted, and the old socialist goal of workers' control is a chimera. The emphasis switches to reducing the hours spent in heteronomous activities and widening the scope and significance of autonomous activities.

The conceptual distinction between heteronomy and autonomy as it applies to the work experience is extremely important for Gorz.[90] The origin of this conceptual distinction has been wrongly attributed to Fromm's close friend Ivan Illich, because in fact it belongs to Fromm.[91] In *Man For Himself* (1947), he describes the psychological process of the replacement of a true sense of self by the experience of the self as the sum total of others' expectations as "the substitution of autonomy by heteronomy."[92] However, Fromm does not apply the distinction to two separate forms of activity, and the danger in doing so is that there is a tendency to dismiss the sphere of heteronomously determined production as beyond reclamation from a humanist point of view. Indeed in *Farewell to the Working Class*, Gorz claims that any power gained by workers in that sphere is bound to be "of a negative and subordinate sort."[93] Fromm, on the other hand, is concerned with humanizing work in whatever context we find it, in a broad struggle to subordinate the system of production to genuine human needs.

In order to show that there is a real possibility of reducing our dependence on heteronomous activity, Gorz argues that structural changes in the labor process are actually undermining work-based society. He also needs to demonstrate that real progress can be seen in the emergence of autonomous activities. So, in the first place he constantly reasserts that the system itself is abolishing work and that work has ceased to be the major factor in defining our identity. Employment has "a much smaller place" in everyone's life than it did in the not so distant past.[94] And in the second place he points to the emergence of a new non-class of postindustrial proletarians who are able to demonstrate a variety of ways of escaping from the patterns of work imposed by the dominant economic logic. Let us examine these claims.

What does Gorz mean when he says that work is abolishing itself, or it has a much smaller place in our lives? The abolition of work could refer to the development of production processes, which are more and more capital intensive. In the richest countries, fewer workers are now employed in blue-collar manufacturing jobs, and if we operate from the definition of a proletarian as a worker who directly produces surplus value, we can see where Gorz finds his title, *Farewell to the Working Class*. However, as Fromm reminds his readers toward the end of *To Have or To Be?*, even though the blue-collar working class may be even more of a minority than it was in the mid-nineteenth century, the vast majority of people are now dependent on the sale of their labor power.[95] Globally, it is the case that there are more people in employment than ever before and the numbers are growing; the idea that the spread of part-time jobs or the reduction of hours in some industries is indicative of the disappearance of work is plainly untrue. The changing nature of work should not be mistaken for the contraction of work *per se*. As "evidence" that paid employment is on the decline, Gorz cites business consultants who predict a large net loss of jobs, but these predictions, made in 1993, have proved false.[96] While it is true that there are fewer "jobs for life" in the modern world economy, the experience of new "non-standard" forms of work often mirrors that of old forms. For example, the call center is symbolic of the enhanced mobility of capital in the era of globalization and is frequently regarded as a new or non-standard form of employment. Yet anyone who has seen King Vidor's 1928 film *The Crowd* will immediately connect the call-center experience to his amazing shot of never-ending rows of clerks at their desks with the supervisors on hand to ensure they are meeting their quotas.

On the question of working time, it is true that in most industries in the "core" of the world economy there have been official reductions in hours worked, but this reduction has not been so dramatic as Gorz suggests. And there are a number of factors working against the trend of reduced hours. For example, the extra time needed for most workers to travel to and from work does not "count" as work time but is nevertheless a heteronomous activity. Furthermore, the number of jobs in which hours are meaningfully counted is decreasing in comparison with task-based jobs involving working very long, uncounted hours, which are necessary if the individual is to succeed in an ultra-competitive internal market. The proliferation of short-term contracts also contributes to the intensified pressure on workers to work longer and harder to justify extensions or win permanent positions. And the pressure of finding a new job once the old contract is finished means that the question of work is more intrusive than ever. The increase in "on call" working also means that although fewer hours may be worked, the worker is at the employer's beck and call for longer periods. If we take a "one world" view of hours, of course, the hours worked in the peripheral and semi-peripheral parts of the world economy are not reducing at all.

When the changes that have taken place in the world of work in the last two decades are taken into consideration, it becomes clear that work could not possibly occupy a "much smaller place" in most people's lives. Even for those thrown out of work, its absence remains central to their lives, with the search for work a necessary condition for their receipt of welfare. The return of mass unemployment gave employers a free hand to impose conditions designed to increase productivity, with employees for the most part powerless to resist the increased intensity of the labor process. The overall picture is one of chronic insecurity, and the contraction of the welfare state and the erosion of pensions add to the pressure to find employment, often late in life. In *Reclaiming Work* Gorz recognizes this problem of the "generalized insecurity," which follows from the "unfettered power of capital" to impose the centrality of work on everyone's lives, but he still insists that work has been eliminated, saved, or abolished at all levels of production throughout the world.[97] His conclusion that this central problem of generalized insecurity will be confronted only when work loses its centrality in everyone's minds is a wholly idealist formulation.

What is left, then, of his claim that work plays a much smaller part in our life? Perhaps he means that we identify less positively with work than we used to, but even this assertion is slippery. Given that the intensity of work has increased, and that there is much greater flexibility over work-time, it is to be expected that more full-time workers say that they would prefer to work part-time. Gorz cites findings that indicate this, and recent studies have confirmed this trend.[98] But complaints about excessive work or the stress of work cannot be taken as a rejection of work as such. Gorz's assertion in *Farewell to the Working Class* that employees regarded work only as a means of earning money[99] is a gross exaggeration, which is simply not borne out by empirical studies. Many people are enthusiastic about the general nature of their work but unhappy about the specific organization of it.[100] But even where there is little enthusiasm for the work activity itself, there is often satisfaction derived from the social aspects of the work experience and from the confirmation of esteem that work gives. This becomes most noticeable when the work suddenly disappears, or when people take early retirement or accept voluntary redundancy and feel bereft at their sudden lack of "usefulness."

Gorz in fact recognizes the importance of the psychological need to fulfill our social obligation, which is why he initially ties in his demand for a guaranteed income with the duty to work and the right to work.[101] He wants income to be independent not of work itself but of work-time. The difficulty of calculating and administering a scheme that ties the guaranteed income to the obligation to work would be immense,[102] and for a number of reasons Gorz drops the condition of the obligation to work from his call for the guaranteed income in *Reclaiming Work*.[103] But the recognition of the social obligation involved in work sits uncomfortably with a dismissive attitude to heteronomous activity, which means that radical action is focused almost exclusively on the reduction of hours rather than tackling the problem of the work experience in people's everyday lives. Gorz is also interested in the development of alternative forms of autonomous activity, such as the Local Exchange Trading Systems, which he extols in *Reclaiming Work*,[104] but they are simply too marginal to bear the weight of Gorz's hope that they can play a major role in transforming society. This becomes clear in the conclusion to his chapter on "Moving Beyond the Wage-Based Society" which is headed "Reverting to the Political" but which unfortunately is bereft of political content.

Nevertheless, the goal of a de-alienated society is always present in the work of Gorz, and in *Reclaiming Work*, he moves closer to Fromm's position on a number of issues. The removal of the obligation to work as a condition for the guaranteed income implicitly accepts that the progressive nature of the scheme would be undermined by having an authoritarian "check" that people are doing their duty.[105] Significantly, in his engagement with the development of postfordism Gorz at last connects with the transformative possibilities of changes in the pattern of work. He is rightly skeptical of the nature of the "flexibility" introduced into labor practices, and his analysis of the "sale of self" involved in the postfordist encouragement of a superficial autonomy for the worker within the wider control of the firm[106] is very close to Fromm's portrayal of the marketing character. When Gorz talks of professional warmth corroding the "art of living," he unwittingly adopts Fromm's vocabulary.[107] When he warns against the cyborg cult as the total victory of capital, he echoes Fromm's revulsion at "cybernetic religion."[108]

Gorz now begins to see the possibility that the "passively suffered" discontinuity of employment and the imposed flexibility of working time might be transformed into opportunities to "choose and self-manage discontinuity and Flexibility," and he cites examples from Germany, France, Holland, and Denmark of practises which open up this possibility.[109] For example, in Denmark a law of 1993 allows for "year off" schemes to be adopted to allow workers timer for self-development, and in Aarhus, Denmark, the refuse collectors organized themselves in such a way as to increase the work force by 25 percent in exchange for shorter hours and reduced pay. The consideration of practical initiatives of this sort is a major step forward in Gorz's work, but it throws into question his previous reluctance to discuss the possibility of humanizing work in the sphere of heteronomy. Gorz, like Fromm, now sees that it is imperative that in order to change society we need to change work, and vice versa, "to change it with a culture of daily life, an art of living, which it would extend and nourish, instead of being cut off from them."[110]

There are other points of sympathy between Fromm's approach and the revised approach adopted by Gorz in *Reclaiming Work*. The contrast between the world of work as it is and as it could be is couched in strikingly similar ways. Gorz plays with a variation of the having/being distinction when he speaks of the fact that we talk of "having" a job rather than "doing" work,[111] and his presentation of the struggle for human freedom as a contest between the power of the living against the dead hand of the system conjures Fromm's distinction between biophilia and necrophilia:

> ...we can either subordinate the apparatus and the social process of production to the power of living activities, or we can enslave those activities the more completely to that apparatus and that process. Behind the question of power over time, it is power *tout court* that is at issue: the distribution of power throughout society, and the direction in which society is to move.[112]

The rhetoric of a "change of direction" is common to them both, and they both posit stark choices, in Gorz's case between "the black hole of non-society and individual meaningless" on the one hand and "new forms of solidarity" on the other, in Fromm's case between "madness" and "robotism" on the one hand and "the birth and self-realisation of humanity" in "brotherliness and solidarity" on the other.[113] Gorz even adopts messianic metaphor when talking about an Exodus out of capitalism that invents its own "promised lands" as it goes along.[114] The final goal is expressed by Gorz in terms of a shift toward relations of cooperation regulated not by the market and money but by "reciprocity and mutuality,"[115] and visualized in terms of a proliferation of cooperatives, Clubs, and societies through which we exercise competitive cooperation and we all pursue excellence.[116] Gorz's late recognition of the potential for advancing the cause of freedom within the world of organized work effectively loosens the strict dichotomy which he had drawn between the spheres of heteronomy and autonomy. In the process, he comes much closer to Fromm's position of the need to transform all forms of work as a prerequisite for the achievement of a de-alienated society.

## Life in Work

Because Fromm insists that productiveness is a quintessential human quality, work is a central issue in his social thought. From this perspective, it is misguided and futile to think of work as merely a means to an end, for to do so would be to consign an activity that is so important to our experience of life to the status of a penance. There are no romantic illusions about the imminence of Fourier's utopian vision of "attractive work" for all here,[117] for Fromm is well aware that the work experience for most workers is tedious or oppressive. For workers in the less developed countries who are taking on more of the basic manufacturing tasks in the world economy, the conditions of work are more like those described so vividly by Marx in the first volume of *Capital* in 1867. Clearly in an age of advanced division of labor the technical problems of overcoming the alienation from the product and process of work are immense, but Fromm is not inclined to circumvent the problem by advocating nothing more than strict limits to the time devoted to unavoidably repetitive tasks.

Fromm considers it of the greatest importance that the experience of work should be satisfying as possible, and in doing so he opens up the scope of what we understand by "politics," for the majority of people have some involvement in discussing the general organization of work or the particular problems that affect them. His call for the humanization of the work experience introduces an ethical dimension to the debates and struggles that affect us all. For Fromm, the experience of cooperation in the workplace can be productive, even within the antagonistic structures of super-capitalism.

The demand for a basic guaranteed income is conceived from a desire to transform the context in which people think of work, whether they are employers or employees. In diminishing the compulsion to work, the onus would be on employers to make work as attractive as possible. In cases were there is scope for the development of creativity in the tasks performed, spontaneity can be encouraged, although in practice the tendency is to minimize it through standardization. Even where tasks are repetitive and undemanding, the social organization of the work can provide opportunities for self-expression. Workers' participation in decision-making is considered essential in developing an active involvement in the organization of the work process. It is resisted by tradition-bound hierarchical managements because it is seen as a threat to their specialized competence, an anti-democratic argument which, if used in the political sphere, would readily be recognized not just as unfair but as inefficient as any dictatorial arrangement. Fromm's work challenges the lack of trust endemic to authoritarian management systems that implicitly operate on the assumption that people will produce better work if they are made more insecure and anxious. His approach demands at least a social partnership approach, an intermediate demand in an economy still driven by the logic of capitalist accumulation. Fromm's long-term goal, like Gorz's, is to reduce the domination of that form of economic rationality and to subordinate it to the fulfillment of human needs. But in the world as it stands, Fromm is sympathetic to all measures that could make the work experience more satisfying. Strong and democratic trades unions play a vital role in this conception, particularly when working for the improvement in the quality of the work experience by ensuring that their members are treated with respect at all times.

# CHAPTER SIX
## CONSUMPTION

In focusing on alienation in the sphere of consumption, Fromm addresses a distinctly modern concern. The dawn of the age of mass consumption can be symbolized by the Model T Ford, which made the motor car available to a mass market, so that by the end of the 1920s, 27 million Americans owned a car. That decade also saw the spread of cinema and radio to millions of people, opening a vast market for advertisers. The potential for social manipulation was apparent to the novelist Aldous Huxley after visiting the United States in the late 1920s, so much so that his dystopia, *Brave New World* (1932), depicts a world of total social control through programming, drugs, and instant gratification.[1] Fromm regarded the book as so prophetic that he devotes five pages to it in *The Sane Society*,[2] which appeared as the United States was experiencing its second phase of mass consumption, with the spread of television and the expansion of cars and consumer durables. It is now commonplace in sociology to consider the ideological impact of patterns of consumption stimulated through the techniques of mass advertising, but Fromm was one of the first to note the potential significance of consumption as a form of social control. In *Escape From Freedom* he bemoans the emergence of what he calls "hypnoid suggestion" through advertising techniques, but, ever the dialectician, he also identifies the nascent consumer movement as a means through which the consumer may restore a capacity for discernment and a sense of significance. The consumer movement, he argues, can play a role equivalent to that of the trade unions in the sphere of production.[3] This was a remarkably prescient observation for 1940, as the first Consumers Union in the United States had been formed only four years earlier by Colston Earne.[4]

The process of consumption in modern capitalist societies is regarded as a major contributory factor to a loss of autonomy, conceptualized by Fromm as the "loss of self," a strong and controversial claim that is examined in the next section of this chapter. Yet despite his assertion that the typically modern person has developed into a *homo consumens* trying to compensate for inner emptiness through voracious and passive consumption,[5] he never regards the manipulation of needs as an irreversible phenomenon. The second section follows some of his suggestions for "sane" consumption, particularly in *The Sane Society* and *The Revolution of Hope*. The pattern of consumption has changed considerably since those books were written, as has the social structure of advanced capitalist societies, but Fromm's major arguments nevertheless still offer relevant insights into the sociological significance of consumption. The third section contrasts his radical humanist perspective with a leading contemporary theorist of postmodern consumption, Zygmunt Bauman, who is typical of those sociologists who tend to view consumerism as an all-embracing and inescapable net. Although Bauman offers some new insights into the development of consumerism, he is less open to the possibility of an effective opposition to the manipulative power of the retail industry. Finally, Fromm's position will be considered in relation to the postmodern argument that modern consumption patterns offer a positive way to express self-identity.

## Consumption and the Loss of Self

Fromm argues that although "modern man" believes himself to be motivated by self-interest, his life is devoted to aims that are not his own. The "self" in question is in fact an alienated self constituted by the social role the individual is obliged to play, a "subjective disguise for the objective social function" of man in an alienated society.[6] In other words, the system of production requires customers to identify strongly with its products and promotes that identity through advertising, but the consumers are convinced that they have made an autonomous decision. Fromm laments a world in which autonomy has been superseded by heteronomy.[7] He illustrates the theoretical possibility of the manipulation of needs by reference to a hypnotic experiment in which the subject is induced to believe that his acquaintance has stolen the subject's nonexistent manuscript.[8] As directed, the subject becomes angry, but the anger the subject feels causes him to supply reasons for the theft, which had not been directly suggested by the hypnotist. In a formal sense these rationalizations are the subject's own invention, but in fact they are a consequence of the initial implantation of the untruth. Furthermore, an outsider walking into the dispute would have no real way of knowing who was telling the truth. This is, of course, an extreme example of manipulation, but Fromm asserts that an equivalent phenomenon is widespread in modern society, and that what pass for genuine mental acts are in fact induced extraneously. Modern advertising methods play a significant role in this manipulation:

> All these methods are essentially irrational; they have nothing to do with the qualities of the merchandise, and they smother and kill the critical capacities of the customer like an opiate or outright hypnosis. They give him a certain satisfaction by their day-dreaming qualities just as movies do, but at the same time they increase his feeling of smallness and powerlessness.[9]

He argues that the suppression of critical thinking starts from early childhood, when the child is persuaded to accept certain statements that contradict his or her real experience, until eventually he or she ceases to notice the discrepancy between claim and reality. Fromm suggests that "pseudo" thinking, feeling, and willing are common, but that as long as there is no discernible force by an outside power we continue to think that we are thinking, feeling, and willing with genuine autonomy; he comments that this is a great illusion.[10]

In what specific ways does consumption contribute to alienation, to loss of self? Interestingly, Fromm begins his discussion of the alienating aspects of consumption in *The Sane Society* by focusing on money itself and endorsing Marx's views on money contained in his early writings.[11] The stress here is on the perverting effects of money, so that a person with no artistic sense may nevertheless buy a beautiful picture and claim to have good taste, or someone who does not read books can buy an expensive library and claim to know good literature. Consumption here substitutes for the exercise of genuine qualities. This lack of appreciation of the product is not confined to conspicuous consumption by the rich but manifests itself in the ignorance concerning where the products come from or how they are made. Consumption becomes a thoughtless process. Why are certain products consumed? The power of advertising means that we buy an image, or, in Fromm's terms, a phantasy, as in the mass consumption of Coca Cola. Despite the fact that the new consumer durables such as cars, televisions, and refrigerators have a genuine use value, what is paramount is the prestige attached to owning them, for these goods confer status. To buy the latest model becomes the dream of everybody, in comparison to which the pleasure in use is secondary. Before the age of mass consumption, the idea of consuming more and better was to give us a happier, more satisfied life, but consumption has changed from being a means to an end into an end in itself.[12] It precludes satisfaction, for, as Fromm argues in *To Have or To Be?*, "I can never be satisfied, because there is no end to my wishes; I must be envious of those who have more and afraid of those who have less."[13] Fromm likens the process of consumption in modern affluent societies to incorporation, the practice of eating things in order to gain their qualities, as in cannibalism. He talks of symbolic incorporation in which the consumer is the eternal suckling crying for the bottle; pathological addictions such as alcoholism, drug dependency, and smoking are only extreme examples. The act of consuming may relieve anxiety but it also requires us to consume ever more, because previous consumption quickly loses its power to satisfy.[14]

If our potential freedom is thwarted in the spheres of production and consumption, is there hope for an autonomous space in the gradual extension of free time? On the contrary, according to Fromm, if we work without a genuine relatedness to what we are doing, and if we consume in an alienated way, then we will be a passive and alienated consumer in our leisure time. Rather than participating in productive and spontaneous activity we tend to "take in" a variety of entertainment and cultural events and items that are determined by industry. Entertainment is an industry like any other, and in buying "fun" our tastes are manipulated so that what we want to see and hear is what we are conditioned to see and hear.[15] In authentic activity, we transform ourselves, we learn and develop; in the alienated form of pleasure nothing is changed within the consumer.[16] In *The Sane Society*, Fromm dwells at some length on a report in *Fortune* magazine from 1953, which describes the social pressure on individuals to conform in a new middle-class settlement in Illinois. The stereotypical norms of the community frown on "odd" intellectual interests such as listening to Mozart or reading Plato and demand instead an easy sociability within very clear and suffocating limits.[17] However, social pressures can be resisted, and people can consume the same objects in radically different ways. Fromm uses the example of reading Balzac, which could be done either critically or as a diversion in which the only pleasure is in knowing the outcome of the plot.[18]

According to Fromm, in both the sphere of production and the sphere of consumption the emphasis is on continuous and limitless acceleration. The vast amounts of money spent on advertising may appear to be a waste of human talent and other resources, but within the logic of the capitalist system it is perfectly rational, for it is necessary to create the demand without which the economy would slide into recession. Nevertheless, advertising, in Fromm's view, constitutes "the most important offensive against the consumer's right to know what he wants."[19] The consumer is encouraged to demand that his or her every desire must be satisfied immediately, and the extension of personal credit makes this possible. Fromm sees the triumph of the "principle of non-frustration" as confirming the dystopian vision of *Brave New World*, in which the children are psychologically conditioned by repeating slogans, one of which is "never put off till tomorrow the fun you can have today."[20] The fun is to be found in consuming, whether it be objects or people, but Fromm suggests that in seeing the world as simply an object to be swallowed, the consumer becomes like a baby at the mother's breast, never becoming weaned, always tied to the receptive orientation, and eternally disappointed.[21] Fromm's strongest denunciation of advertising comes in *To Have or To Be?*, in which he claims that we are not in full control of our minds because "hypnoid" forms of propaganda in both the sphere of commodities and politics amount to a form of brainwashing. He even goes so far as to say that the damage done by advertising is far more serious than the damage done by drug addiction. The bombardment of purely suggestive methods, which pursues us everywhere and at any time, is stultifying and promotes a loss of our sense of reality.[22]

In the craze to consume, driven by economic reason, everything is reduced to monetary value and its worth calculated accordingly. "The whole process of living is experienced analogously to the profitable investment of capital," writes Fromm, arguing that as a result the *quality* of lived experience is reduced to the quantitative calculation of "value for money."[23] In the world of the "having mode" everything is commodified, at least symbolically. Indeed, in the time that has elapsed since Fromm's death, actual commodification has been extended greatly as services previously provided by the public sector have been privatized. But it is the alienating effect on social character that most concerns Fromm. On the one hand, the modern consumer is viewed as essentially passive, as in the receptive orientation, but on the other hand, the consumer is also very active, constantly adjusting to the requirements of the market. However, Fromm regards the "activity" of the marketing character as outward busy-ness which conceals an inner passivity, in the sense that the characters lack a deep attachment to themselves or to others. The marketing characters, according to Fromm, lack goals except those of moving and increasing efficiency, and when asked why they must move and become more efficient, can respond only by referring to the requirements of the system in which they are employed or else to taken-for-granted social expectations.[24] The phenomenon of the marketing character helps to explain why the avid consumers are so little attached to what they buy, for the marketing characters' general lack of attachment extends also to their indifference to the particularity of things:

> What matters is perhaps the prestige or the comfort that things give, but things *per se* have no substance. They are utterly expendable, along with friends or lovers, who are expendable, too, since no deeper tie exists to any of them.[25]

The marketing character in the consumer society displays not reason in the sense of understanding but only "manipulative intelligence" orientated to the achievement of practical purpose, a quality that we share with other animals. Manipulative intelligence without reason is, in Fromm's view, dangerously self-destructive.[26]

There is more than a whiff of the old ascetic in Fromm's condemnation of the culture of consumers in which we passively "drink in" our pleasures. In *The Sane Society* he questions what we can expect from the young generation who have no meaningful, shared artistic experiences and as a result feel impelled to drink alcohol or commit crime, or suffer from neurosis or even insanity.[27] Compulsive consumption compensates for anxiety and evades the difficult responsibility of facing its sources. Even when people know that consuming cigarettes is bad for their health, they continue to smoke rather than forego their escape habit.[28] For Fromm the "trick" of consumerism's suppression of authenticity lies in the feeling of power that it succeeds in conveying to the consumer, the "fake freedom to be the king in the supermarket." Fromm asserts that the consumer develops a sense of potency as the retailers "woo his favour," but essentially there are no meaningful differences between the various products.[29] In fact this view is now rather dated, since the producers have been forced to respond to the radical criticisms of consumer culture which developed during that period by moving toward greater diversity and even customization. The differences between products have been accentuated, and although in many cases the differences may be superficial rather than substantial, there is also a developed consciousness about the advantages and disadvantages of different product designs even in relatively inexpensive items. However, this does not invalidate Fromm's general thesis, and indeed it may well be that the manipulative effect of the whole social package of consumption is even greater when the consumer develops a keen sense of discernment at the expense of a sense of understanding life itself.

It is important to note that although Fromm places a great deal of emphasis on the passivity of the consumer who has plenty of resources, he recognizes that there are millions of people in affluent societies who do not have their basic needs met. For them the effect of the consumer culture is to encourage not simply the legitimate aspiration to a higher standard of living but also a desperation to acquire an ever-increasing quantity of goods.[30] Here Fromm glimpses the danger that atomization may reach even the poorest sections of society, and that the cult of consumption will take the place of social struggles for recognition and respect. Decades on from *The Revolution of Hope* the problem of the "new poverty" riddles the affluent societies, and the attendant problems of crime and violence reflect an anger at the society that seemingly offers everything to everyone—except them.

## Sane Consumption

There are occasions in which Fromm's alternative to the deleterious effects of consumerism appear to be romantic. His appeal to ensure that handicraft production and basic technical skills be taught in schools and his call for the generation of new forms of collective art is reminiscent of the great nineteenth-century English utopian William Morris.[31] Similarly his call for a complete ban on "hypnoid" or suggestive advertising is a long-term goal, and it would be more realistic to suggest specific areas in which the power of the advertisers could be regulated.[32] However, as always with Fromm, the utopian suggestions are present to jolt us into thinking of the possibility of radical change, and they coexist with more immediately realizable suggestions. However, before looking at those suggestions it is vital to understand Fromm's conception of the "self," which needed to be recovered from the consumerist assault. He believes that what passed for happiness in affluent society is the fulfillment of purely subjective needs, irrespective of whether those needs are healthy or conducive to the social good. Fromm's idea of happiness is closer to the Ancient Greek conception of happiness as the fulfillment of those needs "which have an objective validity in terms of the total existence of man and his potentialities."[33] This is, in effect, an endorsement of Aristotle's view that the happy person is "one who is active in accordance with complete virtue, and who is adequately furnished with external goods."[34] Aristotle's term *eudemonia* is often translated as "flourishing" rather than "happiness" in order to differentiate it from the modern popular view of happiness, which in Fromm's view, is delusory. Modern happiness implies a superficial, contented state of satiation, whereas the fullness of human experience involves being active and alert and emotionally open to the richness of life, both its joys and its tragedies.[35]

True happiness, in Fromm's view, is possible only if we achieve a change from alienated consumption into human or "sane" consumption.[36] The old socialist formula of production for use rather than production for profit is inadequate to answer the problem posed by consumerism, since it fails to distinguish between healthy and pathogenic use.[37] But who will make that distinction? Fromm offers a number of possibilities, of which the least convincing is the setting up of a body of experts comprising psychologists, sociologists, economists and consumer representatives who would be able to make authoritative recommendations about what constitutes life-affirming as opposed to life-denying consumption.[38] Such a body would publish studies and make recommendations that may then be adopted through the normal political process, building on existing state agencies such as the U.S. Food and Drug Administration. Although this appears to be a naïve and unrealistic aspiration, it has become increasingly common for professional experts of various sorts to provide invaluable advice in identifying harmful products and educating a wide section of the public about the benefits of healthy consumption. Often this advice has come from disaffected scientists and executives from major corporations who have lent their services to consumer groups and have managed to exert pressure on governments to introduce favorable regulation. However, it may be argued that this pressure is more than counterbalanced by the power exerted on government by the major corporations. In 1968 Fromm thought that a revolution of the consumer against the domination of industry was feasible "unless industry takes control of the state and enforces its right to manipulate the consumer,"[39] but later he perceives the giant corporations' big hold on the government becoming stronger, and he appeals to the American trust-busting tradition to help redress the balance.[40] As long as the influence of the corporations on government remains powerful even an effective consumer movement will not be in a position to challenge the whole pattern of production and consumption and the social–psychological malaise which accompanied it.

The issue of the role of the state in shifting to a "healthier" pattern of consumption is contentious. Herbert Marcuse's analysis of the ideological role of modern consumption in *One Dimensional Man* is very close to Fromm's outlook,[41] but Marcuse could never contemplate the possibility that the state could be used to effect a radical change, operating as he did from the Marxist assumption that the state power was an "engine of class despotism."[42] From this perspective, to imagine that the state could be used positively is to succumb to bourgeois reformism, and this jibe *was* directed at Fromm from many Marxists. However, rejecting the state *in toto* greatly circumscribes effective political action. This produces an analytical paralysis, which, as Roberto Unger warns, leaves us with either a dogmatic commitment to a revolution that is unavailable, or else a timid, defensive reformism.[43] Fromm's discussion of the wider governmental implications of more humane consumption should not be dismissed as naïve idealism but rather as an attempt to encourage us to think more radically about sociopolitical change. In particular he talks about the need for planning production in more sustainable ways, which prefigures much radical environmental thinking, and he also stresses the importance of the public provision of more and more goods, or progressive decommodification. In the years since his death the development of global capitalism has taken us in the opposite direction in both these areas, but the enormity of the problems that have accompanied neoliberal economic policies demands a critical response, and Fromm's observations are a useful starting point for such a response.

Fromm recognizes that the state already plays a limited role in the regulation of what can be produced or advertised. Ideally, he wants to see a situation in which all suggestive advertising is banned and laws are passed restricting the production of harmful products, but he acknowledges that such a situation could occur only if there was a radical change in the democratic process.[44] Nevertheless, there is much that could be done to extend the existing forms of regulation, and much progress has been made in this regard in recent years. The cigarette industry is the most obvious example, and the restrictions placed on it have been accompanied by a widespread educational campaign. However, Fromm recognizes that a movement toward humane consumption would require a protracted educational process in which the government would have to play an important role.[45] While there has been some movement in this direction, particularly in those European states in which Green parties have entered government, the educational effort is overridden by a survivalist commitment to maximize competitiveness in the global economy. As Fromm points out, "the aim of maximal economic growth rate is accepted like a dogma."[46] It appears impossible to escape the logic of maximal growth because if one state (or group of states) were to attempt to apply a zero-growth sustainable economic strategy with strong restrictions on the production of harmful goods such as weapons, cigarettes, or gas-guzzling cars, the resulting capital flight would be disastrous.

On the other hand, the logic of the "limits to growth" argument also appears compelling, warning us that we cannot simply carry on producing in the way that we have been doing because the earth cannot sustain it. Uncharacteristically, Fromm introduces classical political economy into the consideration of this problem, citing at some length John Stuart Mill's argument in favor of a "stationary state" of capital and population in his *Principles of Political Economy*.[47] Mill foresees the possibility of ever-increasing production leaving a world in which nothing is left to the spontaneity of nature and the earth has lost its pleasantness. He concludes that it would be better to decide on an end to economic growth, but adds that this would still leave us free to develop moral, intellectual, and social growth; indeed there would be much more chance of improving the "art of living" if we were not fixated with the art of "getting on."[48] Fromm insists that we have to get back to this principle, and that through a process of social planning (a managed labor market, more egalitarian distribution, redeployment of material resources, etc.) it would be possible to achieve a high standard of living on the basis of reduced income, profit, and consumption.

This appeal for humanistic planning has little to call on for precedent, as Fromm rejects the undemocratic and narrowly productivist model offered by the Soviet Union, and also the highly bureaucratic social democracy pioneered by the British Labour Government following the Second World War. In order to ensure that such planning is sensitive to the real needs of people, Fromm wants to see maximum public participation in project development and implementation, with as much diversity as possible.[49] He maintains his strong opposition to bureaucracy in all its forms in *To Have or To Be?*, commenting "neither the old nor the new bureaucrats can coexist in a system of participatory democracy, for the bureaucratic spirit is incompatible with the spirit of active participation by the individual."[50] He calls on social scientists to devise new forms of large-scale administration, which are more responsive to the changing needs of people. To some extent, there has been progress in the development of more flexible forms of administration, but this has taken place against a background of pressure on the public sector to offer better "value for money." However, despite the triumph of neoliberal deregulation in the 1980s and 1990s, the failure of that neoliberalism has been exposed in the crumbling social fabric of affluent societies and the impoverishment of the less developed world. Now that calls for effective re-regulation of the world economy are being demanded, Fromm's global view that peace for the wealthier part of the world is dependent on the economic advancement of the poorer part sounds remarkably apposite, considering it was made in the mid-1950s:

> Peace and liberty in the Western World cannot, in the long run, coexist with hunger and sickness in Africa and China. Reduction of unnecessary consumption is a must if they want to help the less developed countries, and they must want to help them, if they want peace.[51]

Although the global economic institutions have thus far promoted a "growth at all costs" ideology, the fact that there are such global economic institutions makes it possible to imagine that their remits could be transformed to propel a sustainable development program.[52] Even modest developments, such as the European Union's success in implementing effective environmental measures across states and in conformity with world agreements,[53] indicate the possibility of the sort of humanistic planning that Fromm supported.

Another policy initiative that Fromm considers important in reversing our obsessive consumerism is the suggestion for increased public provision of goods and services. Investment in such goods as public transport, housing, schools, parks, and theaters not only promotes the fulfillment of productive needs but also develops a "sense of solidarity rather than one of personal greed and envy."[54] The argument here is that the decommodification of goods and services that provide life-affirming opportunities would encourage our appreciation of the quality of life and induce a more active and aware consumption. Interestingly, after making this point he introduces his argument in favor of a guaranteed basic income, as discussed in chapter five. Although its relation to consumption is indirect, the linkage is clear. If people are given the means to secure their basic needs without the necessity of work, they may reassess what work they want to do and how much of it, and also think more carefully about their needs. As Fromm points out, it would open up the possibility of retraining and adult education so that people could switch careers and exert a greater measure of control over their lives. The educative effect would help people to become more inquisitive about the social narratives behind the products they consume. This would be education in the original Latin sense of *educare*, meaning to lead out, as opposed to its restricted and restricting sense of inculcation.[55] However, although the increased public provision of goods and basic guaranteed income were being actively considered at the time Fromm was writing about them in the late 1960s and early 1970s, they now look part of a social-democratic agenda whose time has passed. In the past quarter of a century there has been a massive squeeze on public expenditure and a worldwide movement toward the privatization of public services, an agenda vigorously pushed by the World Trade Organization through its General Agreement on Trade in Services. Although these developments present formidable obstacles to a revolution in consumption of the sort desired by Fromm, there are some hopeful developments. There has been a massive increase in participation in higher education in the developed world, and this has been a major factor in the development of what Inglehart has termed "postmaterial" values.[56] This has brought environmental and consumer concerns more firmly on to the political agenda than in Fromm's days of activism, and has witnessed a proliferation of pressure groups that help to counter the strength of the large corporations. And although there has been a reduction in direct state provision of goods and services, there is still an active local politics with greater participation in schemes that have a significant effect on local communities.

The emergence of effective consumer groups constitutes an immense challenge to the power of corporations to manufacture and advertise in damaging ways. In the United States, the champion of sane consumption has been Ralph Nader, who won almost three million votes in the 2000 Presidential election, 2.47 percent of the total, a remarkably high figure for a candidate who had no chance of winning. Nader sprang to fame in 1965 with his exposure of the automobile industry's disregard for safety, which helped to produce a raft of safety regulations and the formation of the National Highway Traffic Safety Administration.[57] There are now multiple organizations and publications campaigning for healthier consumption. Consumer strikes, as proposed by Fromm,[58] have had a dramatic impact. In 1995, when Shell proposed to dump an oil-storage platform in the Atlantic, Greenpeace organized a consumer boycott and sales of Shell petrol fell by 50 percent in Northern Europe, forcing the company to recall the platform and eventually put its parts to useful purpose.[59] Some consumer groups, such as the Multinational Resource Center in the United States and Corporate Watch in the United Kingdom, specialize in monitoring the shady practices of transnational corporations. Others attempt to counter the power of corporate advertising by providing counter information, sometimes with startling success, as in the case of Helen Steel and Dave Morris, who were prosecuted by McDonald's corporation for alleged libel after distributing leaflets claiming that the products were unhealthy, relied on cruelty to animals, and that company exploited its workforce and damaged the environment. The longest trial in British history found in favor of the corporation on some issues and against them on others, but McDonald's suffered very badly from the publicity, which exposed them as corporate bullies.[60] The worldwide success of Naomi Klein's book *No Logo* reflects a massive mobilization of consumers against the power of multinational corporations, using an array of imaginative methods:

> Ethical shareholders, culture jammers, street reclaimers, McUnion organizers, human rights hacktivists, school-logo fighters and Internet corporate watchdogs are at the early stages of demanding a citizen-centred alternative to the international rule of the brands.[61]

She emphasizes the emergence of a resistance, "both high-tech and grassroots, both focused and fragmented," that is as global in its reach and as capable of coordinated action as the multinational corporations it opposes. What is notable about this movement of resistance is its strong and explicit ethical content, which epitomizes Fromm's ideal of a radical humanist commitment to sane consumption.

## Bauman's Irresistible Consumerism

Much has changed in the spheres of production and consumption in the years since Fromm was commenting on their social psychological aspects, but have those changes invalidated his central argument that modern capitalism is deeply alienated? A useful comparison can be made with the eminent British based sociologist Zygmunt Bauman, who deals with consumerism in two recent books, *Work, Consumerism and the New Poor* (1998) and *Society Under Siege* (2002). There are some clear similarities with Fromm's understanding of consumerism and also useful additional points that help to account for changes in consumption patterns in the developed world in the past two decades. Ultimately, however, Bauman neglects the positive side of the dialectic of human freedom that Fromm always insisted on.

Bauman argues that in this age which might be called late modernity or post-modernity, society "engages its members *primarily* in their capacity as consumers," whereas in the past it had engaged them primarily as producers; although the difference is one of emphasis it is so deep and ubiquitous that it fully justifies the epithet "consumer society."[62] The extent to which the developed states have moved away from producer-intensive economies is illustrated by the sharp fall in the proportion of people employed in industry between 1970 and 1994—from 28 percent to 16 percent in the United States and from 30 percent to 20 percent in the European Union.[63] Just as the producer society had to prepare people for their role as workers by instilling discipline, routine, and the limitation of choice, people now have to be prepared for their role as consumers. Now what is needed is the absence of routine and a readiness for constant choice, and, from the viewpoint of economic reason, the instant satisfaction of desires that are shallow and ephemeral. The ideal is best achieved "if the consumers cannot hold their attention nor focus their desire on any object for long; if they are impatient, impetuous, and restive, and above all easily excitable and equally susceptible to losing interest."[64] Like Fromm, Bauman considers it is essential for the smooth-running of the consumer society that, despite the fact that the consumers are compelled by internalized pressure, they nevertheless consider their consumption to be "a free exercise of will." The market may groom them into being unable to ignore its temptations, but on each visit to the market they feel in command of the process because they have the power to choose one brand rather than another, and through this, forge a sense of self-identity.[65] Bauman qualifies this by stating that in fact we need to speak of identities in the plural, as the consumer discards and loses identities and adopts others, all of which remain incomplete and conditional. Indeed, he concludes, very much in the spirit of Fromm, that the term "identity" appears to have lost its usefulness—"more and more often concerns with social placement are fed by the fear of an identification too tough and stiff to be revoked if need be."[66] Although modern consumption is conducted conspicuously, in the cathedral-like shopping malls, the act of consumption is essentially an individual, solitary, and lonely activity; we choose with others but each choice restates and reconfirms our individuality.[67]

Although Bauman shares Fromm's concerns about the effects of built-in obsolescence and the ephemeral and volatile nature of modern consumption, he places much greater emphasis on the volatility and impermanence of the lived experience of consumerism. He argues that the needs that are being met in the consumer society are not "solid" or enduring, like the genuine material needs of people who have few possessions and who value them. Needs are replaced by desires that are insatiable and ultimately narcissistic,[68] and this distinction is fully in line with Fromm's separation of the necessary from the desirable.[69] Bauman goes one step further and endorses Harvey Ferguson's argument that desires have been discarded and replaced by an addictive "wishing," where purchases are made capriciously with a dream-like quality and "nothing underlies the immediacy of the wish."[70] Referring to Freud's theory that the pleasure principle was always reigned back by the reality principle and therefore always at odds with it, Bauman argues that the pleasure principle is now completely liberated and at the service of the reality principle. Consumer society has achieved a feat never before contemplated, the reconciliation of the two principles by "putting the thief in charge of the treasure chest."[71] Bauman observes that there is no deep and longer-lasting satisfaction to the moments we live, that everything is quick and impermanent, and that society is unstable and erratic.[72] Like Fromm, Bauman is convinced that modern consumption involves an addictive dependence on the market, which involves people constantly failing to face the real challenges of life itself. Consumption in the postmodernist age is an evasion; all problems have an easy answer in the market place, and yet these easy answers are provided in a world of increased uncertainty and anxiety.[73] The certainties of jobs for life and secure pensions disappear, but the ability to consume is a consolation as well as a reflection of a shifting, impermanent culture. We cannot think about the things we cannot control, but we can exert choice as consumers:

> Modernity has discovered that the condition of volatility which results in the perpetual insecurity of actors may be made into the most reliable of pattern-maintaining conditions.[74]

Indeed the condition of generalized anxiety directly contributes to the onward march of consumerism, as products are thrust at us that promise to protect us from harm while at the same time fueling our fears.[75]

One significant way in which Bauman takes his analysis further than Fromm is in associating the consumer society with institutional erosion. We noted above that Fromm saw the state as having a role to play in wresting power from the major corporations, through the public provision of more and more goods, the regulation of what was permissible to produce and advertise, and, ultimately, through human-istic planning. Yet in the years since his death there has been, in a number of areas, a "rolling back" of the state, and Bauman associates this directly with the develop-ment of the consumer society. The sort of normative regulation embodied by the welfare state is now considered "dysfunctional" for a prosperous consumer society, and a consensus develops around lowering taxes to give more freedom to the consumer, who has more money to make more choices. The "consumer spirit" rejects all regulation, all attempts to limit choice, and Bauman claims that a society of consumers is resentful of all legal restrictions imposed on freedom of choice and resolutely opposed to legal restriction on potential objects of consumption. There is, he states, widespread support for most "deregulatory" measures, and he even goes so far as to say that in the United States approval has been given to reducing social serv-ices if it goes hand in hand with lowering taxes.[76] Bauman is right to see the close connection between the attack on the welfare state and the acceleration of those features of consumerism first identified by Fromm. The move toward the commod-ification of everything, including water, education, and health care, makes the task of moving closer to sane consumption even more difficult, and the fact that some consumers favor lower taxes at the expense of good social services may indicate a shift to greater individualization. But here, I suggest, Bauman exaggerates the grip of consumerism.

In an article responding to an earlier piece by Bauman on the irresistible attrac-tion of the consumer society, Conrad Lodziak argues that the influence of consumer culture has been exaggerated and that most of what is consumed "can best be explained in terms of practical responses to contemporary living conditions rather than cultural factors."[77] Lodziak points to a number of life-satisfaction studies that show that once basic needs have been met most people give priority to "non-commodifiable" values such as family relationship, love, and friendship. The evidence suggests that the attractions of consumption are trivial and important only to a minority of people.[78] Lodziak also expresses deep skepticism about the claim that majority of people in affluent societies create and recreate their identities through the act of consumption.[79] For the majority of people, most acts of consump-tion are rational responses to the changes confronting them, and it is an exaggeration to make the generalized claim that the people are complicit in the curtailment of their freedom by their compulsive consumption of products that are surplus to their real needs. Rather it is "institutional consumption," by industries, businesses, shops, government departments, and so on that is largely responsible for the manipulation of needs and for wasteful and damaging production.[80] Lodziak's argument is a powerful corrective to Bauman's tendency to portray certain trends as forming part of an inescapable condition, which is so diffuse that we can neither locate its power centers nor hope to control it anymore. In Bauman's metaphorizing discourse, society moves from a "solid" to "liquid" condition, with a new emphasis on speed and acceleration as its principle strategies.[81] While there is a sprinkling of hope in Bauman's work, it is by no means "dialectical" in the sense that Fromm insisted on in *Escape From Freedom*. Lodziak's critique of the ideology of consumerism perhaps bends the stick too far the other way, in underestimating the extent to which the consumer society requires and reproduces the marketing character, but, like Fromm, he finds a place for resistance. Bauman, on the hand, does not see resistance; there is no mention of *No Logo* in *Society Under Siege*.

There is, however, another aspect of consumerism in which Bauman throws new light, and that is its impact on the "new poor." Although Fromm addressed the position of people who were in a condition in which their basic material needs were not being met, he could not have expected, writing in the mid-1970s, that the poor would get poorer and that there would be relatively more of them. Bauman, quoting Lynn Karoly, an economist of the Rand corporation, states that in the United States in the 20 years up to 1996 the total income of the 20 percent most poor American families fell by 21 percent, while the total income of the 20 percent richest rose by 22 percent.[82] He also points to the fact that in Britain, the most neoliberal state in Europe during the 1980s and 1990s, the poorest 20 percent are able to buy less than their counterparts anywhere else in the affluent world, while the richest 20 percent are among the richest in the world.[83] In pre-Modern Europe, the poor had a unique role, their suffering being seen as repentance for original sin, and their presence serving as a reason to practise charity and thereby gain salvation. Under industrial capitalism, the poor became the reserve army of unemployed who could better themselves by the adoption of the work ethic.[84] But when it became apparent that even those who worked regularly were impoverished, the institutions of the welfare state developed to offer a new form of security. Now, Bauman argues, for the first time in history "the poor are now purely and simply a worry and a nuisance."[85] They are not really needed in the work force, and in a society that addresses people primarily as consumers they are "flawed consumers," condemned to lick their wounds in solitude or in gangs of other "nuisances," with no hope that society can help them. The question of poverty turns into the question of law and order; the poor threaten social stability and inhabit a dark world of mean streets, drugs, theft, and violence. The "usual suspects" are rounded up and the poor become redefined as criminals.[86] The jails fill up and new jails are built; indeed this becomes one of the major expanded areas of institutional consumption, as, in the United States alone, there are two million prisoners.

Bauman is short on solutions and far less open to see the ideas and movements that can resist the negative tendencies he depicts. However, he does focus on one idea for resolving poverty that was championed by Fromm, namely, the basic guaranteed income. Endorsing a version suggested by Claus Offe, Bauman notes its essentially conservative nature. By this, he means that it seeks to preserve ethical values and social arrangements that have graced Western civilization against the assault on welfare and equality. Bauman also calls for the decoupling of work from the labor market, so that all contributions to communal life are recognized equally, whether paid or unpaid employment, and he appeals for the work ethic to be replaced by an ethic of workmanship.[87] These sentiments at least offer a glimpse of a radical humanist alternative, but for the most part, Bauman limits himself to developing a better understanding of today's society rather than identifying the ideas and social forces that may open up new possibilities as well as the weaknesses of the social forces that uphold the *status quo*.

In *Society Under Siege*, he offers two reasons for the continued importance of sociological study. First, he asserts that the present condition of "liquid modernity" offers a "perpetual fluidity of shapes" that therefore offers "a standing invitation to human ingenuity and good will." The problem here is that his analysis indicates precisely the opposite conclusion, that no social forces are capable of generating the collective will and strength to move us forward to something better. This idea of "something better" constitutes his second reason for the importance of sociological study, namely, that the only "settlement" possible is the humanity's reconciliation with its own incorrigible diversity. He argues for the urgent need to "reforge the human diversity that is our shared fate into a vocation of human solidarity."[88] The vision here is identical to Fromm's, and even the language is similar, but without the concrete analysis of real alternatives Bauman's hopes fall into Fromm's category of a "dreaming" utopianism.[89] In his final chapter Bauman comments on the redundancy of old forms of utopian vision modeled on More's original *Utopia* (1516). They had a fixity, a confident prescriptiveness and a view of collectively achieved happiness, which has no chance of purchase in a world in which happiness has become a private affair and a matter for the here and now. The modern equivalents to the "solid" utopias, he suggests, are linked to mobility, not to a space, and they are about "speed and acceleration."[90] In Fromm's terms, this is not so much a utopian vision as a surrender to egotism. Nor is it justified by the apparent irresistibility of neoliberal forces, for there is an increasingly articulate and sporadically effective resistance, at a variety of levels including the global. Fromm could never be accused of starry-eyed optimism, but he was sufficiently realistic to recognize that there remains a spirited resistance to the pressures that produce the marketing character.

## "Branding" Ourselves

Fromm recognizes the seriousness of obsessive consumerism, but unlike Bauman he believes that we are not helpless to resist it. What Fromm could never have accepted, however, is the postmodern view that celebrates consumption as a positive expression of self-identity. This argument, presented by James Twitchell in *Lead us Into Temptation*, denies that there are any such things as "false needs."[91] Certainly it is true that for many people in affluent societies, the consumption of goods has become an indicator of our social identity, but for Fromm this was an ineffably sad development. It is true that most acts of consumption are perfectly rational choices taken to improve the quality of life of the purchaser, but there is also the phenomenon of buying primarily to impress or outdo others. Here the goods confer status and that status is derived primarily through the illusion of exclusivity projected by the manufacturers through the techniques of mass advertising.

This has important implications for the individual consumer and for society as a whole. First, we need to ask how "free" the consumer is when buying, for example, an item with a designer label. In most cases, the consumer has no awareness of the "story" behind the item, that is to say, the conditions under which it was produced, the marketing and advertising that has gone into making it desirable. So, in this formally free exchange there is a completely asymmetric power relationship between the buyer and producer. The "conditioning" that the consumer is subjected to from childhood is reminiscent of Huxley's *Brave New World*, with television advertisements being directed at three-year-old children in order to encourage them to pressurize their parents into purchasing toys. Such a process, where it to take place in any other sphere of social life apart from the "free" market, would be readily recognized as propaganda or brainwashing. Next, we need to ask what sort of identity is being bought when the purchase is motivated primarily by the desire to impress or outdo others. What is sought may be understood as the assertion of self-identity, but in fact the identity has been created by Gucci or Rolex or whatever firm is concerned. So much so, indeed, that in the United States, children are now being named after brands such as Chanel and Armani.[92] The "self" here is a self that conforms to an image of exclusivity created extraneously; it means, essentially, conforming to the requirements of a "cool" group. Unlike traditional forms of exclusive and excluding consciousness, such as nationalism and racism, the group is constantly shifting and in process of redefinition, but this process has very little to do with the consumer. Flared trousers for young women do not come back into fashion because of mass petitions and demonstrations by deprived potential consumers.

There is also an element of fear involved in the process, namely, the fear of ostracism if the consumer's taste does not fit in with the dominant, prescribed taste. Wearing flared trousers when they are not in fashion or even to have the "wrong" haircut is to court derision. Again, this sort of competitive pressure is now commonplace in childhood in affluent societies. The "self" in the self-identity achieved through consumption is therefore not an authentic self at all, and from a virtue ethics perspective there is no virtue in it. There are a number of "vices" stoked up by the process, such as envy and false pride, whereby the consumer is proud not of something he or she has achieved but of what his or her money has bought. Are such needs, then, "false"? Clearly not in the sense that they are really felt, but that is a trivial point. In psychoanalytical terms, there is a range of neuroses that provide "answers" to deep-seated problems, but these are precisely "false" answers which need to be revealed as such for damage to be avoided. The "no false needs" argument is as unconvincing as the idea that alcoholics drink just to celebrate the wonder of life.

In social terms, the role of consumption in fostering the marketing character encourages a competitiveness that is wholly lacking in creativity or productiveness. Furthermore, in its fulfillment of economic "rationality" it contributes to social "irrationality" by fueling growth that the planet will not be able to sustain. The pressure to consume encourages the development of a society geared to perpetually responding to market signals. Combined with the competitive pressures in the world of work in the age of super-capitalism, people's lives are filled with the busy-ness of responding to stimuli over which they have little control. They are simply too busy to think about the conditions under which the goods they buy are produced, and, in any event, such issues do not appear on the agenda of the popular media.

So there is, in Fromm's perspective, a real problem in modern patterns of consumption. His concern is captured rather chillingly in the 1998 film *The Truman*

*Show*, in which the eponymous hero spends his entire life unaware that he has been adopted at birth by a media corporation and is living in a community of actors for a constantly running "reality" television show.[93] The director disclaims moral responsibility for the lie that is Truman's life by observing that "we accept the reality of the world with which we are presented." Happily, Truman discovers the truth and opts to face the real "reality," and, even if such an outcome is rather contrived it chimes nicely with Fromm's appeal to resist the manipulative power of the corporations. As in the case of his approach to work, his consideration of consumption widens the scope of what we understand as "political." Even individually we can and do act against unhealthy consumption by changing what we buy, being explicit about why we act in that way, and advising others about the implications of our choices. In the past, consumer movements have scored major victories against corporations on a range of issues since the car-safety issue highlighted by Ralph Nader in the 1960s. Movements for ethical consumption play an important role in educating people about the social effects of the operation of the global market. In encouraging people to think about the conditions under which the goods on sale are produced they help to develop compassion and point to a wider solidarity. They expose forces that are utterly indifferent to the well-being of people, and in doing so they bring into public debate a range of issues that the corporations would much prefer to remain "private."

# CHAPTER SEVEN
## DEMOCRACY

Democracy, for Fromm, is the framework within which social freedom could develop, or, rather, it *ought* to be. Democracy, in his view, is a system that creates "the economic, political, and cultural conditions for the full development of the individual."[1] However, as a democratic socialist he wants to see the deepening of democracy in the political sphere and the extension of the democratic principle to the economic sphere, thereby ensuring that the "secret rule" of those who exert economic power is replaced by a more transparent and responsive form of self-government. Although political democracy is a tremendous step forward in human freedom from authoritarian forms of rule, he is convinced that it needs to be enriched and extended by greater participation. His central criticism of the nature of existing democracy is that it does not live up to its promise of giving real power to people. It is dominated by elites competing for endorsement by a largely uninformed and passive electorate. He wants to recover the potential inherent in the democratic ideal by exploring ways in which democracy can be extended and revivified, making bureaucracy serve people rather than control them. The first section of this chapter concentrates on his criticisms of political democracy, while the second focuses on his suggestions for institutional reform. The third will examines analysis of "old" political movements, which have tried and failed to carry forward the goal of human solidarity, as well as the implications for present-day political practice. The fourth section compares Fromm's approach to that of Roberto Unger in *Democracy Realized* (1998), whose ideas for "democratic experimentalism" roll out a radical humanist agenda in a highly sophisticated and imaginative way. Finally, there is a consideration of how social forces may develop to turn the sort of democratic renovation promoted by Fromm and Unger into a real possibility.

## The Critique of Existing Democracy

In *Escape From Freedom*, Fromm argues that we cannot afford to lose basic democratic achievements such as universal franchise and guaranteed citizen rights, and that the more recent principle of social responsibility for the welfare of all its members should be strengthened and extended.[2] Fromm's first decade in the United States saw him witness President Roosevelt's "New Deal" program, pulling the country out of economic depression and representing the high point of American social liberalism. However, for Fromm this was not enough to overcome the material and spiritual problems that he perceived. His preceding analysis of the social character in capitalist society led him to conclude that despite the veneer of optimism and initiative, most people were overcome by a sense of powerlessness in the face of the irrational and planless nature of society. His immediate answer was to call for the extension of democracy to the economic sphere to curb the power of the propertied elite. As long as modern political democracy restricts itself to the purely political sphere, it "cannot sufficiently counteract the results of the economic insignificance of the average individual."[3] However, socialization of the means of production alone was no guarantee that people would be genuinely empowered, as the example of the Soviet Union showed. He restates a central contradiction bequeathed by Marx; on the one hand a planned economy requires centralization and a highly developed bureaucracy, but on the other the active control and cooperation by each individual requires radical decentralization. A resolution of this contradiction could be achieved only with a radical, "bottom up" democracy and will happen only if "we clearly recognize the necessity of doing so and if we have faith in the people, in their capacity to take care of their real interests as human beings."[4] He argues that victory over all forms of authoritarianism will occur only if democracy takes the offensive and society subordinates the economic machine to the purposes of human happiness.

This vision may seem unrealistically utopian, but it is important to recall that it is premised on his hopes for a defeat of fascism and a renewal of socialist ideas. At the end of the Second World War there was a wave of hope and a great many political programs, in Europe at least, which embraced similar ambitions. Millions fleetingly glimpsed the possibility of the socialization of democracy and the democratization of communism. The United Nations, founded in 1948, appeared to seal the permanence of the world community's commitment to social security with Article 40 of the *Declaration of Human Rights*. In practice, of course, there was no democratic reform of communism and although the social-democratic parties gained support in many parts of Western Europe their radical drive seemed exhausted by the establishment of the welfare state and in practice they reached an accommodation with the capitalist mixed economy.[5] From a left-wing perspective, the situation in the United States worsened dramatically when Harry Truman became President following the death of Roosevelt in 1945, with the onset of the Cold War giving rise to a virulent anticommunism, which tainted the entire "old Left" of the country with the accusation that its activities were un-American.

It was during these years of McCarthyite anticommunism that Fromm researched and wrote *The Sane Society* (1955), in which he draws on the influential account of modern democracy provided by the economist Joseph Schumpeter in *Capitalism, Socialism and Democracy*, originally published in 1942.[6] Schumpeter laid bare the illusions inherent in what he termed the "classical" model of democracy, questioning the idea that the common good is realized by the people deciding issues through the election of representatives charged with realizing the will of the people.[7] Not only is there no consensus on what might be the common good, says Schumpeter, but also the idea that "the people" really decide issues is entirely fictional. Schumpeter portrays the average citizen as completely uninterested and uninformed about political issues, dropping down to a lower level of mental performance when entering the political sphere. The citizen's ignorance is such that he talks in a way that he would readily recognize as infantile within the sphere of his "real" interests, and he becomes "a primitive" again.[8] Developing what became known as the "competitive model of democracy,"[9] he draws a picture of elites competing for people's votes in the way that corporations compete for sales, with great importance given to advertising and image-making at the expense of detailed consideration of the choices available. Advertising, through repeated assertion, is an "attack on the subconscious," which undermines rational thinking.[10] Furthermore, just as the great corporations dominate the market, the established parties dominate the political scene, thereby limiting the degree to which the agenda can be altered either from popular movements or smaller parties. Fromm extends the analogy to include the acquiescence of stockholders who are not interested in the management of the corporation as long as the financial returns are adequate. He recognizes that there is *some* relationship between what voters think and political outcomes, but he argues that this relationship is very tenuous and it is hardly surprising that people feel a deep sense of powerlessness in political matters.[11]

Fromm argues that democracy cannot work effectively in an alienated society, and the processes of representative democracy actually serve to strengthen that alienation.[12] Democracy should involve free individuals expressing their convictions and their free will, but alienated people express prejudices rather than convictions, and their likes and dislikes do not amount to the expression of an autonomous will. Manipulated by powerful propaganda machines using modern advertising techniques, the voters are poorly informed and regard political issues as irrelevant to their daily lives. However, Fromm, having witnessed three crushing electoral victories by Roosevelt, recognizes that political choices are not entirely irrational, and takes this to be a "sign of resilience and basic sanity." There is a tension here in Fromm's picture of a society that is fundamentally alienated but which also displays the potential for informed political participation. According to Fromm the majority voting system adds to the process of "abstractification and alienation," simplifying choices between options selected by the political elites and discouraging participation outside of elections. The elections themselves take on the character of a plebiscite, registering general approval or disapproval at decisions or policies that are made without consultation.[13] Both Fromm and Schumpeter tend to ignore the role played by pressure groups in involving citizens in the policy-forming process, and this could be a crucial element in resting political initiative away from the political oligarchy. This aspect of democratic politics was emphasized in the 1950s by the American political scientists David Truman and later Robert Dahl.[14] In fact Fromm does mention the importance of pressure groups in *Escape From Freedom*, but fails to relate their significance to the overall political process. Although the pluralist approach of Truman and Dahl was intended to refute the rather pessimistic picture supplied by Schumpeter, its argument that power is diffused throughout society conveniently overlooked the fact that in pressure politics those with economic power are normally able to exert decisive political power.

Whereas Schumpeter considered that the weak form of democracy that he identified was the best available mechanism for choosing a government, Fromm was looking to replenish the ideal of classical democracy, and he identifies the process of bureaucratization as the enemy of self-government. The bureaucratic impulse reduces the people to be administered to objects and leaves them in the hands of people who are supposed to apply the rules rather than have feelings.[15] In a speech written for Eugene McCarthy, the radical Democratic candidate for the Presidency of the United States in 1968, Fromm reiterates this attack on the bureaucratic method, arguing that it deprives individuals of all sense of initiative and makes them feel that they could achieve nothing without the planning and organization of the bureaucrats. Somewhat vaguely, he calls for a new bureaucratic procedure, which would enable people to control the bureaucrats, thereby releasing new energies.[16] He considers the alienated bureaucratic method to have a number of features. It is a one-way system with orders streaming down from above, impersonal to the extent that people becomes "cases." It is also irresponsible, in the sense that it does not respond to individual needs or views, but also in the sense that the individual bureaucrat acts only within the prescribed rules and, when confronted by an awkward case, will merely pass the case on to another bureaucrat. Fromm concludes that the alienated bureaucratic method "creates a deep sense of impotence."[17]

## Transforming the Political Process

Fromm's concrete suggestions about how to combat political quiescence now appear to be overoptimistic, but in the late 1960s there was an energetic movement for renewing democracy by increasing participation and improving accountability, particularly in the workplace. Fromm's ideas on democratic renewal were first set down in *The Sane Society*, a decade before the resurgent interest in participatory democracy. Their radicalism is remarkable when the context is considered, for the public face of America in the years of the Eisenhower Presidency was one of superconfidence in the strength of American democracy and its leading role in defense of the Free World.

In order to overcome the passivity that accompanied the simple majority voting system, Fromm suggests the initiation of a network of "face-to-face groups" of approximately 500 citizens to discuss local and national political issues and convey their findings to the state and federal legislatures in order to shape their agendas.[18] The information required to inform their monthly discussions could be supplied by a "cultural agency" independent of government. The results of the votes of these groups could be conveyed to the legislatures using modern technology, presumably public service television. Fromm's defense of the feasibility of such a system is not unreasonable. If we think about subsequent developments in information technology we can see how it might work. The Open University in Britain has shown over the past three decades how complex information, responses, and feedback can operate successfully. The development of computerization eases greatly the technological problems, and Fromm goes on to identify its potential for facilitating democratic planning in *The Revolution of Hope* in 1968.[19]

There are, however, major problems in his ideas for stimulating participation. Fromm models the groups on the Town Meetings that took place in the infancy of the United States and which constituted the framework for local democracy and also welfare provision.[20] However, this spontaneous form of democratic life occurred in a context of nation-building by a population of largely independent means, when cooperation was an urgent need and a strong sense of egalitarianism prevailed. According to Fromm's own analysis, the perceived needs of the people were now to do with money, status, and consumer goods. Like many participatory democrats, he seems to assume that once the citizens had a taste of real democracy they would clamor to take advantage of their new rights, but without some material incentive this seems unduly optimistic. There is, then, the problem of which political force could introduce such a radical innovation, one that would threaten the power of existing political elites and prove a nuisance to corporate interests. In practice instead of face-to-face groups, we now have selected "focus groups" that are used by political parties to test their policies, in the same way that corporations use them to test products. But in this case there is no presumption of an informed opinion, constructive debate, or power from below. The process of consultation blurs into a process of wider manipulation.

The schemes for democratic renewal and humanistic planning are developed in much greater detail in *Revolution of Hope*, written at the height of 1960s radicalism after Fromm had spent more than a decade in energetic political action. Three types of organization are envisaged in an attempt to revivify American political culture and reorientate it toward humanistic ideals. The National Council of the Voice of the American Conscience, consisting about 50 people "whose integrity and capability are unquestioned," is designed to promote the humanization of technological society.[21] It would be tasked with clarifying issues, showing real possibilities and alternatives, recommending solutions, and responding to other bodies such as political parties, and to criticisms of their own statements. Although there would be no formal link with government, Fromm argues that the impact of the findings of such an egregious body would be considerable.[22] The suggestion here is effectively for a humanist "think tank," but Fromm greatly overestimates the difficulty in obtaining consensus on social issues, which, after all, tend to become "issues" precisely because there is no consensus. For example, one issue he mentions is the Vietnam War, but the battle lines within American society were already clearly drawn and expert opinions were not in short supply. In addition, the idea of having a separate organization to act as the "conscience" of a vast country is problematic. Not only is its elitism at odds with his desire for a "bottom up" democracy, but it implies that one body of people can remedy the failings of all the other elites. Fromm is vague as to how the members of the National Council might be selected, although on a brief questionnaire issued with the book he calls for nominations, and presumably a small number of the most popular choices could then select the rest so that a representative section of interests could be included. In fact the response to the questionnaire was extremely disappointing; by the end of March 1970 fewer than 3,000 had been received, and only Fromm himself and Senator McCarthy received substantial support.[23]

For all that Fromm's project is over-ambitious and unrealistic in its specified form, a number of expert bodies with a humanist orientation have produced influential reports on a number of issues, particularly in the field of managing globalization. For example, The Brandt Commission on North–South global relations had an enormous impact in generating discussion about the crisis of underdevelopment.[24] Similarly the Brundtland Report, *Our Common Future*, played a significant role in prompting political elites to think urgently about the need for sustainable development.[25] More recently, the American-based World Order Models Project helped to set up an international Global Civilization Initiative, which, after a number of workshops around the world, produced a report written by Richard Falk, *On Humane Governance*, that not only reached a wide readership but also generated concrete suggestions for achieving social justice and democratization, which have contributed to the emerging debates and protests over the "management" of world affairs.[26] Indeed the normative project outlined in the conclusion to that book is distinctly Frommian in nature and is far more radical than that of Commission on Global Governance, whose 28 members were nearly all former Ministers or top bureaucrats.[27]

The original idea of "face-to-face" groups is amended in *The Revolution of Hope* and "Clubs" are suggested instead, comprising between 1,000 and 300 citizens. Fromm notes the desirability of having a mix of classes and ages but recognizes that this may not be possible, in which case he recommends cooperation between groups of different social composition.[28] He advocates weekly meetings in a permanent meeting place, which would also be social center and a forum for cultural life with movies being shown and discussions of books, music, and art. The main business would be to exchange information on the issues of the day, discuss them fully and, when a consensus was found, plan for the dissemination of the ideas. They should also discuss relevant practical work, which might include participating in local or national political campaigns. Indeed, the spontaneous movement that flourished around Eugene McCarthy's 1968 Presidential campaign reflected many of the features that Fromm was advocating. However, Fromm suggests two prohibitions. First, the Clubs should be free from all bureaucratic procedure, and second, they should avoid any permanent political affiliation. The Clubs would have a humanistic philosophy incompatible with the ideologies of existing political parties, and their scope would be greater:

> Their function would be not simply to inform people, but to demonstrate new ideas as they appeared in the flesh, as it were, of many groups of people, and thus to influence other people more effectively than is possible by political concepts. The new movement would be a cultural movement, aiming at the transformation of persons and of our whole culture.[29]

However, the Clubs would not be indifferent to politics but rather seek to transform the nature of what it is to be political, "to encourage a new spirit in politics."[30] He hoped that these Clubs could form the basis for a mass movement, and his determination to do what he could to encourage it can be seen by his insertion of the postcard asking for positive responses. It may seem to today's reader as hopelessly idealistic, but it was written at a time of high politicization when groups were spontaneously developing. For the most part their *raison d'être* was to protest particular issues, such as the War, racial discrimination, the oppression of women, the degradation of the environment, or the manipulation of the consumer. Fromm's idea of large, well-organized groups forming around a broad humanistic disposition did not materialize, but new social movements did, with an explicit appeal for society to change its values.

Fromm also advocates smaller "Groups" of about 25 people, which would be sufficiently intimate to challenge the mores of alienated life, freeing themselves from old divisive cultural attachments and openly aiming for personal change and development. Such groups would practise a "philosophy of the love of life" and "speak a new language," which cuts through obscurity and inhibiting conventions.[31] However, in reply to his questionnaire supplied with every copy of *Revolution of Hope*, only just over a 1,000 respondents said they would be prepared to serve in Clubs or Groups, and due to the low level of response Fromm concluded that neither the National Council nor the Clubs or Groups were feasible at that time.[32]

When Richard Nixon was elected President in 1968, Fromm retreated from political activity. Although apparently becoming more pessimistic in the 1970s about the possibility of moving toward a sane society,[33] he maintained his theoretical commitment to the development of non-bureaucratic participatory democracy and humanistic socialism. In *To Have or to Be?*, he revives the idea of the "face to face groups," rejecting the idea that opinion polls constitute an adequate substitute for informed opinion based on participation and discussion.[34] He insists that decentralization in politics (and economics) is a prerequisite for a humanistic society, and reasserted his hostility to the tendency of bureaucratic management to treat people as though they were things.[35] He also revives the idea of the Voice of the American Conscience, now re-named the Supreme Cultural Council. This was to be a body of leading intellectuals and artists who would offer information and advice to the government and politicians, and also to citizens. In fact, Fromm envisages one of its major roles as supervising the work of a properly funded independent public service media.[36] *To Have or To Be?* is a summary text that outlines his basic arguments developed in the preceding years in accessible language, with a deliberately inspirational tone. Its widespread popularity made it an important resource for new, "alternative" forms of radical politics, particularly in Germany and Italy. However, in general, by this time the radicalism of the late 1960s and early 1970s had lost a great deal of its energy. What had gone wrong with the old movements of the Left, and what were the prospects for new emancipatory movements?

### Old Socialism, New Humanism

Fromm's most sustained discussion of the nature of the politics that might move us toward a de-alienated society occurs in *The Sane Society*. Fromm here reasserts his adherence to socialism as the only theory that has historically offered the prospect of a world living in peace without exploitation or oppression:

> It has, even after 1914, been the rallying moral idea for millions of European workers and intellectuals, an expression of their hope for the liberation of man, for the establishment of new moral values, for the realisation of human solidarity.[37]

However, Fromm is highly critical of the major socialist movements of the twentieth century and some of the ideas that fired them. In his view, democratic socialism must return to the human aspects of the social problem, criticizing capitalism for what it does to people and offering a vision of socialism, which stresses the ending of alienation and subservience to the economy and the state.[38]

Although he freely acknowledges his debt to Marx throughout his writings, it is clear from the discussion in *The Sane Society* that he considers Marxism in its various forms to have been flawed. He admires the contributions of the social anarchists, specifying Fourier, Proudhon, Bakunin, Kropotkin, and Landauer. He is impressed with their attempts to insert an overtly ethical aspect into their social theory, in particular Proudhon and his moral maxims of self-respect and respect for one's neighbor.[39] He also endorses the anarchists' consistent determination to resist the power of the state. It might be argued that the anarchists were limited because they lacked the analytical sophistication of Marx, but this is not the point. Rather the point is that with the historic victory of Marxism within the socialist movement many of the ethical and anti-authoritarian elements of the rich anarchist tradition were marginalized. Fromm draws on the work of the British "guild socialist" G. D. Cole in order to flesh out the ideal of communitarian socialism, with an emphasis on the extension of liberty through self-government in work and in society in general. The guiding vision is emancipation from enslavement rather than the purely economic goal of a higher standard of living.[40]

Fromm's appreciation of Marx's contribution is tempered by important reservations. He enthuses over Marx's conception of human potential and human freedom, and argues that for Marx economic development was never an end in itself but rather a means to the self-realization of all individuals.[41] He notes the ambivalent attitude of Marx and Engels to centralization and state power. He claims that although they shared with the anarchists the commitment to the abolition of the state, which they defined as an instrument of class rule, they offered few insights into how this would be achieved. Indeed the focus on the necessity of seizing state power and defending it, and the need for a central authority to plan the economy seemed to infer a strong statist orientation, as Bakunin pointed out to Marx and his followers.[42] The emphasis on the need to seize the state power produced, in Fromm's view, an exaggerated concentration on political power and force at the cost of neglecting the social prerequisites for emancipation.[43] Fromm endorses the greatness of Marx's theory of historical materialism but laments Marxism's inability and unwillingness to extend it and apply it imaginatively, relying instead on repeating its formulas as "sterile dogmatism."[44] Moreover, he accuses Marx of a romantic idealization of the working class, a result of a purely theoretical scheme rather than of "an observation of the human reality" of the class. Marx was guilty of a "profound psychological error" in asserting that the workers had nothing to lose but their chains, for they had also to lose "all those irrational needs and satisfactions, which were originated while they were wearing their chains."[45] This is, of course, precisely the area in which Fromm tries to shed light with the help of psychoanalytical knowledge.

According to Fromm, Marx makes three fundamental errors. The first is his neglect of the moral factor in man, of the need for the liberators of mankind to develop that liberation in their own lives. The second is the overoptimism in anticipating the success of the socialist project, which produced an impetuosity that was to have disastrous consequences. The third error is the belief that the socialization of the means of production is a necessary *and* sufficient condition for the transformation of capitalism into socialism.[46] The first two criticisms are powerful ones, the third is somewhat dubious. Fromm had already quoted Marx's severe criticisms of vulgar communism, which treated the annulment of private property as the simple solution to all problems.[47] It is also clear that Marx's conception of human freedom entailed a radical democratic society, and as far back as the 1848 *Manifesto of the Communist Party* Marx and Engels had proclaimed that the task of the working class to "win the battle for democracy."[48] However, Fromm clearly considers that Marx places insufficient stress on the importance of retaining democratic institutions and the necessity of a transformation of consciousness among working people. This lacuna allowed Lenin to act undemocratically in the hope that the radical democracy could follow the seizure of power. For Fromm, the theoretical and political errors of Marx and Engels opened the way for "the destruction of socialism which began with Lenin."[49]

Fromm views the work of Stalin and his epigones as a thorough perversion of the idea of socialism, but unlike many other humanist socialists he holds Lenin fundamentally responsible for creating the standpoint that produced it. He argues that the idea of the vanguard party of professional revolutionaries, articulated by Lenin at the beginning of the century, demonstrates a lack of faith in the spontaneous action of the workers and peasants, and this lack of faith flowed from the fact that "*he had no faith in men.*"[50] As we saw in the introduction, Fromm considers that it was Rosa Luxemburg who identified the dangers of this trend most clearly, seeing bureaucratism as the antithesis of social democracy and spelling out the dangers of vanguardism to her Russian comrades.[51] Not only were Stalinist methods of repression more brutal than the Czarist ones, but also they were so complete that they precluded the emergence of effective opposition or even individual dissent. Even before the emergence of full political democracy in the West, new ideas and movements—Fromm cites Chartism in Britain—had been able to organize and protest against their exclusion and oppression, but this was not permitted in the Soviet Union.[52] In terms of the exploitation of the worker, Fromm likens Stalinism to the early exploitative stages of capitalism in the West, with obsessional striving for industrial advance, ruthless disregard for the individual, and greed for personal power as its mainsprings.[53] In his view, the decisive difference between the West and the Soviet world is that in the West there is freedom to express criticisms of the existing system, whereas in the Soviet system, such criticism is suppressed with brutal force. For Fromm, the West is moving in the direction of Huxley's *Brave New World* and the East *is* Orwell's *1984*; he adds, somewhat enigmatically, that both systems tend to converge.[54]

Given the uncompromisingly critical stance that Fromm adopted to Bolshevism or Marxism–Leninism, it may seem strange that some have considered him to be a closet Trotskyist. Gershom Scholem first suggested that he had moved to Trotsky's position in 1927,[55] while Burston reports David Riesman as saying that late in life Fromm expressed his admiration for Trotsky.[56] We also know that Fromm maintained a long correspondence with Raya Dunayevskaya, once Trotsky's secretary and leader of the Marxist-Humanist *News and Letters* group in the United States. It is, of course, possible that Fromm did admire Trotsky for his bravery in standing against Stalin and exposing the degradation of Soviet "socialism," and, indeed, for arguing for a genuine soviet democracy. Furthermore, Trotsky was a humanist and fully aware of the need for cultural transformation. However, Trotsky never faltered from his conviction of the need for the vanguard party since his "conversion" in 1917, and he was one of the military leaders who suppressed the Kronstadt mutiny, the act that Fromm identifies as the point at which all hope for progress in the Russian revolution died. Furthermore, the various Trotskyist groups that developed around the world, engaged in the sort of sectarian infighting that Fromm regarded as utterly incompatible with the building of a humanist movement. Fromm was certainly attracted to Trotsky's personality, but in terms of? political outlook he was closer to Rosa Luxemburg.

Luxemburg and Landauer were victims of the suppression of the German and Bavarian revolutions of 1919, and, as the right-wing leadership of the Social-Democratic Party was complicit in the suppression of those movements, those sympathetic to the revolutionary cause held an often bitter hostility to social democracy as a political movement. At one stage, Fromm blames the right-wing of the German Social-Democrats for permitting the rise of Hitler,[57] but in general his approach lacks bitterness and there is a willingness to acknowledge the potential of social democracy and its achievements in securing the welfare state. To reach a stage when the basic physical needs of people could be met was a necessary basis for building a society in which people could fulfill their psychological needs. His attitude to social democracy is therefore a mixture of negative findings and cautious hope. He comments that both communism and social democracy were expressions of deep disillusionment following the overoptimism of the earlier phase of Marxism. The communists in Russia took a "jump of despair," and in concentrating on the seizure of state power and the socialization of the means of production they neglected the social sphere, thereby completely contradicting "the very essence of socialist theory." The consequences of this brought "more frightful results" than the loss of faith suffered by the social democratic parties.[58] Now that we are able to look back on the Bolshevik "experiment" after its demise, it is apparent that Fromm was correct in his assessment of the damage it did for the idea of socialism. The social democratic loss of faith often led to "the acceptance of nationalism, to the abandonment of a genuine socialist vision, and of any radical criticism of capitalistic society." Within a few years of the publication of *The Sane Society*, both the German Social-Democrats and the British Labour Party moderated their old socialist programs to indicate their long-term acceptance of capitalism. So, for Fromm, social democracy tended to mean higher wages for the workers at the expense of the loss of its "messianic pathos, its appeal to the deepest longings and needs of man."[59]

For Fromm, the old socialist emphasis on the ownership of the means of production had led to a neglect of the bigger question of providing a happier and more just existence for the mass of the people. "The principal point here," he argues, "is not ownership of the means of production, but participation in management and decision-making."[60] This naturally drew criticism from Marxists, but it would be a mistake to think that Fromm considered the question of ownership irrelevant. In those passages where he calls for an emphasis on co-management rather than nationalization he is at pains to point out that a certain amount of state intervention and socialization is necessary.[61] In *To Have or to Be?* he reiterates "what matters is the power to direct production, not ownership of capital," but this is still a very radical demand. He insists on the drastic restriction of the right of stockholders and the management of corporations to determine production solely on the basis of profit and expansion, and at the same time demands strict control on the nature of advertising to limit its function to imparting information.

Fromm argues that the fundamental choice that we face is not that between communism and capitalism but between *robotism* and humanistic communitarian socialism.[62] The emphasis is on "bonds of brotherliness and solidarity" in which everyone gains a sense of self through the experience of being the true subject of one's powers rather than by conformity, and in which "a system of orientation and devotion exists without man's needing to distort reality and to worship idols."[63] In *To Have or to Be?*, he comments that the experience of the Soviet Union had produced such a corruption of socialism that the terms "socialism" and "communism" had been compromised,[64] but in the conclusion he continues to invoke the goal of "genuine humanistic socialism."[65] The pursuit of this form of socialism also requires a cultural transformation.[66] This would involve a change of direction in education with the emphasis on human development rather than in training for the needs of the economic system, as well as the development of new forms of communal art, through which the population could shed its passivity and create a new social productiveness. Finally, he insists that any movement toward the solidarity of man must be an explicitly ethical movement, devoted to the "spirit of reverence towards life and the solidarity of man." He hopes for the long-term development of a new, humanistic, non-theistic "religion" that would have a universalistic character in keeping with the emerging unification of mankind, embracing the humanistic teachings common to all great world religions, with an emphasis on the practice of life rather than on doctrinal beliefs.[67]

*To Have or To Be?* offers a broad endorsement of what we would now recognize as the politics of new social movements. Fromm sees more than a glimmer of light in the movements protesting ecological degradation, sexism, racism, and the exploitation of the less developed world that were in their infancy when he wrote his book. For all the reverses of the social democratic agenda that have taken place since then, there has been a steady progress in these movements, which have staked out a permanent place in local, national, and global politics. In Europe, in the form of Green and Left Libertarian parties, they regularly secure representation in parliaments and occasionally enter government as coalition partners. It is this kind of movement that carries forward Fromm's radical humanist hopes.

## Democratic Experimentalism

Social and political theory is more often than not extremely circumspect when it comes to the consideration of political practice, but Fromm insists that "insight separated from practice remains ineffective."[68] Convinced of the possibility of the emergence of a "new humankind living in solidarity and peace, free from war and class struggle," he comments that it would require all the energy, intelligence, and enthusiasm that had been expended in achieving the technical utopias of conquering the skies and electronic communication. He enjoins sympathetic readers to produce a multitude of designs and experiments of new social forms in order to "begin to bridge the gap between what is necessary and what is possible."[69] For the most part, however, social and political theory has been much more cautious than Fromm when it comes to predicating democratic paths to emancipation. Recent debate about democracy has been dominated by what is often referred to as the "deliberative" turn, with the emphasis on improving the quality and scope of political decisionmaking so that it overcomes the irrationality induced by manipulative propaganda.[70] Two of the world's best-known social and political theorists, John Rawls and Jürgen Habermas, associated their work with deliberative democracy.[71] However, although there are some radical variations of deliberative democracy, for the most part its advocates remain wedded to a liberal constitutionalist framework and tend to play down the difficulties posed by existing economic relations for democratic revival. However, one theorist whose work elaborates a transformative ambition in a sophisticated and detailed manner is Roberto Mangabeira Unger who, in *Democracy Realized*, articulates a bold program of "democratic experimentalism."[72]

Both Unger and Fromm emphasize the gap between what democracy is and what it ought to be. Fromm once said that democracy today is "consent by the governed, achieved by manipulation," when it ought to be "active participation and responsibility of each citizen in the whole social life."[73] For Unger, ordinary American citizens are likely to feel like angry outsiders "powerless to reshape the collective basis of the collective problems they face."[74] Toward the end of his book he contrasts this with a normative vision of a republic of citizens who become "a nation of prophets, seeking prophetic power in the genius of ordinary men and women" forging a reconciliation between individual self-development and social solidarity.[75] Although Unger does not discuss expressly the ethical postulates of his take on the "is" and the "ought" it is clear that he is operating from a strong humanist perspective. Toward the beginning of his book the language takes on a distinct Frommian tinge, as Unger argues that "our capacity for love and solidarity grows through the strengthening of our ability to recognize and to accept the otherness of other people." Love that is least dependent on idealization or similarity leads to accepting each other as context-transcending beings rather than passive recipients of processes imposed upon us. We are clearly not there yet, but for Unger it is essential that we make ourselves into such beings through the deepening of democracy, and in so doing "democratic experimentalism draws energy and meaning from concerns outreaching politics and economics."[76] So, unlike most radical democratic theorists today who rely entirely on pragmatic arguments, Unger affirms a strong normative foundation for his work, and, like Fromm, this is shown by his emphasis on the importance of character development and the educative aspect of social development.

Unger seeks institutional innovation that can soften the tension between the need to engage in group life and the need for individual self-assertion and self-development, and holds that this is the core of the good of human liberation. Key to this endeavor is the lifting of entrenched divisions, which weigh heavily on social relations.[77] Some of the suggestions for advancing this goal are broadly in line with Fromm's thoughts, particularly his emphasis on a revolution in education and a commitment to continuous education and permanent reskilling.[78] Fromm's insistence on the literal reading of education as "leading out" (*educare*)[79] led him to take a deep interest in A. S. Neill's experimental school at Summerhill in England. Fromm wrote a foreword to Neill's book on the school, praising its emphasis on promoting the happiness, freedom, and independence of its pupils and its rejection of force either by overt or anonymous authority.[80] Similarly Unger prescribes an equally radical departure from the rote-learning, authoritarian and nationalistic aspects of traditional education. He envisions a school that would rescue the child from its family, class, country, historical epoch, giving children the powers "of insight and action and the access to alien experience enabling them to become little prophets," an experience that requires "a large measure of detachment from the dominant culture."[81] Schools, he considers, must break the dependence on sameness and agreement and encourage children to "think differently."[82] He wants schools to give children the instruments to overcome social and historical circumstance and to strengthen the idea of the possible greatness of ordinary men and women and even the "greatness of humanity."[83] At the postschool level, he suggests a scheme of social inheritance, partly financed by heavy taxes on personal inheritance, whereby a social endowment account would enable adults to engage in further and higher education and retraining programs.[84]

There are also points of similarity in some of the economic measures designed to strengthen public participation. Unger lends his support to the idea of a basic guaranteed income, conditioned upon demonstrated willingness to train and work.[85] He also emphasizes the importance of a strengthened public sector, but, like Fromm, is insistent that the central issue is not the public or private ownership of the means of production but that the economy operates for the public good rather than for the private gain of entrenched elites. Unger emphasizes partnerships between the public and private sectors and a much wider dispersal of ownership and profits.[86] However, he recognizes the imbalance that has developed between capital and labor, particularly under the last two decades of neoliberalism, and demands that capital should now have less freedom so that labor may now have *more* freedom.[87] He points out the contrast between the mobility of capital and the restrictions of the mobility of labor, speculating that the one reform that would bring about world revolution today would be the global removal of barriers to labor mobility. In the long term, this could be achieved and it would undermine the conservative nationalism that Unger, like Fromm, considers regressive.[88]

Unger also emphasizes the importance of the unions and their role "beyond economism" in struggling for the dignity of labor and the establishment of fairness in the world of work. Even more radically, Unger deals with the problem that the interests of core workers may be represented by the unions at the expense of nonunionized peripheral workers by suggesting that all members of the workforce and those seeking work must be automatically unionized, thus producing a "more solidaristic union movement."[89] In this way, he posits a strengthening of the social forces in the "middle space" between the macropolitics of institutional change and the micropolitics of personal relations, which would support more effective collaboration and social partnership.[90] A final point of similarity between Fromm and Unger lies in their commitment to combating wasteful consumption. However, Unger does not dwell on the psychological damage of contemporary consumption patterns but rather sees the taxation of consumption as the best way to increase the tax yield (and therefore public expenditure) and restore a measure of control over the economy, which is denied in neoliberal political economy. He suggests that initially a flat rate indirect tax could be imposed, leading later to a direct tax on consumption, which could be steeply progressive (the Kaldor tax).[91] This would clear the way for penalties against socially damaging consumption, following consultation and discussion through whatever new democratic institutions that were developed.

In other respects Unger offers far more detailed and sophisticated suggestions, particularly in respect of economic reform and the legal framework of democratic innovation (at the time of publication Unger held the position of Professor of Law at Harvard University). Crucial to his antidote to neoliberalism is an emphasis on massively raising the amount of savings to strengthen the public sector and create a variety of new economic agents to invest, both public and private and a combination of both.[92] A high level of savings wards off speculative runs on the currency and is preferable in every respect to the old Keynesian dependency on borrowing as well as the neoliberal indifference to saving.[93] Unger argues in some detail that the neoliberal preference for government-induced private spending overestimates its capacity to ward off slumps and underestimates the importance of retaining more economic and political autonomy at the level of the state. It also cuts off new sources of investment funding, which could be operated through new democratically accountable institutions and provide for a more inclusive society. Greater access to investment and production opportunities as well as a great variety of new spending institutions for the provision of public goods are vital to his solidaristic model. The object is to develop the "vanguard" parts of the economy not at the expense of the "rearguard" but in such a way as to bring the two together productively. Old redistributive strategies, both in rich countries (welfare state redistribution) and poorer countries (diffusion of small scale property) have failed to provide the innovation and growth necessary to outweigh the burdens they impose, but innovative, decentralized public investment schemes could do so.[94]

Politically, much of the democratic innovation envisaged by Unger would take place at the level between the existing public institutions and the micropolitics of personal relations, but clearly there would have to be a major change of attitude among existing political parties for such a program to be launched and continually refreshed. There is no one master plan here, as different innovations would be needed according to the specific situations in which "politics" finds itself atrophied. So, an intensification of politics might be achieved by the introduction of proportional representation in those countries in which office is contested by two major parties with small policy differences, as in the United States and Great Britain. However, in other instances a strong, directly elected President may be able to introduce the sweeping changes needed, as, for example, in Brazil. Above all, Unger claims that elements of direct democracy must be brought into representative democracy, and that vetoes provided for by liberal checks and balances should not be permitted to prevent democratic innovation.[95] Political alliances need to reach out to new social alliances, which overcome the conservative defense and assertion of narrowly defined interests and instead emphasize the transformative and solidaristic aspects of refashioned interests.[96] The strength of Unger's text is the pragmatic and persuasive nature of the program; in other words there are schemes that could overcome the ossified divisions of interests in modern societies, both rich and poor. However, we are left to ponder just why the elites in those countries would feel the need to move from their rather comfortable myopia, or how the relatively powerless multitude could find the power to force them to feel that need.

Both Fromm and Unger seek to break an impasse, rejecting not just the *status quo* of capital domination but also the failed alternatives of communism and bureaucratic socialism. There is a sense in which both writers are implicitly directing their comments to the socialists or social democrats of their time. Unger comments that the disillusioned ex-Marxists have become institutionally conservative social democrats. Real change, they know, would be revolutionary, but revolution is not an option and would be too dangerous even if it were so, so we are left to "humanize the inevitable." They threw out the good part of Marxism, the transformative aspirations, to keep its bad part, the historical fatalism, changing its political significance, so that "lack of ideas soon made room for lack of character."[97] The progressive way forward would be to forge a broad popular alliance with a solidaristic political strategy, which roots redistributive claims to a productivist vision.[98] Politics must be made to work, because there is no other way forward. This too was Fromm's conviction. To deny the possibility of change, on the grounds that capitalist power relations would never permit it, is dogmatic and fatalistic. There remains a possibility, no matter how small, that radical humanist politics can emerge out of the mire of constitutional politics. There remains the stubborn problem of identifying the social and political forces that might act as catalysts to this change of direction.

## The Problem of Agency

The central problems of *why* people should mobilize in movements of this sort and *how* they can exert an impact on political and economic decisions remain. In *The Revolution of Hope*, Fromm outlines four conditions for the development of a real possibility for radical social change:

- Widespread dissatisfaction with our way of life;
- The maintenance of a functioning democratic system;
- The emergence of a critical consciousness among significant sections of the middle class;
- The emergence of alternative ideas, which, he argues, are not entirely dependent on the mass media and may be disseminated in the future via "new technical factors."[99]

It may be useful at this point to make some observations on each of these points, in the light of social, economic, and political developments since the book was published in 1968. However, it is important to be clear about the context of these questions. Too often social and political theory assumes that the arena for the developments and changes that need to be considered is "society," without specifying which sort of society and how the scope of social and political action in that society is constrained by its position in the world economy. Fromm clearly had the United States in mind when writing *The Revolution of Hope*, and he had been energized by the breadth of radical support for the presidential candidacy of Eugene McCarthy. Now we have to be more specific when talking about the prospects for radical change, as Unger does in *Democracy Realized* when he shifts his attention between core countries to less developed countries in discussing concrete applications of broad principles.

In terms of general dissatisfaction with our current way of life, there can be little doubt that for the vast majority of people in the less developed countries the quality of life has diminished greatly after two decades of global neoliberal policies. With large proportions of their national product devoted to servicing heavy debts, and International Monetary Fund imposed structural adjustment programs moving them away from self-sufficiency and undermining public provision of basic services such as health, education, and water, the peoples of the less developed world are in no doubt that there has to be radical change in the world system. In the "core" countries of the world economy, the situation is less clear. A few years ago the liberal American economist J. K. Galbraith talked about a "culture of contentment" enjoyed by the majority even as the plight of the poorer sections of the community becomes steadily worse.[100] The alliterative elegance of the phrase gave it a popular, shoulder-shrugging appeal for pessimists, but "contentment" is surely wide of the mark in describing the experiences of the majority of people in the affluent societies. As we saw in chapter five, even the "successful" competitors in the new capitalism suffer from what Richard Sennett describes as the "corrosion of character."[101] The development of what Ulrich Beck calls the risk society in "second modernity" brings with it insecurities, uncertainties, and loss of boundaries for clear majorities in the core states; they are in no way "satisfied" societies.[102]

Fromm's insistence on the continued functioning of the democratic system appears to be so obvious and fundamental that it requires no further remark. However, it brings to our attention the problem of a widening democratic deficit. As we see in chapter eight, as a result of the success of neoliberalism in a globalized world, many important areas of economic policy are effectively dictated by bodies such as the World Trade Organization, which are largely operating in the interests of giant corporations and finance houses. In both the United States and Great Britain, first-past-the-post voting systems ossify the party system because it is virtually impossible for smaller parties to break through into legislature. Millions are left with no effective representation of their concerns, and they either vote for the least unacceptable candidate or stay at home. In Britain, this has resulted in an alarming drop in voter turnout and a situation in which the Prime Minister can take the country to war even though a clear majority of citizens opposed such action. In addition, the huge fortunes spent on electioneering further protect the power held by the "cartel" parties and their corporate sponsors. In the United States, the problems of the electoral system for the election of the President were highlighted spectacularly in 2000 when voting irregularities in Florida turned the state's votes over to George Bush and secured him victory, even though he had a minority of the popular vote. Grassroots participation in party politics is diminishing everywhere, in inverse proportion to the power of major donors. Democracy still functions, but it is weaker than it was when Fromm wrote his book. The introduction of proportional representation systems of voting in all legislatures is a *sine qua non* for the renovation of political democracy.

As for the development of a critical consciousness among the middle class, here we are able to point to the emergence of new social movements since the 1970s and their impact in raising consciousness on a variety of issues such as gender and racial oppression, environmental degradation, consumer rights, and the preservation of peace. More recently, as we see in chapter eight, the development of a global anticapitalist movement has shown the ability of groups to address the issue of the global management of the world economy at the appropriate level, as a global politics begins to emerge. It has to be conceded that the advocates of this new politics are often fragmented and sometimes marginalized within their own polities, but there can be no doubt that they have had a considerable impact on political agendas and have occasionally scored notable successes in moving the old social and political movements to respond to new issues. This is perhaps the most optimistic development when considering Fromm's four conditions.

Finally, on the possibility of circulating radical ideas that give people a hope that significant change may yet be heard, the situation is again unclear. On the one hand, the domination of television by a small number of huge corporations means that the diet of news and information, as well as the ideological content of much mass entertainment, is in conservative hands. On the other, the globalization of news coverage can sometimes help progressive forces in unexpected ways. In the coup of 2002 against Hugo Chavez, the democratically elected left-wing President of Venezuela, the control of the national media by the usurpers was undermined by the availability of satellite reports that there was resistance to the coup, and this was decisive in rallying the democrats and securing the release and restoration of Chavez. Perhaps more significantly, the use of the Internet has produced immensely sophisticated networking by radical groups and the dissemination of ideas has been instant and global.

"Ideas," wrote Fromm, "become powerful only if they appear in the flesh; an idea which does not lead to action by the individual and by groups remains at best a paragraph or a footnote in a book."[103] From where can the motivation come to advance a politics of liberation? The communication of new values through the exemplary actions and theories of the new politics is vital. Inglehart has provided sustained empirical evidence to suggest that the development of this new politics is based on the development of "post-material values,"[104] demonstrating that social and political discourse is not a closed universe. However, to add to the problem of atrophied political systems there is also the problem of the erosion of the autonomous power of nation-states in the age of globalization. In the absence of world government, what possibility is there for the development of radical humanist ideas such as those espoused by Fromm? This is considered in chapter eight.

# CHAPTER EIGHT
## ONE WORLD

The imminent arrival of "one world" was predicted by Fromm in a lecture in 1962 at which he declared that it would be probably the most revolutionary event in the history of mankind.[1] Pointing to the internationalization of production and the innovations in communications as indicators of this emergent globalization, the problem he poses is whether this world will be a place we can live in harmoniously or whether it will end as one great battlefield. His response turns on a dichotomy that he describes between a humanist tradition and a tribalist one. He identifies the humanist tradition with an affirmation of the equality of all people in the world, and quotes Cicero as stating, "you must now conceive of this whole universe as one commonwealth, of which both gods and men are members."[2] According to Fromm, the humanist task is to find a new harmony in life through the development of human powers, to achieve the realization of the essence of humanity. This language of human essence and its realization would have been no less strange to the audience in 1962 than it is today, and Fromm recognizes and laments the evanescence of the humanist tradition. He comments that the essence of man will become important only at a time when the experience of man is alive again.[3]

What does it take to restore the living experience of humanity? For Fromm, it would mean the restoration of human flourishing as the central purpose of our existence, rather than the present fixation with the maximization of economic wealth and the exercise of social and political power over others. He insists that as long as human needs remain subservient to the imperatives of unfettered capitalist economic competition there will be a continual reproduction of the myriad social divisions that have thwarted progress toward the ideal of human solidarity. Ultimately, if this ideal is to stand a chance of making tangible progress, radical change will have to occur at the global level, requiring the benign revision of our programmed national identities. Fromm argues that only when a condition of human solidarity is reached will the contradiction between "universal" and "socially immanent" ethics be resolved. Universal principles such as "thou shalt not kill" or "love thy neighbour as thyself" have endured across space and time, but there are also principles that are specific to particular cultures and even social classes within cultures whose rules need to be adhered to if the social entity is to survive.[4] Ultimately, the tension between the two different types of ethics will be resolved only when we build a global society in which the interest of society as a whole has become identical with that of all its members.

The contradiction between absolute and immanent principles will tend to disappear only if existing society becomes progressively free and human.[5]

In that 1962 lecture, Fromm approvingly quotes the injunction from Leviticus (19: 33), which commands the Israelites to "love the stranger, for you have been strangers in Egypt and hence you know the soul of the stranger."[6] However, he concludes that the tribalist response to the challenge of life, with nationalism as its modern form, appears to have prevailed. In tribalism one has confidence only in the people of your own tribe and feel an obligation only to those who speak the same language, sing the same songs, and eat the same food. The stranger is treated with suspicion, a potential scapegoat for the failings of the members of the tribe. Modern nationalism poses, for Fromm, the greatest obstacle to the emergence of a harmonious one world. It becomes clear that the dichotomy between humanism and nationalism is at the heart of the question as to whether progress can be made toward the goal of human solidarity. This is what is examined in the rest of this chapter, with the next section focusing on Fromm's strong anti-nationalist standpoint and some of his suggestions for an internationalist alternative. The second section relates this to more recent debates in the area of "liberal nationalism" involving Yael Tamir, David Miller, and Stephen Nathanson. The final section looks at the relevance of Fromm's appeal for international human solidarity in the light of developments since his death in 1980.

## Fromm's Antinationalism

As we saw in chapter one, Fromm's revulsion against nationalism originated in his experience as a teenage boy in Germany during the First World War. It was then that he realized that millions were being slaughtered for no good reason other than the irrational thirst of political elites for national selfglorification.[7] In *The Sane Society* he concedes that most people obtain their sense of identity from belonging to a nation rather than from belonging to our global species. As a result, he claims, objectivity is warped and the stranger is judged by different criteria than fellow "clan" members. Fromm sees nationalism as an "incestuous fixation," which poisons the relationships not only of the individual to the stranger but also to members of the clan and to himself/herself; the person who is still in thrall to ties of blood and soil is not yet fully born, as the capacity for love and reason is crippled. Fromm, having lived through the rise of the Nazis and the hysteria of the McCarthyite "un-American activities" witch-hunts, leaves the reader in no doubt about his opposition to nationalism:

> Nationalism is our form of incest, is our idolatry, is our insanity. "Patriotism" is its cult. It should hardly be necessary to say that by 'patriotism' I mean that attitude which puts . . . nation above humanity, above the principles of truth and justice; not the loving interest in one's own nation, which is the concern with the nation's spiritual as much as with its material welfare—never with its power over other nations.[8]

He goes on to assert that love for one's country that is not part of one's love for humanity is not love at all, but idolatrous worship. However, it is important to note the qualification in his antinationalist position, for he allows for a love of one's country that extols the "local" manifestations of social and cultural practices which are valued universally but expressed in different ways. He recognizes the validity of an emotional attachment to the culture and tradition of one's community, for if we did not have that feeling for the particular forms in which we celebrate our living together it would be difficult to develop the active interest in other cultures that is necessary if human solidarity is to be developed. However, while most versions of liberal nationalism would like to make a similar distinction between nationalist supremacism and active community affiliation, none go so far as Fromm in his condemnation of nationalist sentiment.

Let us look more closely at the graphic way in which Fromm expresses his deep suspicion of nationalism. As a psychologist he is struck by the power of the emotional attraction of nationalism and its irrational basis. He points out that the rage felt by patriots when a person is deemed to have betrayed his or her patriotic duty is at the level of an uncontrollable deep-seated indignation of the sort that is not experienced in any other situation.[9] In Fromm's view, nationalism offers a feeling of security that is unnatural, for the free person is, of necessity, insecure, and the psychic task that people should set for themselves is not to feel secure but to be able to tolerate insecurity "without panic and undue fear."[10] In psychological terms, regression to the incestuous fixation of nationalism can be reversed only through the development of love and reason toward the goal of "human solidarity and justice," a new form of rootedness that will transform the world into a truly human home.[11] Later in the chapter we discuss whether there are grounds for thinking that progress might be made toward this ideal, but for now we concentrate on Fromm's analysis of the pathology of nationalism.

Fromm recognizes that the development of strong groups has played a vital role in the evolution of humankind, and that the survival of the group depends to some extent on the strong sense of identity of the members and their willingness to place the collective above themselves. This "group narcissism" can be benign or malign. In the case of the former the group sets out to achieve something creative and leaves behind the "closed circle of group solipsism" in the act of focusing on the external goal. It becomes malign when the focus is on conquest or the constant symbolic reiteration of the superiority of the nation.[12] This distinction is useful because it allows for a differentiation between a nationalist resistance to the oppression exerted by a more powerful state, when the goal of national political autonomy may be a justifiable remedy to historic injustice, and great-power nationalism of an aggressive or suppressive character. This is not to say that one form of nationalism is good and another bad, but simply that political movements seeking national independence may have a just cause, a cause that could be justified in non-nationalistic terms.[13] In the case of aggressive nationalism, he argues that prejudices are deliberately inflamed by political elites when the state lacks the means (or political will) to provide adequately for the majority of its members; instead it provides them with narcissistic pride that compensates for their economic and cultural poverty.[14] In practice, both forms of group narcissism are blended, and Fromm is suspicious of them all.

He wants to expose the prevalence and danger of the irrational outpourings of nationalist rhetoric that are part of everyday discourse. He asks us to consider a person who claims that his family is the most admirable in the world, the only clean, intelligent, good, and decent one. Most would consider such a person crude, unbalanced, or insane, but when a fanatical speaker addresses a mass audience and substitutes the nation or race for "family" he will be praised for his love of country by those within the group.[15] Although Fromm clearly has the image of Hitler in mind here, the point can be extended beyond the obvious cases of demagogy to the mainstream of liberal democratic politics. As long as the politician is addressing an audience within a particular state it is quite normal that the rhetoric will slide into nationalist banalities such as "making our country great again" or "drawing on our finest traditions," or even puerile playground claims that "our" armed forces are the greatest in the world. It passes virtually unnoticed because an unconscious consensus has developed whereby the innate superiority of the nation is built into everyday discourse. National identities are historically constructed in such a way that they buttress the power of socioeconomic elites of each nation-state, resting on myths that frequently have no rational basis.

Political groups of the extreme Right display an aggressive nationalism that is not an aberration from a more tolerant and benign patriotic political culture. Rather it feeds on a deeply embedded cult of patriotism that has been propagandized in all the major liberal-constitutional states for the past 200 years. This tribal mentality has been described by the British social psychologist Michael Billig as "banal nationalism," in which he argues that the rhetoric of nationalism is constantly reinforced in linguistic iteration, through the use of words like "we," "this," and "here."[16] Given the virtually uncontested inculcation of national symbols, myths, and the rhetoric of assumed community in the areas of education, information, and entertainment, and in their ubiquity through flags, anthems, honors, and public discourse, what is surprising is that so many people in fact identify themselves in ways other than by nationality. Nationalism, adopted by many in the nineteenth and twentieth century as an ideology based on principles such as the right of self-determination, is now transformed into what Pierre Bourdieu has termed *doxa*,[17] a disposition adopted without conscious choice, which exerts a powerful social control over its recipients.

Worship of the nation is, for Fromm, a form of idolatry, and the struggle to free ourselves from the worship of this false God is at the same time the fight against narcissism. The full maturity of humanity is achieved by complete emergence from narcissism, both in its individual and group forms. In cases of individual narcissism the individual will normally have some doubts about his or her personal image, but in cases of group narcissism there is no space for doubt to enter, since the narcissism is shared and reinforced by the majority and becomes one of the most important sources of human aggression.[18] Fromm identifies a sharp discrepancy between our intellectual development, with its tremendous scientific and technological advances, and our emotional development, which has left us in a state of marked narcissism with all its "pathological symptoms."[19] Perhaps the most serious pathology is that which Fromm terms "incestuous fixation" in which the subject cannot overcome the tie to the mother figure.[20] This leads to impairment of judgment, for if mother cannot be wrong how can we judge any person or movement or state that is in conflict with "mother" or is disapproved of by her.[21] The second most important pathological trait associated with incestuous fixation is the failure to experience another human being as fully human, for only those within the nation command respect and the stranger is despised. But if we recognize humanity only in that "crippled form" in which it is shared with fellow nationals then we become strangers to our selves and our capacity to love is impaired or destroyed. Finally, if we remain tied to the mother image of the tribe or nation we are unable to develop independence and integrity, for it is possible to realize our true selves only if we are open to the world and free from all forms of incestuous fixation. Fromm accepts that the tendency to remain bound to our primal ties is inherent, but it is constantly in conflict with the opposite tendency to progress and to grow, and the latter is the progressive and healthy path. We must choose the latter and transcend the group narcissism that is nationalism if we are to move closer to the goal of human solidarity.

Fromm poses the question, "is there any hope that narcissistic madness will not lead to the destruction of man before he has had a chance to become fully human?" At an abstract level he identifies the need for an alternative, radical humanist, object of devotion. Fully aware of the power of what Freud termed the "narcissistic core" within humanity, he suggests two ways in which we could move toward a benign narcissism without reducing the narcissistic energy in each person. The first is that the object of narcissism be changed to that of mankind, the entire human family, so that the creativity of the species is celebrated and shared. The second is a feature common to all benign narcissism, namely the development of an emphasis on achievement, through common goals for the eradication of hunger and disease and for the dissemination of knowledge and culture.[22] However distant these possibilities may appear, Fromm considers that the advancement of the philosophical idea of the equality of all human beings enables us at least to post these goals on the global political agenda of the future.

Is it possible to advance the cosmopolitan ideal at a more concrete level? In *The Heart of Man* Fromm offers some hopeful ideas for promoting a consciousness of common humanity, celebrating it through symbols, holidays, and festivals under the auspices of the United Nations. He also suggests the teaching of world history and geography in textbooks in order to counter the distorted glorification of national accounts. However, he concedes that such a development can occur only when all nations are willing to reduce their national sovereignty in favor of the sovereignty of mankind. The need for a strengthened United Nations with effective power to resolve disputes between nations is an obvious condition for the possibility of a new cosmopolitanism.[23]

In his many campaigns and interventions Fromm displayed a willingness to engage in the concrete task of identifying the ideas and movements that may lead to a more peaceful and harmonious world order. During the Cold War he worked energetically for peace, giving interviews and making speeches to plead for the thawing of the tension between the two superpowers and the negotiated reduction in their nuclear arsenals. This is set down in detail in *May Man Prevail*, which first appeared in 1961, but his argument that the Soviet Union under Khrushchev was genuinely seeking peaceful coexistence was undermined by the Cuban missile crisis of October 1962.[24] As a leading member of the pressure group SANE he campaigned for nuclear disarmament in the 1950s and 1960s, advocating the strategy of negotiated reciprocal disarmament sparked by a unilateral initiative, the line of action eventually adopted by Mikhail Gorbachev. In the mid-1960s he campaigned vigorously against the Vietnam War, and in a speech prepared for the SANE Madison Square Garden rally in December 1966 he pleads for the cessation of hostilities because of the "indifference to life" and the "brutalization of man" that the slaughter was encouraging. He warns that unless the killing stops people will lose the capacity to ever stem "the tide of death and de-humanization." He also warns that the indifference to life is not confined to South East Asia but finds its way back home—"how do we expect our young generation to respect life, if they witness daily destruction taking place with the consent of their elders?"[25]

Fromm was also convinced that the huge discrepancy in wealth between the affluent countries and the less developed parts of the world constitutes an insuperable obstacle to world peace. "Peace and liberty in the Western World cannot, in the long run, coexist with hunger and sickness in Africa and China," he concludes in *The Sane Society*.[26] In *To Have or To Be?* he issues a prophetic warning about the consequences of not closing the gap between the rich and poor nations. Building a "white fortress" of rich countries could create epidemics of a global nature, or international terrorism using small nuclear or biological weapons:

> What will happen if nothing crucial is done to close the gap? Either epidemics will spread into the fortress of the white society or famines will drive the population of the poor nations into such despair that they, perhaps with the help of sympathizers from the industrialized world, will commit acts of destruction, even use small nuclear or biological weapons, that will bring chaos within the white fortress.[27]

This warning of terrorism was based not simply on an assessment of the reaction to economic hardship but to the imperialist attitude displayed by the rich to the poor. The international relations context may have changed dramatically since Fromm wrote these words, but the end of the Cold War has not diminished the threat that he identified. The corporate interests that he regarded as a major obstacle to human solidarity have benefited from two decades of neoliberal economic policy, but the deregulation of the markets of the less developed countries has deepened their impoverishment. Similarly Fromm's warning that the giant corporations' "big hold" on the government is growing stronger has been confirmed,[28] and this combination has produced an aggressive imposition of neoliberal principles that have sharpened global antagonisms. However, as we shall see in the concluding section, neoliberalism has given rise to a countervailing power, the anticapitalist movement, which could be the beginning of a movement for human solidarity.

### Liberal Nationalism and Cosmopolitanism

Despite his anti-nationalism, Fromm is not at all opposed to the positive attachment to elements associated with the nation, such as literature, music, art, customs, or traditions, provided that this attachment is not contaminated by group supremacism in any shape or form. It might seem that Fromm's approach is compatible with liberal national positions that point to the indispensable role of national feeling in the building of strong communities and argue that it is possible to combine this with the liberal commitment to tolerance and equal rights between and within nations. However, Fromm's cosmopolitanism resists any accommodation with liberal nationalism, primarily because of the gulf between their positions on the question of moral obligation, but also, I suggest, because of Fromm's complete opposition to the irrationalism that permeates and perpetuates itself in nationalist feeling.

Even the moderate defense of nationalism accords a moral priority to fellow nationals, which is unacceptable to a radical humanist perspective. Stephen Nathanson has argued for a moderate nationalism that could satisfy the criticisms of what he terms "global humanism." He argues that when a commitment to a particular nation is combined with a recognition of the duty to treat all people decently, then "nationalism is a morally legitimate pursuit of group goals and group well-being." He still insists that moderate nationalists "recognize a primary duty to their own nation,"[29] a discrimination that Fromm could never accept. The global humanist objection to the claim that nationalism is in itself a morally legitimate pursuit of group goals is that the moral legitimation for those group goals does not reside in the fact of nationality, an inherited given, but rather in terms of universal rights and wrongs involved in such things as resisting oppression. The experience of that oppression may take on the form of nationalist consciousness, but that is different from saying that nationalism is morally legitimate. Nathanson argues that if global humanists accept that there can be valid nationalist claims, for example to statehood, then there is no real difference between the two positions. But even the moderate nationalist position is making far greater claims than the global humanist position could accept, for if the moral legitimation lies with nationalism rather than in some universal norm, then how are we to judge its moral claims?

Yael Tamir, from a similar perspective, insists that nationalism offers "a set of moral values worthy of respect and serious consideration."[30] Tamir rightly emphasizes the importance of a strong sense of community in learning and discharging our moral duty, but then draws the dangerous conclusion that we owe a greater moral obligation to the members of our own community than we do to the stranger. This involves a double confusion. First, while rightly crediting communities for developing our sense of right and wrong, a *universal* moral sense, it overturns the universality of the moral sense by asserting the priority of the particular communal obligation. Second, it venerates one type of community, the nation, over the many other forms in which we develop our moral sense of what it takes to live together harmoniously. Tamir unwittingly supplies an example of how a "national" outlook runs roughshod over all others. In arguing that individual self-esteem is bound up with the successes and failures of fellow members of their "group" he cites the delight of the Israeli country when the Israeli representative became Miss Universe.[31] The many Israeli feminists and their male supporters who would have been appalled by the entire sexist spectacle are simply erased from this image of the country united in its triumph.

Similar claims to priority accorded to members of the nation are made by David Miller, who states, "I owe special obligations to fellow members of my nation which I do not owe to other human beings."[32] The form of ethical particularism that he adopts to defend his nationalism is based on the ties of affection, sympathy, or loose reciprocity that can be found in strong communities.[33] When it comes to justifying why that community should ideally be a nation, however, Miller's claim rests on arbitrary assertions about human identity and motivation. The nation just *is* "the only possible form in which overall community can be realised in modern societies,"[34] and social divisions based on such identities as class and religion have been overcome as "national identities have triumphed over such divisions, as the historical record shows."[35] The fact that social divisions can be accommodated is arbitrarily regarded as a triumph of nationality rather than a triumph of democracy or rational, social cooperation. However, Miller is right to argue that it is extremely difficult to justify the principle of nationality from the perspective of ethical universalism, and that therefore there needs to be a "more heroic" version of universalism that attaches no intrinsic significance to national boundaries.[36] Miller points out that Sidgwick, writing in the *Elements of Politics* in 1897, called cosmopolitanism the "ideal of the future," which could not yet be realized because the strength of national sentiments was too great. Is it too much to ask that the validity of this judgment may at least be questioned in the twenty-first century, now that the age of "one world" is upon us?

Fromm insists that xenophobia will be overcome only when one fundamental truth is triumphant, namely, that ethical principles stand above the existence of the nation.[37] However, while his forthright universalism might well be regarded as "heroic," it is instructive to note Fromm's distinction between two images of heroism, for he relates this typology explicitly to the contradiction between humanism and nationalism. In *To Have or To Be?* he approvingly cites a number of cosmopolitan epithets, such as Goethe's "above the nation is humanity" and Edith Clavell's "patriotism is not enough" as instances of a European humanist tradition—both theological and nontheological—which reached its zenith in the Renaissance.[38] He suggests that in this period when thinkers treated seriously the idea that all are equal in the sight of God and that the humblest person has infinite worth, the Christian hero was the martyr, the hero of love, the opposite of the pagan hero of Greek and Germanic legend. The pagan hero aims to conquer and destroy, and fulfillment in life comes in pride, power, fame, and combative skill, with Homer's *Iliad* being its finest poetic expression. In short, the character of the hero as martyr is that of *being*, giving, and sharing, while that of the pagan hero is having, exploiting, and forcing.[39] It is the latter model of heroism, symbolized in the idea of "manliness," which was seized upon not just by political leaders but also infiltrated itself into the social character of citizens who went to war with such enthusiasm in the nineteenth and twentieth centuries, risking national suicide in order to protect the image of the strongest power, of honor, or of profits.[40]

Is there, then, no place for a legitimate patriotism in Fromm's radical humanism? Does patriotism *have* to be the cult of idolatry? Although Fromm was clearly suspicious of the term he nevertheless contributed to debates about the general direction "our" society was taking and the choices "we" felt when talking as a citizen of the United States about his adopted country. To some writers, such as Charles Taylor, this would be a normal part of patriotic discourse, distinguishable from nationalism because it relates to laws and the structure of the state and civil society rather than to a common political allegiance based on some ethnic, linguistic, cultural, or religious identity. On this reading, patriotism predates modern nationalism, although Taylor admits that nationalism has become "the most readily available motor of patriotism."[41] One can see why the distinction between nationalism and patriotism would have resonance in the United States, where the majority of the population are conscious of originating from other nations, with a variety of ethnic and religious backgrounds, and where the process of assimilation has been the defining achievement of the new country. But the concern remains that the discourse of patriotism is bound up with insularity, paranoia, and, in the worst case scenario, hatred of those outside the *patria* or those inside who see it as their duty to criticize their government even during times of war. Even the left-leaning liberal philosopher Richard Rorty feels moved to anger against those who take no pride in their country, unwittingly illustrating the sort of aggressive intolerance that Fromm was trying to warn against.[42] Rorty's position mirrors that of Isaiah Berlin, in that both consider that we need the connectedness of nationhood to feel not only pride but also shame, the implication being that if we feel shame for certain social problems we will be more impelled to rectify them.[43] Again it is not clear why this should work at the level of the nation rather than at a local level, or, why, if it can work at both, it cannot work at the global level too. Ultimately this is a defense of irrationalism, for we are being asked to feel pride in something that is not our achievement, or shame about something that is not our fault. Nor is there any indication that such pragmatic irrationalism produces more integrated nation-states, as the continued presence of extreme poverty in some of the richest countries in the world testifies. Adopting Fromm's perspective, we should feel anger at extreme poverty everywhere, and address the issue at each appropriate level.

A crucial question arises if Fromm's ideal of human solidarity is to be more than just a votive prayer. Is it possible for cosmopolitanism to develop? Miller argues that internationalist humanism is "misguided" because the majority of people are too deeply attached to their national identities to make the "obliteration" of those identities an "intelligible goal."[44] Similarly Rorty rejects the idea of human solidarity as the identification with "humanity as such" as simply "impossible—a philosopher's invention, an awkward attempt to secularize the idea of becoming one with God."[45] There can, I suggest, be two kinds of response to this negativity, and these are explored in the final section. The first is to point to developments in the world system that may place a strain on nationality as the principal form of identity and provide opportunities for the development of a cosmopolitan consciousness. This raises a serious question mark against pragmatic defenses of nationalism that emphasize how the nation overcomes the isolation of localism, replaces irrational myths with society-building myths, and offers "appropriate" territorial boundaries in which politics can operate. If, in the twenty-first century, it makes more sense to think of global governance doing these positive things that nations used to do, the pragmatic defense of nationalism begins to dissolve. The second response to the skeptics is to identify the ideas and movements that place the idea of human solidarity on the horizon of political possibility.

## The Conditions for Human Solidarity

Fromm's prediction of "one world" is well on its way to being realized. In the years since his death there has been a massive expansion of international trade in goods, capital, and services, as tariffs and other protective barriers have come tumbling down. Multinational corporations have come to dominate the world market, spreading production to all areas of the globe, assisted by the revolution in electronic communications. This intensification of international competitiveness has diminished the capacity of the governments of nation-states to choose their own paths to economic development while simultaneously increasing the significance of decisions made at a global level about world trade and other issues in the management of the world economy. In other words, nation states have less autonomy in the management of their economies, and greater interdependence is reflected in the emerging processes of global governance.[46] Objectively, then, these developments suggest that the "big" questions concerning the future of the global community will form the primary agenda for the politics of the twenty-first century.

In practice, however, the investiture of greater powers in institutions of global governance, such as the World Trade Organization and the International Monetary Fund, has led to the triumph of neoliberal policies, which have delivered benefits primarily to multinational corporations. In the affluent states the drive to free-up trade and investment has involved the elimination of many of the regulatory and redistributive powers previously used to ensure the social protection of citizens, and the obligation to present the most attractive conditions for the accumulation of capital has forced down tax levels and placed a severe squeeze on social expenditure. In affluent countries such as the United States and Britain this has led to a widening of the gap between rich and poor, and, it may be argued, to a weakening in the popular belief that government can make a difference. In the less developed countries, chronic indebtedness and their inability to export to the highly subsidized economies of the United States and the European Union has forced them into the hands of IMF "adjustment" programs, leading to the privatization of staple services such as education, health care, and water supply. The gap between these poorest countries and the most affluent in the world economy continues to grow. We have then, an economic globalization that has not been matched by the development of democratic governance in the political sphere. However, there is no serious argument that this problem can be dissolved by the restoration of greater autonomy for nation-states (or blocs) through the introduction of protective measures. It is a global problem that has to be addressed globally, and a prerequisite for progress in this area is the development of a global ethic of the sort advocated by Fromm and, more recently, by the theologian Hans Küng.[47]

The negative effects of globalization have provoked liberal nationalists to cling to the community-building power of national identity. In particular liberal nationalists warn against the obliteration of rich national cultures and their replacement by a cheap and/or nasty corporate-controlled flow of information, entertainment, and goods. Tamir, for example, foresees the disappearance of national identity as presaging the "nightmare" future in which "all share in one shallow universal culture, watch soap operas and CNN, eat MacDonalds [sic], and take the children to the local Disneyworld."[48] Likewise Miller dreads the coming of "a lowest-denominator mass culture exemplified by Disney, McDonalds, and Australian soap operas."[49] These warnings miss the point, in two ways. First, the development of a shallow mass culture has not occurred because of the weakening of nationality, and often coexists in and adjusts to societies with strong nationalist traditions. It is the power of the corporations and their regulation that is key here, and this is the sort of issue that would have to be addressed at a global as well as at local level. The second thing that the liberal nationalist argument ignores is that the cultural flow is far from one-sided, and that the combination of local cultures with other cultures can be a powerful mix that can break down barriers and contribute to a cultural internationalism that is not dictated by powerful vested interests. Capitalist modernity, as Tomlinson has argued, is technologically and economically powerful but culturally it is weak.[50] It may well be that only in the twenty-first century will the prediction of Marx and Engels be realized that "national one-sidedness and narrow-mindedness become more and more impossible, and from the numerous national and local literatures there arises a world literature."[51] Fromm's radical humanism seeks a culturally strong and ethically explicit redress to the neoliberal version of progress, not by bunkering down in outdated nationalist mentalities but by actively seeking to redirect the "one world."

Fromm was completely and consistently clear that the power of major corporations must be confronted and reined back to give us the chance to prioritize human needs and open a way to the development of human solidarity. In his first major work, *Escape From Freedom*, he berates the anarchic nature of capitalist production and insists that the economy must be managed for the welfare of the people. "All that matters," he asserts, "is that we establish a rational economic system serving the purposes of the people."[52] The central point is to replace the manipulation of citizens by active and intelligent cooperation, and expand the principle of "government of the people, by the people, for the people, from the formal political to the economic sphere."[53] In his final major work, *To Have or To Be?* he is even more insistent that the power of the giant corporations must be curbed:

> For even the remnant of democracy that still exists is doomed to yield to technocratic fascism, to a society of well-fed, unthinking robots—the very type of society that was so much feared under the name of "communism"—unless the giant corporations' big hold on the government (which becomes stronger daily) and on the population (via thought control through brainwashing) is broken.[54]

The transformative ambition is clear, and in identifying the key issue of control of economic life Fromm identifies the forces against which solidarity movements can mobilize.

We now turn to the question of whether or not it is possible to identify the ideas and social forces that may lead to a more enlightened and egalitarian globalization, without which Fromm's quest for human solidarity would be rendered forlorn. He conceived solidarity primarily as affinity with our fellow human beings, a feeling that what we share in emotional and intellectual capacities far outweighs the things that divide us in a fundamentally irrational social system. But this solidarity has to be grounded in daily practice in terms of identifying with others in the pursuit of common goals, establishing reciprocity with other groups, and recognizing that our efforts are complementary with a range of other causes. Peter Waterman, one of the few writers to have attempted to theorize solidarity, has written that "Affinity Solidarity" is concerned with values, feelings, and friendship and allows for "global linkages within or between ideologies or movements, including between people without contact but acting in the same spirit."[55] He rightly emphasizes the need for other practices of solidarity such as identity, substitutionism, complementarity, reciprocity, and restitution to be operationalized if an effective international solidarity is to be developed. It seems to me that this is entirely consistent with the sort of thing that Fromm was trying to do in the reconstructive parts of *The Sane Society*, *The Revolution of Hope*, and *To Have or To Be?* and in his many sociopolitical interventions.

Fromm prided himself on being a hard-headed realist who did not harbor illusions and was fully aware of the difficulties involved in the pursuit of genuine freedom. Yet he was, most certainly, a utopian, not fixated on the minutia of social reconstruction but on the "real possibility" of human beings taking responsibility for the direction of their own lives, as individuals, as members of organizations and political societies, and as citizens of the world. The normative goal is the realization of the expression of the unique human qualities of love, reason, and productiveness in a condition of human solidarity. But is this, in his own terms, a real possibility? According to Fromm "the real possibility is one which *can* materialize, considering the total structure of forces interacting in an individual or in a society."[56] Despite the divisiveness and ruthless that flow logically from the neoliberal agenda, the emergence of globalization has given rise to both the ideas and social forces that open up the possibility of a change of direction in global governance, even if the obstacles are formidable. In recent years there has been an explosion in the literature arguing for the development of new forms of cosmopolitan democracy and more accountable and humane management of the global economy.[57] Although the aggressive unilateralism of the Bush administration has pushed these ideas off the short-term agenda, they are very much part of the long-term agenda for the twenty-first century. Indeed the breakdown of the ministerial meeting of the World Trade Organization in Cancun in 2003 following a determined resistance by a group of 21 states (G21) led by Brazil, India, and China, is an early indication that the status quo is unsustainable.

In terms of the social forces that can carry forward the demand for global justice, movements have emerged that challenge the neoliberal worldview and which embody Fromm's commitment to an ethical revolution. The first instance is the Zapatista revolt in one of Fromm's homelands, Mexico, which began on January 1, 1994, to coincide with the launch of the North American Free Trade Association. Faced with the imminent destruction of their community by the economic threat of cattle ranchers, oil producers, and paper manufacturers, the people of the Chiapas declared their willingness to take up arms "For Humanity against Neoliberalism."[58] The Zapatistas brought their local struggle to an international audience and universalized their concerns, projecting not simply the image of defensive victims but the positive message of "dignity, hope, and life."[59] Here ideological purity is less significant than universalizing the demands of the oppressed through open dialogue via the new forms of electronic communication.[60]

The same subversive use of electronic communication has also been a feature of the global anticapitalist movement, which heralded its arrival as a force of resistance at the ministerial meeting of the World Trade Organization at Seattle in December 1999 and has continued around the world since at meetings of the World Trade Organization, the International Monetary Fund and the World Bank, the Group of

Eight, and the World Economic Forum at Davos. At a time of neoliberal triumphalism, when European social democracy appears to have jettisoned its historic adherence to equality, it is remarkable to hear of massive "anticapitalist" demonstrations around the world, involving a truly global array of protesters who represent an array of interests, not all of which are compatible, but who share the ethical conviction that global governance as presently exercised is manifestly unjust. It is a measure of the concern of the authorities that there has been a concerted campaign within the media to redesignate the "anticapitalist" protestors as "antiglobalization" protestors. This move simultaneously deflects attention away from the systemic injustice of the mode of accumulation and implies that the protestors are standing in the way of progress, like the Luddites who smashed up factory machinery in early-nineteenth-century Britain. The anticapitalist movement is loosely organized in the World Social Forum, which met for the first time at Porto Alegre in Brazil in 2001. The second meeting, also at Porto Alegre, in 2002, was attended by over 50,000 delegates from over a thousand organizations.[61] The future forms of this global protest are unpredictable, as is the extent to which they can articulate their concerns sufficiently to jolt the global elites into rethinking global governance, but the emergence of this anti-systemic phenomenon is of the greatest significance, for it shows that there is "real possibility" for change. This is expressed in the single slogan, "Another World is Possible."

Fromm was not prone to wild optimism, but he simply refused to accept that nothing could be done about affluent alienation in the rich countries and extreme poverty in the less developed parts of the world. The forces that he identifies as corruptors of the human spirit appear to have grown stronger and more entrenched since his death, and the traditional movements for egalitarian reform appear to have acquiesced to the imperative of retaining competitiveness in the global economy. However, in the new politics of the new social movements and in the global anticapitalist movement we see manifestations of what he took to be a precondition for an effective emancipatory politics, namely, a strong ethical conviction that the world could be changed to meet authentic human needs. "Our only hope," he writes in *To Have or To Be?*, "lies in the energizing attraction of a new vision."[62] Piecemeal reform is not sufficient because it does not carry with it the impelling force of strong motivation:

> The realization of the new society and the new Man is possible only if the old motivations of profit, power, and intellect are replaced by new ones: being, sharing, understanding; if the marketing character is replaced by the productive, loving character; if cybernetic religion is replaced by a new radical-humanistic spirit.[63]

The cynics will scoff at such utopianism and point to the overwhelming compulsion of material interest over considerations of social justice, or else they will insist on the inherent destructiveness of humankind. For Fromm, these positions are no more than convenient excuses for doing nothing to make the world a better place. He insists that even though the chances for radical change may be slim, life is too valuable to surrender to the forces of wealth and power. At a global level, millions share that view.

# CHAPTER NINE

# CONCLUSION: RADICAL HUMANISM AND
# HUMAN SOLIDARITY

What is unique about Fromm's social theory is its explicit ethical commitment to the universal realization of human potentials. He is convinced of the need for an ethical turn to be taken in order to open up a real possibility of the achievement of a condition of human solidarity. His humanism is radical because it opposes all antagonistic social structures that reproduce exploitation and oppression. It is universal in a twofold sense; philosophically, in that it is based upon a philosophical anthropology that yields universal norms, and empirically, in the sense that it involves a global vision of overcoming relationships of domination and subordination in all aspects of human life. From an early age Fromm accepted the fundamental truth of Marx's critique of capitalism, placing particular emphasis on the alienation thesis with its stress on *how* capitalism shapes and distorts social relations. His own work attempts to rectify a fault that he identified in Marxist theory, namely, its tendency to analyze socioeconomic development largely in structural terms while paying little attention to the consciousness of those identified as the agents of radical social change. His development of "social character" as an analytical framework enables him to analyze the phenomenon of affluent alienation in terms of the development of the marketing character. Although at times this alienation is presented as being totally pervasive, his emphasis on the question of what we are alienated from opens up the positive questions about the tasks of emancipation in late capitalism. In other words, how can we envisage a de-alienated character in a de-alienated world? In order to develop a positive conception of freedom Fromm draws on his special skills in psychoanalysis, resulting in his pathbreaking exposition of the productive character and the ideal of the being mode of existence.

His overall conception of social freedom draws heavily on Marx, as can be seen in his final major work, *To Have or To Be?* Here he endorses Marx's vision of bringing production under common control in conditions worthy of our human nature, while insisting that real freedom resides beyond this realm of necessity, involving "that development of human power which is its own end, the true realm of freedom."[1] Nevertheless, the political movements developed in Marx's name are anathema to Fromm. He regards the Marxism–Leninism of the communist system as a "vulgar forgery" of Marx's thought[2] condemning the communist regimes of his day as not socialist in any sense, lacking as they did even the semblance of democracy.

As for social democracy, it had reached an accommodation with the status quo and had lost its transformative energy. It is only in the years since his death that new forms of political activity sharing Fromm's radical humanism have developed. The entry of *Die Grünen* into the German Parliament in 1983 heralded the rise of a new form of politics based on the concerns of new social movements. This development has not been confined to formal party political activity but proliferates in nongovernmental organizations throughout the world, often international in their scope. More recently, the entry of the global anticapitalist movement onto the world political stage, with its overtly ethical appeal, offers renewed hope that Fromm's imperative has found a political voice. It demands the subordination of the logic of capitalist accumulation to the authentic needs of human beings in order that all may be able to develop their potential as rational, productive, and loving beings. His message is clear: for the world to change for the better people have to change their "selves" by developing an awareness of the divisiveness of a social system driven by the competitive struggle for the maximization of profit and power. Nothing short of a radical reevaluation of values is required if we are to achieve the change of direction that can make a real possibility of the goal of human solidarity.

What can Fromm's ideas offer to modern social and political theory?[3] Here I suggest two related areas in which his radical humanist approach can challenge existing assumptions shared by most modern and postmodern theorists. The first is his espousal of a strong normative conception of human essence, which provides a foundation and justification for the adoption of an emancipatory perspective. It provides a framework for the critique of existing social practices and the values that support them and a vision of individual and social freedom to pursue. This theory of human nature fills a lacuna left by other theories, as can be seen when looking at recent attempts to theorize the concept of solidarity. The second area relates to the scope of his vision. In searching for ideas and movements that advance a radical humanist agenda across a range of activities his approach supports the potential of a loosely linked yet thematically tuned political engagement. From the daily struggles for respect in everyday life to the protests against the myopia of neoliberal governance of the world economy, the goal of human solidarity begins to lose its nebulous quality.

In order to examine the first claim concerning the value of his normative theory of human essence it is interesting to compare his use of it to support a plea for human solidarity with other theorists who have focused on the concept of solidarity in recent years. Some of these contributions offer valuable insights into how solidarity may develop, but in their determination to avoid the twin "crimes" of universalism and essentialism their work runs into significant difficulties.[4] Richard Rorty, for example, in *Contingency, Irony and Solidarity*, accepts that there is such a thing as moral progress and that it is "in the direction of greater human solidarity."[5] He shows the significance of works of literature in developing an understanding of the privations of individuals and groups unfamiliar to us, thereby encouraging our sympathy and tolerance. Yet Rorty's unwillingness to accept any "metaphysical" grounding of human experience in terms of a common human nature renders him incapable of justifying *why* we should support the idea of solidarity. Furthermore, in his appeal for people to recognize the feelings of pain and humiliation that he claims we all share, he is unwittingly falling back on an essentialist view of human nature, as Norman Geras has convincingly argued.[6] Axel Honneth, in *The Struggle For Recognition*, argues convincingly that moral claims are constantly being made in everyday struggles for recognition, pointing toward the development of social solidarity in which "every member of a society is in a position to esteem himself or herself."[7] However, although he recognizes that there needs to be some way of distinguishing those struggles that take us closer to the goal of societal solidarity from those that are entirely self-interested and even reactionary, he is unable to supply the requisite criteria from within his inter-subjectivist analytical framework.[8] Similarly Alain Touraine, in *Can We Live Together?*, makes an eloquent plea for the emergence of multicultural societies and the renewal of an ethical perspective in our struggles to create a stronger social bond, which also recognizes diversity. However, when it comes to the content of such an ethics we are left with an empty box.[9] What is lacking in all these contributions is what we find in Fromm's radical humanism, a well worked-out conception of human flourishing to serve as a guide to identifying the fertile conditions for the development of human solidarity.

The reluctance in social and political theory to even begin to inquire about what is that makes us human and what is required to enable us to flourish must be confronted. The specific objections to the sort of philosophical anthropology adopted by Fromm were examined in chapter three, but here it is appropriate to comment at a more general level on two fundamental concerns. The first is that a normative theory of human nature is too stipulative to allow for difference, and second, that if it avoids the first objection it must be too vague to serve any useful purpose. In short, it is assumed that general theories of human nature are bound to be either too "thick" or too "thin." If it is too "thick" to accommodate the diversity of interests and aspirations thrown up in the course of late modernity, it will inevitably offer some "totalizing" vision of the ideal community, which will prove inimical to human freedom. In chapter three we saw that this concern has been expressed by Iris Marion Young, who warns of the danger of operating with a definition of human nature because it might lead to exclusion or devaluation of acceptable ways of life, even though she admits that any normative theory relies on a theory of human nature.[10] This amounts to an uncomfortable evasion. Fromm's conception is formulated in such a way that it is difficult to conceive of "acceptable" practices being excluded or devalued. He draws a clear distinction between humanist conceptions of human nature and authoritarian ones, specifying the dangerous social consequences of the latter. His criticisms of the psychological implications of the doctrines of Luther and Calvin are good examples of exposing how authoritarian conceptions of human nature prepare the ground for totalitarian outcome. His own humanism, on the other hand, explicitly rejects such authoritarianism, even in its inner-directed, liberal-humanist form in Kant's idea of duty. The imperative to develop the essential human qualities of rationality, productiveness, and love for all in a social context of human solidarity cannot be thought of as an invitation to totalitarianism. Fromm's radical humanism might, of course, prompt a rejection of certain cultural practices that deny individuals their ability to develop their potential, and this would lend support to those individuals within those cultures who are struggling to amend or abolish those practices. This is surely preferable to a relativism that deems a practice acceptable as long as those who hold the power within a certain culture assert that it is.

Is Fromm's radical humanism too "thin" to serve a useful purpose for emancipatory social theory, or, to put it more provocatively, does it amount to no more than pious pleading for the world to become a better place? It is certainly possible that rational reflection on human nature may yield moral guidelines that are either ambiguous or indeed fail to address issues that any social theory worth its name should not avoid. We cannot, like Aristotle, ignore the question of slavery, or, like Aquinas, accept poverty as natural, allowing only for its alleviation by the virtuous practice of charity. However, in Fromm's case the specificity of the essential human qualities that need to be developed in order to lead a productive life can serve as a guide to discriminate between progressive and regressive responses to social development. Fromm's own exhaustive work in identifying the obstacles to freedom and in seeking solutions is helpful in this respect. In his contributions to the discussion of major issues in such areas as gender relations, work, consumerism, democracy, and international affairs, he gets to the heart of how socioeconomic structures impact on social relations, and he urges the search for humane solutions to those concrete problems.

His radical humanism offers broad but effective criteria to guide our assessment of social developments. Do they help to promote reason, love, and productiveness or do they encourage socially irrational outcomes, inflame hatreds, and reproduce passivity? Do they move us closer to the goal of human solidarity or do they foment social division? In many cases, such as neoliberal economic policy or the existence of sweatshop production, the radical humanist reaction is obvious and the emphasis will fall on finding feasible alternatives. In more specific areas of policy within existing states, the focus on encouraging the development of independent productive and loving powers can serve as a guide in the policy choices in areas such as health care, welfare, education, and planning. Naturally, not all cases are clear and certain social dilemmas will not be easily resolved by the simple application of radical humanist criteria. For example, the debate in France about the display of religious symbols in schools reveals a clash of solidarities in which either a dogmatic secularist or a religious fundamentalist disposition is likely to provoke conflict. In such cases the radical humanist perspective can do no more than urge compromise and accommodation of difference within the context of its long-term goals. Is *any* moral theory able to offer more?

It is the sweep of Fromm's social thought that prompts our second claim for his significance to emancipatory social theory, namely that it can lead to fresh thinking about how the concept of solidarity can be theorized in the age of globalization. The emergence of global politics as an aspect of globalization in the period since Fromm's death in 1980 makes his appeal to human solidarity less of a dream than it may have appeared during his lifetime. The period of accelerated interconnectedness that we know as "globalization" has so ruptured traditional strategies for achieving emancipation that there is now something of a consensus among emancipatory theorists that radical rethinking of alternatives is required. Despite the promise of its name, globalization appears to have inflicted greater divisiveness on the world. Rapid socioeconomic change has weakened or destroyed established communities of various sorts, for example, geographic communities based on old industries, craft-based trades unions, socialist and communist political parties. Not only did solidarity flourish in these "sites," developing a sense of loyalty, self-respect, and purpose, but these "old" solidarities can claim enormous success in areas such as education, health, welfare at a local and national level. In the less developed countries of the world, the solidarity developed around successful struggles against imperialism is now strained to breaking point by economic dependence on the neoliberal guardians of the International Monetary Fund and the World Bank. However, it has also to be recognized that those involved in old solidarities were only rarely simultaneously conscious of the wider goal of human solidarity. Many old movements, set up to resist exploitation and injustice, fell into the paradox of solidarity, whereby their strength is gained through the demonization or exclusion of "the other," thus rendering chimerical the wider aspiration to a more general condition of solidarity. So, for example, although historically the trades union movement has been of tremendous importance in representing the material interests of the working classes, in practice many unions conducted or condoned blatantly racist and/or sexist practices.

There is now an opportunity to broaden the nature of solidarity, even while globalization has extended the gap between rich and poor both within the core countries of the world economy and between the core and peripheral countries.[11] For globalization has, in important respects, brought the world closer together through increased mobility and instant communications. Social and political issues take on an increasingly global aspect, and, as we saw in chapter eight, the issue of the democratization of global governance is now on the agenda and will remain there. New solidarities have emerged in the form of the new social movements, particularly around environmentalism, feminism, and global justice, internationalist in outlook yet strong on local initiatives.[12] In addition the anticapitalist movement has emerged on a global scale since its spectacular impact at the demonstration against the World Trade Organization in Seattle in December 1999.[13]

There is, however, a lag between the sudden ending of established forms of solidarity and the development of newer forms, which might lead to a situation in which we can identify the possibility of a "change of direction" along the lines called for by Fromm. Another, pessimistic way of conceptualizing this "lag" is the "end of politics" thesis, which points to the shrinking remit of the political sphere.[14] Where nation states once enjoyed a modicum of autonomy and the ability to decide on significant issues within their own borders, such as the limits to commodification, economic planning, the redistribution of wealth, and the scope of the welfare state, they now find themselves forced into policies such as privatization and marketization by the imperative of making their economies suitable for the maximum accumulation of capital.[15] This has contributed to a weakening of public life, with symptoms such as low voter turnouts and diminishing membership of political parties. However, established forms of constitutional politics are not the only form of politics, and it is one of Fromm's strengths that he extended the sphere of the political to a wide range of issues while at the same time recognizing the need for a revitalization of public life through constitutional reform.

Fromm identifies the struggle for solidarity at a variety of levels, and this opens up the sphere of the "political" in a potentially exciting way. His contributions on women's emancipation, the work experience, and the social effects of mass consumption point to a politics of everyday life in which a range of strategies can be developed on specific issues, which at the same time highlight common experiences of lack of care or respect from corporate managements or political and administrative elites. There is a great deal of overlap between these issues, and often an international dimension, as with consumer boycotts or international women's actions. Furthermore these issues are by no means confined to the affluent countries, although the form of the struggle is likely to be very different in the less developed countries. For example, perhaps the most pressing demand of workers in the less developed world is the basic recognition of trades union representation, but even this is linked to a broader struggle to press for social clauses in future trade agreements, which would affect all workers and offers the possibility of developing a strategy that could unify all workers.[16] In the sphere of consumption Fromm recognizes the danger to our independence of thought posed by modern consumer culture, but even in the early 1940s he identified the vitally important role that consumer movements could play. Now they constitute a major vehicle of resistance to the power of the major corporations and form part of a new political sphere of action. These spheres of action overflow local and national boundaries and increasingly take on an international nature.

At the global level new forms of solidarity have emerged around the anticapitalist movement and the Social Forums, which now meet annually at a global and continental level. As we saw in chapter eight, the ethical commitment to a humane "one world" has been rediscovered in these new anti-systemic movements. The anticapitalist movement has a range of empirical arguments against neoliberal global governance, but it has a wider significance. It is questioning, in explicitly ethical terms, the direction and purpose of social life in the world. It is myopic to deride the appeal for human solidarity on the basis of our common humanity as "flimsy"; the age of global politics has arrived and Fromm's ethical universalism is highly appropriate for the new politics of emancipation.

Of course it might be said that these new movements are fragmented and marginal to the real decision-making processes at global, national, or even local level, and this objection is a serious one. Yet in many respects these movements are ahead of the game in terms of global politics and it is the area of domestic politics that is marginalized, irrelevant to people's concerns and overwhelmingly administrative in nature. The anticapitalist movement in general, and Lori Wallach of the Public Citizen movement in particular, successfully worked for the defeat of the antidemocratic Multinational Agreement on Investment in 1998 when governments and political parties around the world showed little sign of knowing what was going on.[17] The point here, however, is that global politics will slowly penetrate the domestic agendas and there will be a need for articulation of old and new politics. Fromm had no time for the dogmatic dismissal of the "old" forms of constitutional politics. He did not become fully politically active until his fifties, but he contributed where he felt it could make a difference. This involved a range of interventions, such as addressing the communist-organized Moscow Peace Conference in the presence of Khrushchev in 1962, writing speeches for Eugene McCarthy's presidential bid in 1968, and even delivering a paper to a Senate hearing on détente in 1974. Most revolutionaries would dismiss such interventions, declaring constitutional politics to be a waste of time. Fromm was aware that to create real possibilities it was necessary to engage with the power structures as they existed while never losing sight of the ultimate concern. He was willing to embrace all movements willing to make a priority of the needs and dignity of all human beings irrespective of race, nation, class, or creed, and that spirit of undogmatic humanist conviction is his legacy today.

# NOTES

## Chapter One    Introduction: The Quest

1. For example, Daniel Burston, *The Legacy of Erich Fromm* (Cambridge, MA: Harvard University Press, 1991); Mauricio Cortina and Michael Maccoby (eds.), *A Prophetic Analyst: Erich Fromm's Contribution to Psychoanalysis* (Northvale, New Jersey: Jason Aronson, 1996).
2. See Pamela Pilbeam, *Republicanism in Nineteenth Century France, 1814–1871* (London: Macmillan, 1995).
3. Biographical details of Fromm's life are taken from Rainer Funk, *Erich Fromm: His Life and Ideas* (New York: Continuum, 2000), except where stated.
4. Erich Fromm, *Beyond the Chains of Illusion: My Encounter with Marx and Freud* (New York: Simon and Schuster, 1962), p. 5.
5. Ibid., pp. 5–6.
6. Hermann Cohen, *Religion of Reason: Out of the Sources of Judaism* (New York: Oxford University Press, 1995); Fromm pays tribute to the influence of "that great opus" in *You Shall Be As Gods* (New York: Henry Holt, 1991), pp. 12–13; on Cohen's neo-Kantian socialism see Harry van der Linden, *Kantian Ethics and Socialism* (Indianapolis: Hackett, 1988).
7. The manuscript of the projected work is published as part three of Erich Fromm, *On Being Human* (New York: Continuum, 1998), and comprises discussions of Meister Eckhart, Karl Marx, and their common religious concern.
8. Erich Fromm, *Psychoanalysis and Religion* (Yale: Harvard University Press, 1978), pp. 93–95.
9. Erich Fromm, *The Sane Society* (New York: Henry Holt, 1990), p. 60.
10. Fromm, *Psychoanalysis and Religion*, p. 1.
11. Fromm, *The Sane Society*, p. 140.
12. Terry Eagleton, *After Theory* (New York and London: Allen Lane Penguin, 2003), p. 121.
13. Erich Fromm, *Escape From Freedom* (New York: Henry Holt, 1994), p. 263.
14. Erich Fromm, "Sex and Character" (1943) in Fromm, *Love, Sexuality and Matriarchy: About Gender* (New York: Fromm International, 1999), pp. 114–115.
15. Margaret Canovan, "Sleeping Dogs, Prowling Cats and Soaring Doves: Three Paradoxes in the Political Theory of Nationhood" in *Political Studies* 49 (2), 2001, p. 212.
16. Fromm, *Beyond the Chains of Illusion*, p. 10.
17. For an excellent collection on his work as a psychoanalyst see Mauricio Cortina and Michael Maccoby (eds.), *A Prophetic Analyst: Erich Fromm's Contribution to Psychoanalysis* (Northvale, NJ: Jason Aronson, 1996).
18. Erich Fromm, *To Have or To Be?* (New York: Continuum, 2002), p. 174.
19. Ibid., p. 197 and p. 173.
20. Ibid., p. 174.
21. Ibid., p. 175.
22. Fromm, *The Sane Society*, p. 362.
23. Fromm, *To Have or To Be?*, p. 105.

24. Ibid., parts one and two.
25. Charles Pasternak, *Quest: The Essence of Humanity* (Chichester and Hoboken, NJ: John Wiley, 2003).
26. Erich Fromm, "Psychoanalysis and Sociology" in Stephen E. Bronner and Douglas M. Kellner (eds.), *Critical Theory and Society: A Reader* (London: Routledge, 1989), pp. 37–39.
27. Karl Marx and Friedrich Engels, *Collected Works*, volume four (New York and London: International Publishers and Lawrence & Wishart, 1975), p. 93.
28. Erich Fromm, *The Dogma of Christ* (New York: Henry Holt, 1993), pp. 46–47.
29. Ibid., p. 48.
30. Fromm, *Psychoanalysis and Religion*, pp. 48–49.
31. Fromm, *The Working Class in Weimar* (London: Berg, 1984), p. 228.
32. Max Horkheimer, Foreword to Martin Jay, *The Dialectical Imagination: A History of the Frankfurt School and the Institute of Social Research, 1923–1950* (Berkeley: University of California Press, 1996), p. xxv
33. As reported by Wolfgang Bonss, Introduction to Fromm, *The Working Class in Weimar*, p. 3.
34. Ibid., p. 33.
35. T. W. Adorno, E. Frenkel-Brunswick, D. Levinson, and R. Nevitt Sanford, *The Authoritarian Personality* (New York: W. W. Norton, 1969)—most acknowledgements to Fromm's path-breaking work are provided in Else Frenkel-Brunswick's contribution.
36. This view is convincingly expressed by Jose Brunner in "Looking into the Hearts of the Workers, or: How Erich Fromm Turned Critical Theory into Empirical Research" in *Political Psychology* 15 (4), 1994.
37. Erich Fromm, "The Method and Function of an Analytic Social Psychology: Observations on Psychoanalysis and Historical Materialism" in Fromm, *The Crisis of Psychoanalysis* (New York: Holt, Rinehart, and Winston, 1970), pp. 110–134. This is also published in A. Arato and E. Gebhardt (eds.), *The Essential Frankfurt School Reader* (New York: Urizen Books, 1978), pp. 477–496.
38. Erich Fromm, "Sozialpsychologischer Teil" in *Erich Fromm Gesamtausgbe* (Stuttgart: Deutsche Verlags-Antalt and München: Deutscher Taschenbuch Verlag, 1999), volume one, pp. 139–187—originally published in *Studien über Autorität und Familie*, Schriften des Institut für Sozialforschung 5 (Paris: Alcan, 1936).
39. Erich Fromm, *The Revision of Psychoanalysis*, Rainer Funk (ed.) (Boulder, San Francisco, Oxford: Westview Press, 1992), p. 33.
40. John Schaar, *Escape From Authority: The Perspectives of Erich Fromm* (Evanston, New York: Harper Torchbooks, 1964), p. 8.
41. Fromm, *The Crisis of Psychoanalysis*, chapters 2 and 5.
42. Fromm, *The Revision of Psychoanalysis*, p. 9.
43. Ibid., p. 33.
44. Fromm, *The Revision of Psychoanalysis*, pp. 7–8.
45. The book was first published in Great Britain in 1942 under a different title, *The Fear of Freedom*. Confusingly, this title has been retained in subsequent editions, for example, Erich Fromm, *The Fear of Freedom* (London: Routledge, 1997).
46. Fromm, *Escape From Freedom*, pp. 11–12.
47. Ibid, p. 276.
48. Ibid., pp. 256–257 and 287. In his discussion of social character in *The Sane Society* he emphasizes the interaction between human nature and the nature of the external conditions, stating that humanity is not a "blank sheet of paper on which culture writes its text," p. 81.
49. Fromm, *Escape From Freedom*, p. 296; cf. Erich Fromm, "The Application of Humanist Psychoanalysis to Marx's Theory" in Fromm, *On Disobedience and Other Essays* (New York: Seabury Press, 1981), pp. 29–30.
50. Erich Fromm, *Man For Himself: An Inquiry Into the Psychology of Ethics* (New York: Henry Holt, 1990), pp. 57–58.

51. Michael Maccoby, Introduction to Eric Fromm and Michael Maccoby, *Social Character in a Mexican Village* (New Brunswick and London: Transaction Books, 1996), p. xxii.

52. This aspect of Fromm's work is beyond the scope of this book.

53. In discussion with Jurgen Habermas in "Theory and Politics: A Discussion with Herbert Marcuse, Jurgen Habermas, Heinz Lubasz, and Tillman Spenglar" in *Telos* 38 (1978–1979), p. 127, Marcuse asserts "the real reason for Fromm's departure from the Institute was his castration of Freudian theory, especially the revision of the Freudian concept of instinctual drives."

54. According to Rainer Funk this was $4000, or one year's salary—Rainer Funk, *Erich Fromm: His Life and Ideas* (New York: Continuum, 2000), p. 92, but Rolf Wiggershaus reports a figure of £20,000—Rolf Wiggershaus, *The Frankfurt School: Its History, Theories, and Political Significance* (Cambridge: Polity, 1995), p. 271. On Fromm's involvement and break with the School see Funk, Wiggershaus, pp. 52–64 and 265–273, and Jay, *The Dialectical Imagination*, pp. 88–106.

55. This is discussed in Jay's *The Dialectical Imagination*, pp. 103–105.

56. Herbert Marcuse, "Critique of Neo-Freudian Revisionism" in *Eros and Civilisation: A Philosophical Inquiry into Freud* (London: Routledge, 1998), pp. 238–274. For Fromm's attack on Marcuse see "The Alleged Radicalism of Herbert Marcuse" in Fromm, *The Revision of Psychoanalysis*.

57. For an excellent discussion of the details of the Fromm–Marcuse dispute see John Rickert, "The Fromm–Marcuse Debate Revisited" in *Theory and Society* 15 (3), 1986, pp. 351–399. See also Daniel Burston, *The Legacy of Erich Fromm* (Cambridge, MA: Harvard University Press, 1991), ch. 9, and Jay, *The Dialectical Imagination*, pp. 106–112.

58. "Theory and Politics: A Discussion with Herbert Marcuse, Jürgen Habermas, Heinz Lubasz, and Tillman Spenglar" in *Telos* 38 (1978–1979), p. 127.

59. Fromm, *Man For Himself*, pp. 12–13 and 211–212.

60. Ibid., p. 14.

61. Ibid., p. 20.

62. Ibid., chapter three.

63. Ibid., p. 43.

64. Erich Fromm, *The Heart of Man: Its Genius for Good and Evil* (New York, Evanston and London: Harper and Row, 1964), p. 116n.

65. Ibid., p. 117.

66. Ibid., p. 121.

67. Erich Fromm, *The Art of Loving* (London: Thorsons, 1995), pp. 65–83.

68. Funk, *Erich Fromm: His Life and Ideas*, p. 139.

69. Erich Fromm, *The Art of Loving*, p. 103. Fromm quotes this passage in his posthumously published article on "The Alleged Radicalism of Herbert Marcuse" in Fromm, *The Revision of Psychoanalysis*, pp. 126–127.

70. Erich Fromm, "Psychoanalysis and Zen Buddhism" in Fromm, D. T. Suzuki, and R. De Martino, *Zen Buddhism and Psychoanalysis* (London: Souvenir Press, 1993) [originally 1960].

71. Fromm, *To Have or To Be?*, p. 6.

72. Ibid., p. 109–110. Fromm relates the having character to Ibsen's *Peer Gynt*.

73. Ibid., p. 77.

74. Ibid., p. 78.

75. Ibid., p. 199.

76. Ibid., p. 185. The qualities of the "new man" are listed on pp. 170–172.

77. Fromm, *Escape From Freedom*, p. 268.

78. Fromm, *Psychoanalysis and Religion*, p. 26.

79. Ibid., pp. 33–36 and p. 85.

80. Ibid., p. 37.

81. Ibid., pp. 49–50.

82. Fromm, *Escape From Freedom*, p. 271.

83. Fromm, *The Sane Society*, p. 239. For a sample of Luxemburg's work see Rosa Luxemburg, *Selected Political Writings* (New York: Monthly Review Press, 1971). Landauer, less well-known in the English-speaking world, was a communitarian socialist who emphasized the spiritual dimension of socialism—Gustav Landauer, *For Socialism* (St. Louis: Telos Press, 1978).

84. Fromm, *The Sane Society*, p. 240.

85. Fromm, *To Have or To Be?*, p. 160.

86. This is from a recently discovered review by Fromm of Trotsky's *Diary in Exile—1935*, published by Harvard University Press in 1958. See *Science and Society* 66 (2), 2002, pp. 271–273, and Kevin Anderson's introduction, pp. 266–701.

87. Funk, *Erich Fromm: His Life and Ideas*, p. 146; the relevant correspondence is available in the Erich Fromm Archive in Tübingen. Fromm maintained a critical stance toward Israel because of its position toward the Arab population; he makes this clear in a letter to the Italian socialist Angelica Balabanoff of October 29, 1962 (Erich Fromm Archive).

88. They were married in 1944. Fromm had ended the relationship with Karen Horney in 1940—see Bernard Paris, *Karen Horney: A Psychoanalyst's Search For Self-Understanding* (New Haven and London: Yale University Press, 1994), pp. 144–145.

89. Erich Fromm, *May Man Prevail?: An Inquiry Into the Facts and Fictions of Foreign Policy* (New York: Doubleday Anchor, 1964), pp. 190–200.

90. Funk, *Erich Fromm: His Life and Ideas*, p. 145.

91. Stephen Eric Bronner, "Fromm in America" on the CD Rom issued by the Erich Fromm Archive *225 Articles About Erich Fromm*, 2001, pp. 5–6; Fromm's manifesto, "Let Man Prevail," is published in Erich Fromm, *On Disobedience and Other Essays* (New York: Seabury Press, 1981).

92. Fromm was unable to deliver the speech as he had his first heart attack prior to the rally.

93. Erich Fromm, *The Revolution of Hope: Toward a Humanised Technology* (New York and London: Harper and Row, 1968).

94. Erich Fromm, *Marx's Concept of Man* (Continuum: New York, 1992).

95. Bronner, "Fromm in America," p. 7.

96. Erich Fromm (ed.), *Socialist Humanism* (London: Allen Lane Penguin, 1967). In the process of editing the book he enraged the French structuralist Marxist Louis Althusser by rejecting his contribution; Fromm to Althusser (January 8, 1964). When Althusser wrote a stinging complaint about censorship to an intermediary, Adam Schaff, Fromm wrote to Schaff (February 8, 1964) stating that Althusser's paper was "just terribly boring, and without any theoretical thought worth publishing"—the correspondence is in the Erich Fromm Archive.

97. Fromm, *The Sane Society*, p. x.

98. Fromm, who met Huxley in the 1950s, discusses the salience of his novel in *The Sane Society*, pp. 224–228.

99. Ibid., p. 362.

## Chapter Two    Freedom Lost

1. Erich Fromm, *Escape From Freedom* (New York: Henry Holt, 1994), p. xv.

2. Erich Fromm, interview with Oliver Hunkin on the program "You Shall Be As Gods" in the *Doubts and Certainties* series, BBC 1, August 29, 1968.

3. Erich Fromm, *To Have or To Be?* (New York: Continuum, 2002), p. 173.

4. Fromm, *Escape From Freedom*, p. 104.

5. Ibid., p. 74.

6. For a succinct outline of Freud's views on the development of the sexual function see chapter three of his 1940 text, *An Outline of Psycho-Analysis* (London: Hogarth Press, 1973); for Fromm's early treatment of libido theory and character see his 1932 text, "Psychoanalytic Characterology and its Relevance for Social Psychology" in Fromm, *The Crisis of Psychoanalysis* (New York, Chicago, San Francisco: Holt, Rinehart, Winston, 1970).

7. Fromm, *The Crisis of Psychoanalysis*, pp. 129–130.

8. Ibid., pp. 116–117.

9. Fromm, *The Crisis of Psychoanalysis*, pp. 119, 128 and 110–111 respectively.

10. Erich Fromm, *Escape From Freedom* (New York: Henry Holt, 1994), pp. 275–276.

11. Ibid., pp. 277–278.

12. Ibid., p. 282.

13. Ibid., pp. 278–279. Fromm's empirical study of the character of German workers is found in Erich Fromm, *The Working Class in Weimar: A Psychological and Sociological Study* (Leamington Spa: Berg, 1984).

14. This is adapted from Fromm's own diagrammatic presentation in "The Application of Humanist Psychoanalysis to Marx's Theory" in Erich Fromm, *On Disobedience and Other Essays* (New York: Seabury Press, 1981), pp. 29–30 and also Fromm, *Beyond The Chains of Illusion: My Encounter with Marx and Freud* (New York: Simon and Schuster, 1962), p. 87.

15. Fromm, *Beyond The Chains of Illusion*, p. 107n.

16. Fromm, *Escape From Freedom*, p. 294. Fromm accepts that Weber does not suggest that this is the exclusive cause.

17. Ibid., p. 275.

18. Fromm provides a full list of the positive and negative aspects of the nonproductive orientations in *Man For Himself: An Inquiry into the Psychology of Ethics* (New York: Henry Holt, 1990), pp. 114–116.

19. Erich Fromm and Michael Maccoby, *Social Character in a Mexican Village* (New Brunswick and London: Transaction Publishers, 1996), p. 235.

20. Erich Fromm, *The Dogma of Christ* (New York: Henry Holt, 1992), p. 10.

21. Ibid., pp. 81–89, cf. Theodore Reik, *Dogma and Compulsion* (New York: International Universities Press, 1951).

22. Ibid., pp. 17–21, cf. Sigmund Freud, *The Future of An Illusion* (New York: W. W. Norton, 1975).

23. Fromm, *Escape From Freedom*, p. 63.

24. Ibid., p. 74.

25. Ibid., pp. 75–78.

26. Ibid., p. 83.

27. Ibid., p. 82; see also Hans-Jürgen Goertz, *Thomas Müntzer: Apocalyptic, Mystic and Revolutionary* (Edinburgh: T. and T. Clark, 1993), chapter 14.

28. Ibid., p. 84.

29. Ibid., pp. 85–86. Fromm quotes from Calvin's *Institutes of the Christian Religion*, Book III, chapters 14, 11.

30. Ibid., p. 88.

31. Ibid., p. 89.

32. Ibid., pp. 90–94.

33. Ibid., pp. 77–78.

34. Ibid., pp. 69–71.

35. See Norman Cohn, *The Pursuit of the Millennium* (New York: Oxford University Press, 1970), pp. 158–162.

36. Erich Fromm, *The Heart of Man: Its Genius for Good and Evil* (New York, Evanston and London: Harper and Row, 1964), p. 81.

37. Thomas More, *The Sadness of Christ and Final Prayers and Instructions* (Princeton, NJ: Scepter, 2000), p. 153 and 149.

38. On the social implications of the various theological positions see Ernst Troeltsch, *The Social Teaching of the Christian Churches*, volume one (Louisville, Kentucky: Westminster/John Knox Press, 1992), chapter 2, part 9.

39. J. Stanley Glen, *Erich Fromm: A Protestant Critique* (Philadelphia: The Westminster Press, 1966), p. 54.

40. Ibid., p. 196.

41. See, for example, Robert Young, "Luther and the Temporal Kingdom" in David Muschamp (ed.), *Political Thinkers* (Basingstoke: Macmillan, 1986), pp. 71–75.
42. Fromm, *Escape From Freedom*, p. 74.
43. Ibid., pp. 205–206.
44. Ibid., pp. 207–208.
45. Wilhelm Reich, *The Mass Psychology of Fascism* (London: Souvenir Press, 1972), p. 23. Reich's book was first published in 1934.
46. Ibid., p. 209.
47. See Richard Gruenberger, *A Social History of the Third Reich* (New York: Penguin Books, 1974), chapter 13.
48. Fromm, *Escape From Freedom*, pp. 209–210.
49. Ibid., pp. 211–216.
50. Ibid., p. 220, cf. Erich Fromm, *The Anatomy of Human Destructiveness* (London: Pimlico, 1974), p. 498n.
51. Ibid., pp. 531–535.
52. Ibid., pp. 572–574.
53. Fromm, *Escape From Freedom*, pp. 224–225.
54. Ibid., p. 231.
55. Erich Fromm, *The Heart of Man*, pp. 85–86.
56. Ibid., p. 87.
57. Ibid., p. 237.
58. Ibid., p. 238. Fromm's use of the word "exterminate" has a gruesome significance, as the attempted extermination of European Jewry began in the year of the book's publication. The chapter offered readers in the United States a graphic warning of the irrational destructiveness of the Nazi ideology and practise.
59. For a summary of his theory of Instincts see Freud, *An Outline of Psycho-Analysis*, pp. 5–8.
60. Erich Fromm, *Man For Himself: An Inquiry into the Psychology of Ethics* (New York: Henry Holt, 1990), p. 151. Fromm refers to Nietzsche's *The Genealogy of Morals* (New York: Doubleday, 1956) II, 16.
61. Ibid., p. 219.
62. Fromm, *The Anatomy of Human Destructiveness*, pp. 40–41.
63. Konrad Lorenz, *On Aggression* (New York: Harcourt Brace Jovanovitch, 1965). The first edition was published in German in 1963.
64. Fromm, *The Anatomy of Human Destructiveness*, pp. 43–44.
65. Ibid., p. 362.
66. Fromm, *Man For Himself*, p. 216.
67. Ibid., pp. 22–23.
68. Fromm, *The Anatomy of Human Destructiveness*, pp. 52–53.
69. Fromm, *Escape From Freedom*, pp. 118–119.
70. Marcuse's review is published as "The Foundation of Historical Materialism" in Herbert Marcuse, *From Luther to Popper* (New York and London: Verso, 1972), pp. 1–48; his 1941 paper is "Some Social Implications of Modern Technology" in Andrew Arato and Eike Gebhardt (eds.) *The Essential Frankfurt School Reader* (New York: Urizen Books, 1972), pp. 138–182.
71. Erich Fromm, Introduction to *Socialist Humanism* (London: Allen Lane Penguin, 1967), p. xi; in fact in *The Holy Family*, Marx and Engels argue that members of the propertied class are also alienated, but feel "at ease and strengthened" in it because they see it as a product of their own power and they have a "semblance of human existence"—see Marx and Engels, *Collected Works*, volume five (London: Lawrence and Wishart, 1976), p. 36.
72. Fromm, *Escape From Freedom*, p. 240.
73. Ibid., p. 239.
74. Ibid., p. 251; Fromm's emphasis.
75. Ibid., p. 247.

76. Ibid., p. 117.
77. Ibid., p. 253.
78. Ibid., pp. 253–254.
79. Ibid., p. 127.
80. Ibid., pp. 249–250.
81. Ibid., pp. 241–247.
82. Fromm, *The Sane Society*, pp. 124–125.
83. Fromm, *To Have or To Be?*, p. 202.
84. Ibid., p. 118.
85. Fromm, *The Sane Society*, p. 136.
86. Fromm, *Man For Himself*, p. 68.
87. Ibid., p. 73.
88. Fromm, *To Have or To Be?*, pp. 157–158; for a more extensive discussion see Erich Fromm, *On Being Human* (New York: Continuum, 1998), pp. 148–158. For Marx's discussion of the having/being distinction see Marx and Engels, *Collected Works*, volume three, p. 309.
89. Fromm, *The Sane Society*, pp. 141–146.
90. Fromm, *To Have or to Be?*, pp. 148–149.
91. Erich Fromm, "Man-Woman" in Erich Fromm, *Love, Sexuality and Matriarchy: About Gender*, New York: Fromm International Publishing, 1997, p. 124.
92. Fromm, *To Have or to Be?*, pp. 200–201.
93. Fromm, *The Sane Society*, p. 175.
94. Fromm, *Escape From Freedom*, pp. 265–266.
95. Ibid., p. 262.
96. Ibid., p. 263.
97. Fromm, *The Anatomy of Human Destructiveness*, p. 20.
98. His mother fled Germany just before the War and his second wife, Henny, fled the Nazis with the philosopher Walter Benjamin and was fortunate to be allowed into neutral Spain following Benjamin's suicide—see Rainer Funk, *Erich Fromm: His Life and Ideas* (New York: Continuum, 2000), p. 122.

## Chapter Three   Humanistic Ethics

1. Erich Fromm, *Psychoanalysis and Religion* (New Haven and London: Yale University Press, 1978), chapter four.
2. Ibid., p. 74.
3. Ibid., p. 33.
4. Ibid., p. 20.
5. See Daniel Statman (ed.), *Ethics: A Critical Reader* (Edinburgh: Edinburgh University Press, 1997); Roger Crisp and Michael Slote (eds.), *Virtue Ethics* (Oxford and New York: Oxford University Press, 1997); Rosalind Hursthouse, *On Virtue Ethics* (Oxford: Oxford University Press, 1999); Philippa Foot, *Natural Goodness* (Oxford: Clarendon Press, 2003).
6. Alasdair MacIntyre, *After Virtue: A Study in Moral Theory* (2nd edn.) (London: Duckworth, 1995), chapter 5.
7. Ibid., pp. 54–55.
8. Erich Fromm, *Escape From Freedom* (New York: Henry Holt, 1994), p. 114.
9. Fromm, *Man For Himself*, pp. 121–123.
10. Fromm, *Escape From Freedom*, p. 165.
11. Ibid., pp. 114–115.
12. Erich Fromm, *Man For Himself: An Inquiry Into the Psychology of Ethics* (New York: Henry Holt, 1990), p. 7.
13. Fromm, *Man For Himself*, p. 14.

14. This is dealt with in part five of Baruch Spinoza, *Ethics*, A. Boyle (trans.) (London and New York: J. M. Dent, 1910), particularly propositions III and IV, pp. 203–204.
15. Fromm, *Man For Himself*, p. 145.
16. Ibid, p. 24. Fromm comments that we can still learn a lot about human nature from Shylock's speech in *The Merchant of Venice*, which begins "Hath not a Jew eyes?"
17. Ibid., p. 10.
18. The passages that Fromm cites are from Kant's "Metaphysics of Morals"—see Immanuel Kant, *Political Writings*, H. B. Nisbet (trans.), (Cambridge: Cambridge University Press, 1992), pp. 144–147.
19. Fromm, *Man For Himself*, pp. 31–37.
20. Ibid., pp. 25–26.
21. Ibid., pp. 91–92.
22. Ibid., pp. 175–176.
23. Ibid., p. 30. There is an indirect connection here with Fromm's strenuous criticism of Aristotle's logic, for the analytical logic which he founded, resting on the laws of thought, famously stresses either/or choices and therefore leaves open the question of how new knowledge may ever develop. Fromm, as a dialectical thinker, praises the "paradoxical logic" of philosophy from the time of Heraclitus and Lao Tse for its dynamism, its stress of transforming human beings, and its openness—Fromm, *The Art of Loving* (London: Thorsons, 1995), p. 62, cf. Fromm, "Psychoanalysis and Zen Buddhism," in Erich Fromm, D. T. Suzuki, and Richard De Martino, *Zen Buddhism and Psychoanalysis* (London: Souvenir Press, 1993), pp. 101–102.
24. Fromm, *Man For Himself*, pp. 26–27 and 176–177.
25. Fromm, *The Heart of Man*, pp. 143–146.
26. Spinoza, *Ethics* (New York and London: Everyman's Library, 1910), part four, Appendix, pp. 193–194.
27. Ibid., part four, pro. 44, pp. 172–173; Fromm, *Man For Himself*, p. 222.
28. George Santayana, Introduction to Spinoza, *Ethics*.
29. Spinoza, *Ethics*, pp. 193–194.
30. Fromm, *Man For Himself*, p. 27n. The passage from Marx is from the first volume of *Capital*—see Marx and Engels, *Collected Works* (New York and London: International Publishers and Lawrence and Wishart, 1996), volume 35, p. 605n.
31. Erich Fromm, *Marx's Concept of Man* (New York: Continuum, 1992).
32. Lawrence Wilde (ed.), Introduction to Wilde, *Marxism's Ethical Thinkers* (New York & Basingstoke: Palgrave, 2001).
33. Lawrence Wilde, *Ethical Marxism and Its Radical Critics* (New York and Basingstoke: St. Martin's Press and Macmillan, 1998), pp. 28–29.
34. Erich Fromm, *The Revolution of Hope: Toward a Humanised Technology* (New York, Evanston, and London: Harper and Row, 1968), p. 58, and, for a fuller discussion, Fromm, *Marx's Concept of Man*, chapter 4.
35. Besides the discussion in *Marx's Conception of Man* the most insightful reading of Marx's humanism can be found in a paper delivered in Paris in May 1968, "Marx's Contribution to the Knowledge of Man" in Erich Fromm, *The Crisis of Psychoanalysis* (Holt, Rinehart, Winston: New York, Chicago, San Francisco, 1970), chapter 3.
36. Karl Marx and Frederick Engels, "Manifesto of the Communist Party" in *Collected Works*, volume six, p. 506.
37. Fromm, *The Heart of Man*, p. 116n.
38. Ibid., pp. 116–117.
39. This summary of Fromm's concept of human essence is taken from Fromm, *Man For Himself*, pp. 38–50, and *The Heart of Man*, chapter 6; see also Fromm, Suzuki, and De Martino, *Zen Buddhism and Psychoanalysis*, pp. 86–95.
40. Fromm, *The Heart of Man*, p. 117.
41. Fromm, *Man for Himself*, p. 45 and 43.

42. Fromm, *The Art of Loving*, pp. 41–45.
43. Ibid., p. 47. He ascribes this view to the pragmatist William James.
44. James Daly, *Deals and Ideals: Two Concepts of Enlightenment* (London: Greenwich Exchange, 2000), pp. 28–30.
45. Fromm, *The Art of Loving*, pp. 101–104.
46. Daniel Burston, *The Legacy of Erich Fromm* (Cambridge, MA: Harvard University Press, 1991), p. 95.
47. Fromm, *Man For Himself*, p. 91.
48. Karl Marx, *Capital*, volume three (Harmondsworth: Penguin, 1981), p. 959. Marx saw the reduction of necessary work-time as a prerequisite for human freedom.
49. Karl Marx, Preface to *A Contribution to the Critique of Political Economy* in Marx and Engels, *Collected Works*, volume 29, p. 264.
50. Fromm, *Escape From Freedom*, pp. 256–262.
51. Ibid., p. 258.
52. Fromm, *Man For Himself*, pp. 87–88.
53. Ibid., p. 92.
54. Ibid., pp. 97–101.
55. Ibid., pp. 102–107.
56. Ibid., pp. 96–97.
57. Burston, *The Legacy of Erich Fromm*, pp. 73–77.
58. Fromm, *To Have or To Be?* (New York: Continuum, 2002), p. 24.
59. Ibid., p. 199 and pp. 111–112.
60. Michael Maccoby, Introduction (1995) to Erich Fromm and Michael Maccoby, *Social Character in a Mexican Village*, p. xix.
61. Fromm, *The Sane Society* (New York: Henry Holt,1990), pp. 12–21.
62. Fromm, *The Sane Society*, chapter 8; *The Revolution of Hope*, chapter 5; *To Have or To Be?*, part three.
63. Fromm, *To Have or To Be?*, p. 88.
64. Ibid., pp. 170–172.
65. Fromm, *Man For Himself*, pp. 114–117, in which Fromm specifies the positive and negative traits within each nonproductive orientation; cf. Fromm, *To Have or To Be?*, p. 108.
66. Che Guevara, "Man and Socialism in Cuba" in John Gerassi (ed.) *Venceremos: The Speeches and Writings of Che Guevara* (London: Granada, 1972), p. 553. I am indebted to my colleague Mark Weinstein for drawing this to my attention.
67. Maccoby, *Social Character*, p. xx.
68. Fromm, *Man For Himself*, p. 85.
69. Fromm, *Psychoanalysis and Religion*, pp. 21–22.
70. Erich Fromm, "Psychoanalysis and Zen Buddhism" in Fromm, D. T. Suzuki and R. de Martino, *Zen Buddhism and Psychoanalysis* (London: Souvenir Press, 1993, orig. 1960), pp. 113–141.
71. Erich Fromm, *Man For Himself: An Inquiry into the Psychology of Ethics* (New York: Henry Holt, 1990), p. 198, cf. *To Have or To Be?*, pp. 49–51.
72. Fromm, *Psychoanalysis and Religion*, p. v.
73. Ibid., p. 3.
74. Ibid., p. 4.
75. Ibid., p. 26.
76. Ibid., pp. 33–36 and 85.
77. Ibid., p. 37.
78. Ibid., pp. 49–50.
79. Ibid., p. 53. The knowledge of our dependence should add to our sense of social responsibility, as Alasdair MacIntyre has argued in *Dependent Rational Animals: Why Human Beings Need the Virtues* (London: Duckworth, 1999).
80. Fromm, *Psychoanalysis and Religion*, pp. 94–95.

81. Ibid., pp. 111–112. Fromm's next book dealt with the understanding of dreams, fairy tales and myths—Erich Fromm, *The Forgotten Language* (New York: Grove Press, 1951).
82. Ibid., pp. 114–119.
83. Genesis 3:5.
84. Fromm, *You Shall Be As Gods* (New York: Henry Holt,1991), p. 4.
85. Ibid., pp. 24–25.
86. Ibid., pp. 162–163.
87. Ibid., pp. 123–133.
88. Ibid., p. 229.
89. Erich Fromm, *The Dogma of Christ* (New York: Henry Holt, 1993), pp. 42–43.
90. Ibid., pp. 46–47.
91. Ibid., p. 48.
92. Ibid., pp. 38–39.
93. Ibid., pp. 79–81; see Judith Herrin, *The Formation of Christendom* (Oxford: Basil Blackwell, 1987).
94. See Norman Cohn, *The Pursuit of the Millennium* (Oxford and New York: Oxford University Press, 1970), and Gordon Leff, *Heresy in the Later Middle Ages: The Relations of Heterodoxy to Dissent,* (Manchester: Manchester University Press/Sandpiper Books, 1999).
95. Fromm, *Psychoanalysis and Religion*, pp. 48–49.
96. This is published as the third part of Erich Fromm, *On Being Human* (New York: Continuum, 1998), edited with a foreword by Rainer Funk.
97. Ibid., pp. 141–142.
98. Ibid., p. 133.
99. Ibid., pp. 166–168. Marx's discussion of religion is from the Introduction to The Critique of Hegel's Philosophy of Right" in *Collected Works*, volume three, pp. 175–176.
100. Fromm, *You Shall Be As Gods*, p. 44n.
101. See Lawrence Wilde, "The Ethical Marxism of Erich Fromm" in M. Cowling and P. Reynolds (eds.), *Marx, The Millennium and Beyond* (Basingstoke: Palgrave, 2000).
102. Fromm, *On Being Human*, p. 170. Fromm is quoting Bloch's *Atheism in Christianity* (New York: Herder and Herder, 1972). Bloch's work on religion offers many similarities to Fromm's—see Vincent Geoghegan, *Ernst Bloch* (New York and London, 1996), chapter 3.
103. MacIntyre, *After Virtue*, p. 148.
104. Aristotle, *Ethics* (Harmondsworth: Penguin, 1976), J. A. K. Thomson (trans.), p. 76 (Book One of the Nichomachean Ethics).
105. Philip Kain, *Marx and Ethics* (New York: Oxford University Press, 1991), pp. 30–32.
106. Fromm, *Man for Himself*, pp. 16–17. This arises in the course of Fromm's defence of "objectivistic" against "subjectivistic" ethics.
107. Ibid., p. 18. On the science of man, pp. 20–24.
108. Ibid., p. 24.
109. Ibid., p. 16.
110. Fromm, *Beyond the Chains of Illusion*, p. 10.
111. Fromm, *Man for Himself*, pp. 219–221. Fromm acknowledges the similarity with Spinoza's ethics in this respect.
112. Hursthouse, *On Virtue Ethics*, pp. 222–223.
113. For example, Fromm, *The Sane Society*, p. 276 and 344; Fromm, *To Have or To Be?*, chapter 8.
114. For example, John Schaar, *Escape From Authority: The Perspectives of Erich Fromm* (New York, 1964, p. 22). A similar objection, this time to Marx's humanism, is made by Ted Benton, *Natural Relations: Ecology, Animal Rights and Social Justice* (London: Verso, 1993), p. 40.
115. Erich Fromm, *The Crisis of Psychoanalysis* (New York: Holt, Rienhart and Winston, 1970), pp. 33–35; Erich Fromm, *The Anatomy of Human Destructiveness* (London: Pimlico, 1997), Appendix, pp. 581–631.

116. Fromm, *Man For Himself*, p. 218; Fromm, *The Sane Society*, pp. 37–38.
117. Fromm, *To Have or To Be?*, pp. 192–193.
118. Fromm, *The Anatomy of Human Destructiveness*. The second part of the book compiles the evidence against the instinctivist theorists such as Konrad Lorenz.
119. Fromm, *To Have or To Be?*, p. 194.
120. Fromm, *The Anatomy of Human Destructiveness*, p. 575. His discussion of the anthropological evidence forms chapter 8.
121. Seyla Benhabib, *Critique, Norm and Utopia: A Study of the Foundations of Critical Theory* (New York: Columbia University Press, 1986), pp. 132–133—see also p. 57 and 69.
122. Iris Marion Young, *Justice and the Politics of Difference* (Princeton: Princeton University Press, 1990), p. 36.
123. For an eloquent defense of essentialism see Terry Eagleton, *After Theory* (London and New York: Allen Lane Penguin, 2003), chapter five. However, his judgment that "talk about human nature is embarrassingly general" (p. 121) does not apply to Fromm.
124. Ibid., p. 20.
125. Ibid., pp. 18–19.
126. Fromm, *The Heart of Man*, p. 102, and Fromm, *The Art of Loving*, p. 26.
127. I have argued that Marx is respectful of nonhuman nature in Lawrence Wilde, " 'The Creatures, Too, Must Become Free': Marx and the Animal/Human Distinction" in *Capital and Class* 72, Autumn 2000.
128. Fromm, *Man For Himself*, p. 39: Fromm, *The Revision of Psychoanalysis*, pp. 24–25.
129. Fromm, *To Have or to Be?*, pp. 26–28.
130. Michael Maccoby, "The Two Voices of Erich Fromm: Prophet and Analyst" in Mauricio Cortina and Michael Maccoby (eds.), *A Prophetic Analyst: Erich Fromm's Contribution to Psychoanalysis* (Northvale, NJ: Jason Aronson, 1996), pp. 88–89.
131. Ibid., p. 65.
132. Fromm, *The Sane Society*, p. 352.
133. Fromm, *To Have or to Be?*, p. 173.
134. Fromm, *The Sane Society*, pp. 238–239.

## Chapter Four   Toward a Gendered Humanism

1. Carol Gilligan, *In a Different Voice: Psychological Theory and Women's Development*, (Cambridge, MA: Harvard University Press, 1982); J. Trebilcot (ed.), *Mothering: Essays in Feminist Theory*, Totowa (NJ: Rowman and Allanheld, 1984).
2. For introductions to their work see Toril Moi (ed.), *The Kristeva Reader* (Cambridge, MA and Oxford: Blackwell, 1986) and Margaret Whitford (ed.), *The Irigaray Reader* (Cambridge, MA and Oxford: Blackwell, 1991).
3. Johann Jacob Bachofen, *Myth, Religion and Mother Right: Selected Writings*, Ralph Manheim (trans.) (Princeton, NJ: Princeton University Press, 1992)—there is a useful introduction by Joseph Campbell. *Mother Right* was originally published in German in 1861 and republished in 1926.
4. August Bebel, *Women Under Socialism*, Daniel de Leon (trans.) (New York: Schocken Books, 1971) [originally 1879]; Friedrich Engels, *The Origin of the Family, Private Property, and the State* (New York: Pathfinder, 1972) [originally 1884]. Engels's contribution owed more to the work of the American anthropologist Lewis Henry Morgan, whose *Ancient Society* was published in 1877. Morgan's work among the Iroquois supplied independent confirmation of the existence of matrilineal society and was far more influential than Bachofen's. They corresponded but never met.
5. See Gerda Lerner, *The Creation of Patriarchy* (Oxford: Oxford University Press, 1986), pp. 28–31.
6. Robert Briffault, *The Mothers: The Matriarchal Theory of Social Origins* (New York: Macmillan, 1931); Fromm's review appeared in the first edition of volume three of the

*Zeitschrift* in 1934 and it is published in the original German in volume one of Erich Fromm, *Gesamtausgabe* (Stuttgart and Munich: Deutsche Verlags-Anstalt, Deutscher Taschenbach Verlag, 1999), pp. 79–84.

7. First published in English in Erich Fromm, *The Crisis of Psychoanalysis: Essays on Freud, Marx, and Social Psychology* (New York: Holt, Rinehart, Winston, 1970), pp. 84–109.

8. This is now published in a collection edited by Rainer Funk including the two articles from the *Zeitschrift*—Erich Fromm, *Love, Sexuality and Matriarchy: About Gender* (New York: Fromm International Publishing, 1997). All following references will be to this edition. Funk, who found the manuscript of "The Male Creation" among Fromm's papers in the New York Public Library, estimates 1933 as the date of writing.

9. The exchange took place in the journal *Dissent* in 1955. For the definitive discussion of the Marcuse–Fromm dispute see John Rickert, "The Fromm–Marcuse Debate Revisited" in *Theory and Society* 15 (3) 1986, pp. 351–399. See also Daniel Burston, *The Legacy of Erich Fromm* (Cambridge, MA: Harvard University Press, 1991), chapter 9.

10. Fromm, *Love, Sexuality and Matriarchy*, pp. 77–78.

11. Ibid., p. 79.

12. Fromm, *Love, Sexuality and Matriarchy*, p. 80.

13. Ibid., p. 84.

14. Ibid., p. 83.

15. Bachofen, *Myth, Religion and Mother Right*, p. 79.

16. Ibid., pp. 80–81.

17. Ibid., p. 91.

18. Ibid, pp. 109–110.

19. Fromm, *Love, Sexuality, and Matriarchy*, p. 31.

20. Ibid., p. 27.

21. Ibid., p. 26. The argument here bears a close resemblance to Marx's discussion of the relationship between political and human freedom in *On the Jewish Question*, with which Fromm would have been familiar.

22. Ibid., p. 22.

23. J. J. Bachofen, Introduction to *Mother Right* in Bachofen, *Myth, Religion and Mother Right: Selected Writings of J. J. Bachofen* (Princeton, NJ: Princeton University Press, Mythos edition, 1992), pp. 102–103 on mother-based religion and p. 109 on the advance to patriarchy. His suggestion of mother-based religion inspired Charlotte Perkins-Gilman to include this in her feminist utopian novel *Herland*, written in 1915.

24. Ibid., p. 110, cf. Fromm, *Love, Sexuality and Matriarchy*, pp. 24–25.

25. Bachofen, *Myth, Religion, and Mother Right*, pp. 118–119.

26. Fromm, *Love, Sexuality and Matriarchy*, p. 44.

27. Ibid., p. 29.

28. Ibid., pp. 40–41.

29. Ibid., pp. 44–45.

30. Ibid., pp. 38–40.

31. Ibid., p. 41.

32. Erich Fromm, *Escape From Freedom* (New York: Henry Holt, 1994), chapter three.

33. Fromm, *Love, Sexuality and Matriarchy*, p. 43.

34. Ibid., p. 35.

35. Ibid., p. 51.

36. Ibid, p. 48. Horney's articles on distrust between the sexes were published posthumously in Karen Horney, *Feminine Psychology*, H. Kelman (ed.) (New York: W. W. Norton, 1967). Her article, "Culture and Aggression: Some Thoughts and Doubts about Freud's Death Drive and Destruction Drive" was published posthumously in the *American Journal of Psychoanalysis* 20 (1960), pp. 130–138. Horney and Fromm had an intimate relationship in the United States during his tenure with the Institute for Social Theory. She was the third powerful and older woman in his life, following his mother and his first wife, Frieda Fromm-Reichmann.

37. Ibid., p. 51.
38. Ibid., pp. 54–56. In 1966, Fromm published a radical interpretation of the Old Testament which argued for a liberating subtext to the story of the Fall, whereby the serpent is correct in saying that if they eat the forbidden fruit they will know the difference between good and evil and "shall be as Gods." Only in disobedience does humanity create itself. See Erich Fromm, *You Shall Be as Gods* (New York: Henry Holt, 1991), pp. 88–89 and 64.
39. Fromm, *Love, Sexuality and Matriarchy*, pp. 66–72.
40. Ibid., p. 112.
41. Ibid., p. 97.
42. Ibid., p. 115.
43. Erich Fromm, *Man For Himself: An Inquiry into the Psychology of Ethics* (New York: Henry Holt, 1990).
44. Fromm, *Love, Sexuality and Matriarchy*, p. 38.
45. Ibid., pp. 47–48.
46. Erich Fromm, *The Forgotten Language: An Introduction to the Understanding of Dreams, Fairy Tales and Myths* (New York: Grove Press, 1957), pp. 196–231.
47. Ibid., p. 202.
48. Ibid., p. 218.
49. Ibid., p. 213.
50. Ibid., p. 221.
51. Ibid., p. 222.
52. Ibid., pp. 228–231.
53. Fromm, *Escape From Freedom*, p. 8.
54. In Fromm, *Love, Sexuality and Matriarchy*, p. 163 and 170.
55. Ibid., p. 165.
56. Ibid., p. 169.
57. Ibid., p. 189.
58. Ibid., pp. 194–195.
59. Erich Fromm, *Man for Himself*, particularly chapter four, part five; for a more succinct discussion of human essence see Erich Fromm, *The Heart of Man: Its Genius for Good and Evil* (New York: Harper and Row, 1964), chapter six.
60. On Fromm's ethics see Rainer Funk, *Erich Fromm: The Courage to Be Human* (New York: Continuum, 1982), chapter 5; Lawrence Wilde, "Against Idolatry: The Humanistic Ethics of Erich Fromm," in *Marxism's Ethical Thinkers* (Basingstoke and New York: Palgrave, 2001).
61. Rainer Funk, Editor's Introduction to Fromm, *Love, Sexuality and Matriarchy*, p. vii.
62. Erich Fromm, "You Shall Be As Gods," interview with Oliver Hunkin in the "Doubts and Certainties" series, BBC television, August 29, 1968. My thanks to Rainer Funk for access to the videotape.
63. Erich Fromm, *The Anatomy of Human Destructiveness* (London: Random House, 1997), p. 127; see Donald W. Winnicott, *The Maturational Processes and the Facilitating Environment: Studies in the Theory of Emotional Development* (London: Hogarth Press and the Institute of Psychoanalysis, 1965).
64. Erich Fromm, *The Sane Society* (New York: Henry Holt, 1990), p. 45.
65. Ibid., p. 47.
66. Ibid., p. 47; the criticism of Freud's attribution of conscience exclusively to the paternal side is repeated in Fromm, *To Have or To Be?* (New York: Continuum, 2002), p. 192.
67. Erich Fromm, *The Art of Loving* (London: Thorsons, 1995), p. 29; Herbert Marcuse comes up with a similar list of positive female qualities that may be used as a force for liberation—see his interview with Bryan Magee, 1978, in Bryan Magee, *Men of Ideas: Some Creators of Contemporary Philosophy* (Oxford: Oxford University Press, 1982), p. 53.
68. Fromm, *Man for Himself*, part three. Later in the book he comments that if a woman does not fulfill her potential to be a mother she will experience a frustration which can be

remedied only by "increased realisation of her powers in other realms of her life" (p. 219), but this is not central to his argument about the human essence.

69. Fromm, "The Significance of the Theory of Mother Right For Today" in Fromm, *The Crisis of Psychanalysis*, p. 83.
70. Fromm, *To Have or To Be?*, pp. 145–146.
71. Ibid., pp. 191–193.
72. Carol Gilligan, *In A Different Voice, and The Birth of Pleasure: A New Map of Love* (London: Chatto & Windus, 2002).
73. Luce Irigaray, *Je, tu, nous: Toward a Culture of Difference* (London: Routledge, 1993), pp. 12–13.
74. Luce Irigaray, *Democracy Begins Between Two* (New York: Routledge, 2001), p. 54.
75. Irigaray, *Je, tu, nous*, p. 24, cf. p. 17 and 90; she criticises Bachofen for the weakness of his argument that matriarchy is more moral but patriarchy is more spiritual—"what do spirituality and heavenliness mean without ethics?," p. 27.
76. Irigaray, *Je, tu, nous*, pp. 81–92.
77. Luce Irigaray, *This Sex Which is Not One* (Ithaca, New York: Cornell University Press, 1985), p. 29
78. Ibid., p. 122.
79. Irigaray, *Democracy Begins Between Two*, pp. 150–151.
80. Ibid., p. 15.
81. Irigaray, *An Ethics of Sexual Difference* (London: Athlone, 1993), chapter 10, pp. 59–71.
82. Ibid., pp. 62–65.
83. Ibid., p. 69.
84. Ibid., p. 67.
85. Erich Fromm, *Psychoanalysis and Religion* (New Haven and London: Yale University Press, 1978), p. 22.
86. For an excellent discussion of this aspect of Irigaray's work see Alison Martin, *Luce Irigaray and the Question of the Divine* (London: Maney Publishing for the Modern Humanities Research Association, 2000).
87. Luce Irigaray, *Sexes and Genealogies* (New York: Columbia University Press, 1993), p. 61.
88. Ibid., pp. 63–64.
89. Luce Irigaray, *To Be Two* (London: Athlone, 2000), p. 88.
90. She suggests that the word Goddess implies one of many—Irigaray, *An Ethics of Sexual Difference*, p. 68.
91. Irigaray, *To Be Two*, pp. 108–109.
92. Irigaray, *Je, tu, nous*, p. 25.
93. Irigaray, *Democracy Begins Between Two*, pp. 40–41.
94. Fromm, "Man-Woman" (1951) in *Love, Sexuality and Matriarchy*, p. 122.
95. Irigaray, *Democracy Begins Between Two*, p. 9; also p. 72.
96. Ibid., p. 89.
97. Ibid., p. 29.
98. Kate Soper, "Feminism, Humanism, Postmodernism" in Soper, *Troubled Pleasures* (New York and London: Verso, 1990), p. 233.
99. Ibid., pp. 233–234.

## Chapter Five   Work

1. Erich Fromm, *Escape From Freedom* (New York: Henry Holt, 1994), pp. 259–260.
2. Erich Fromm, *The Sane Society* (New York: Henry Holt, 1990), pp. 177–178.
3. Erich Fromm, *The Anatomy of Human Destructiveness* (London: Pimlico, 1997), p. 187n.
4. Fromm, *The Sane Society*, pp. 289–290.
5. Erich Fromm, *The Revolution of Hope: Toward a Humanised Technology* (New York and London: Harper and Row, 1968), p. 127.

6. Erich Fromm, *To Have or To Be?* (New York: Continuum, 2002), pp. 100–101.
7. Fromm, *The Anatomy of Human Destructiveness*, pp. 326–327.
8. Ibid., p. 328.
9. Ibid.
10. Hugh Willmot and David Knights, "The Problem of Freedom: Fromm's Contribution to a Critical Theory of Work Organisation" in *Praxis International* 2 (2), 1982, pp. 220–222.
11. André Gorz, *Reclaiming Work: Beyond the Wage-Based Society* (Cambridge: Polity, 1999).
12. Fromm, *Escape From Freedom*, pp. 58–63.
13. Ibid., p. 95.
14. Ibid., pp. 118–119.
15. Fromm, *Man For Himself: An Inquiry Into The Psychology of Ethics* (New York: Henry Holt, 1990), pp. 67–78.
16. Fromm, *The Sane Society*, p. 180. Fromm refers here to the work of Peter Drucker who, at the time of writing, continues to argue for a humanistic approach to work relations.
17. Ibid., p. 182.
18. Gorz, *Reclaiming Work*, chapter 2.
19. Richard Sennett, *The Corrosion of Character* (New York: W. W. Norton, 1999), chapter four, in which he looks at the computerization of a bakery.
20. Fromm, *The Sane Society*, pp. 293–294.
21. Ibid., p. 295.
22. Ibid., pp. 296–297.
23. Sennett, *The Corrosion of Character*, chapter one.
24. Fromm, *To Have or To Be?*, p. 147–154.
25. Ibid., p. 146.
26. Fromm, "Let Man Prevail" (originally 1960) in *On Disobedience And Other Essays* (New York: Seabury Press, 1981), p. 62.
27. Fromm, *Man For Himself*, p. 69.
28. Ibid., p. 147.
29. Sennett, *The Corrosion of Character*, p. 115.
30. Ibid., pp. 150–151. The study was later published as Michael Maccoby, *The Gamesmen: The New Corporate Leaders* (New York: Simon and Schuster, 1976).
31. Fromm, *The Sane Society*, pp. 241–244; James Lincoln, *Incentive Management* (Cleveland: Lincoln Electric, 1951).
32. Ibid., pp. 245–246.
33. Fromm, *To Have or To Be?*, p. 199.
34. Fromm, *The Sane Society*, p. 276. Kant's practical imperative requires that we act so that we use humanity always as an end, never *merely* as a means—Immanuel Kant, *Groundwork of the Metaphysics of Morals* (Cambridge: Cambridge University Press, 1999), p. 38.
35. Fromm, *The Sane Society*, p. 276.
36. Ibid., pp. 287–289.
37. Ibid., pp. 283–284.
38. In Erich Fromm, *The Crisis of Psychoanalysis* (New York, Chicago, San Francisco: Holt, Rinehart, Winston, 1970), p. 67.
39. Erich Fromm, *Psychoanalysis and Religion* (New Haven and London: Yale University Press, 1978), p. 1.
40. Fromm, *The Revolution of Hope*, p. 96.
41. Ibid., p. 97.
42. Lawrence Wilde, *Modern European Socialism* (Aldershot: Dartmouth, 1994), chapter 4.
43. Fromm, *The Revolution of Hope*, p. 98.
44. Ibid., pp. 98–99.
45. Kenneth Morgan, *Labour in Power, 1945–1951* (Oxford: Oxford University Press, 1985), pp. 366–368.
46. Fromm, *The Revolution of Hope*, p. 99.

47. Ibid., pp. 100–106.
48. Lawrence Wilde, *Modern European Socialism*, pp. 59–60.
49. Fromm, "Humanist Socialism" in *On Disobedience and Other Essays*, p. 88.
50. For the most coherent statement of this strategy see Stuart Holland, *The Socialist Challenge* (London: Quartet Books, 1975).
51. Philippe Van Parijs (ed.), Introduction to Parijs, *Arguing for Basic Income* (London: Verso, 1992), pp. 11–12.
52. Ibid., p. 3.
53. Fromm, *The Sane Society*, p. 335.
54. Ibid., p. 337.
55. Ibid., p. 336.
56. Fromm, *To Have or To Be?*, p. 186.
57. Fromm, *The Sane Society.*, p. 338.
58. Fromm, "The Psychological Aspects of the Guaranteed Income" in Fromm, *On Disobedience and Other Essays*, pp. 98–99.
59. Ibid., pp. 96–97.
60. Ibid., p. 100.
61. See, for example, Ulrich Beck, *The Brave New World of Work* (Cambridge and Malden, MA: Polity and Blackwell, 2000), particularly the final two chapters.
62. Fromm, *The Revolution of Hope*, p. 127.
63. Ibid., p. 128.
64. See Daniel Moynihan, *The Politics of a Guaranteed Income: The Nixon Administration and the Family Assistance Plan* (New York: Random House, 1973).
65. Van Parijs, Introduction to *Arguing for Basic Income*, p. 30 n4.
66. Friedman's position at this time can be found in his "The Case for a Negative Income Tax: The View from the Right" in J. H. Bunzel (ed.), *Issues of American Public Policy* (Englewood Cliffs, NJ: Prentice Hall, 1968), pp. 111–120.
67. Gorz criticises the right-wing version of basic income in Gorz, *Critique of Economic Reason* (London: Verso, 1989), pp. 203–212.
68. Gorz, *Reclaiming Work*, pp. 84–93.
69. Brian Barry, "Equality Yes, Basic Income No" in Van Parijs (ed.), *Arguing for Basic Income*, pp. 139–140.
70. Fromm, *The Sane Society*, pp. 302–305; Elton Mayo, *The Human Problem of an Industrial Civilisation* (New York: Macmillan, 1946).
71. Fromm, *The Sane Society*, pp. 306–320.
72. Ibid., p. 313.
73. Fromm, note to the third impression of *The Sane Society* (London: Routledge, 1991), pp. xii–xiii. He cites the Yugoslav system of workers' self-management as a possible model to be adopted within the framework of a state.
74. Fromm, "Humanist Socialism" in *On Disobedience and Other Essays*, p. 78.
75. Ibid., p. 89.
76. See Wilde, *Modern European Socialism*, pp. 29–30.
77. Fromm, *The Anatomy of Human Destructiveness*, p. 328.
78. Fromm, *Escape From Freedom*, p. 123.
79. Fromm, *The Sane Society*, p. 325. He cites F. Tannenbaum, *A Philosophy of Labour* (New York: Alfred Knopf, 1952).
80. See Lawrence Wilde, "Swedish Social Democracy and the World Market" in Ronen Palan and Barry Gills (eds.), *Transcending the State-Global Divide* (Boulder and London: Lynne Reinner, 1994).
81. Fromm, *The Sane Society*, p. 326.
82. Fromm, "Humanist Socialism" in *On Disobedience and Other Essays*, p. 89.
83. Jo-Ann Mort (ed.), *Not Your Father's Union Movement: Inside the AFL-CIO* (London: Verso, 1998).

84. Alexander Cockburn and Jeffrey St. Clair, *Five Days That Shook the World: The Battle for Seattle and Beyond* (London: Verso, 2000).
85. Ronaldo Munck, *Globalisation and Labour: The New Great Transformation* (London and New York: Zed Books, 2002).
86. There is no indication that Gorz has read Fromm's discussions of work, although he mentions *Escape From Freedom in Reclaiming Work*. Gorz was influence by Herbert Marcuse and Ivan Illich, both of whom were theoretically close to Fromm.
87. Ibid., p. 59.
88. André Gorz, *Capitalism, Socialism, Ecology* (London: Verso, 1994), p. 53.
89. Ibid., p. 57, cf. Gorz, *Reclaiming Work*, p. 3.
90. André Gorz, *Farewell to the Working Class* (London: Pluto Press, 1982), pp. 5–6.
91. Conrad Lodziak and Jeremy Tatman, *André Gorz: A Critical Introduction* (London and Chicago: Pluto Press, 1997), p. 93. Gorz may well have taken the distinction from a 1976 book by Illich, but the distinction originates in Fromm, as Illich would have been well aware. Illich visited Fromm frequently in Switzerland in the 1970s.
92. Fromm, *Man For Himself*, p. 158.
93. Gorz, *Farewell to the Working Class*, p. 49.
94. Gorz, *Reclaiming Work*, p. 64.
95. Fromm, *To Have or To Be?*, pp. 195–196.
96. Gorz, *Reclaiming Work*, p. 49.
97. Ibid., pp. 52–54, the section on "generalized insecurity."
98. Ibid., pp. 63–64; for example, the findings of a survey of 2,500 employees in the United Kingdom undertaken by the Policy Studies Institute and the London School of Economics for the Economic and Social Research Council, reported in *The Guardian*, June 13, 2001.
99. Gorz, *Farewell to the Working Class* (London: Pluto Press, 1982), p. 2.
100. The case of nurses in the British National Health Service offers a good example. See Isobel Allen, *Stress Among Ward Sisters and Charge Nurses* (London: Policy Studies Institute, June 2001).
101. Gorz, *Critique of Economic Reason* (New York and London: Verso, 1989), pp. 206–208.
102. Gorz outlines the scheme in ibid., pp. 209–212.
103. Gorz, *Reclaiming Work*, pp. 85–93.
104. Gorz, *Reclaiming Work*, pp. 102–108. See also Jim Shorthose, "Micro-Experiments in Alternatives" in *Capital and Class* 72, Autumn 2000.
105. Fromm, *The Revolution of Hope*, p. 127; Gorz's reasons for dropping the condition are both pragmatic and principled, but although he claims they are reflect the new realities of postfordism this is unconvincing.
106. Ibid., pp. 39–43.
107. Ibid., p. 71, cf. Fromm, *Man for Himself* (New York: Henry Holt, 1990), p. 18.
108. Gorz, *Reclaiming Work*, p. 115; cf. Fromm, *To Have or to Be?*, p. 151.
109. Gorz, *Reclaiming Work*, pp. 94–98.
110. Ibid., p. 98.
111. Ibid., p. 2.
112. Ibid., p. 73.
113. Ibid., p. 59, cf. Fromm, *The Sane Society*, pp. 360–363.
114. Gorz, *Reclaiming Work*, p. 79.
115. Ibid., p. 65.
116. Ibid., p. 78.
117. Charles Fourier, writing in the early nineteenth century, identified the need for attractive work ("*travail attractif*") as a fundamental aspect of human freedom. See Charles Fourier, *The Utopian Vision of Charles Fourier*, introduced by Jonathan Beecher and Richard Bienvenu (London: Jonathan Cape, 1975), part six.

## Chapter Six   Consumption

1. Aldous Huxley, *Brave New World* (Harmondsworth: Penguin, 1967); on the American influence see David Bradshaw, Introduction to Aldous Huxley, *Brave New World Revisited* (London: Harper Collins, 1994).
2. Erich Fromm, *The Sane Society* (Henry Holt: New York, 1990), pp. 224–228.
3. Ibid., pp. 127–128.
4. David Bollier, *Citizen Action and Other Big Ideas: A History of Ralph Nader and the Modern Consumer Movement* at www.nader.org/history_bollier.html, chapter one, p. 4. Bollier also points to the significant impact of two books, Frederick Schlink and Stuart Chase's *Your Money's Worth* (1927) and Schlink and Arthur Kallet's *100,000,000 Guinea Pigs: Dangers in Everyday Foods, Drugs and Cosmetics* (1933).
5. The "Homo consumens" formula is found in: Erich Fromm, *The Revolution of Hope: Toward a Humanised Technology* (New York: Harper and Row, 1968), p. 38; Erich Fromm, *On Disobedience and Other Essays* (New York: The Seabury Press, 1981), p. 95; Erich Fromm, *To Have or To Be?* (New York: Continuum, 2002), p. 176.
6. Fromm, *Escape From Freedom*, pp. 116–117.
7. Fromm, *Man For Himself: An Inquiry into the Psychology of Ethics* (New York: Henry Holt, 1990), p. 158. Gorz first develops this conceptual dichotomy in *Farewell to the Working Class* (London: Pluto, 1982), p. 97 and retains it in his subsequent works.
8. Fromm, *Escape From Freedom*, pp. 185–188.
9. Ibid., p. 128.
10. Ibid., p. 197.
11. Erich Fromm, *The Sane Society* (New York: Henry Holt, 1990), pp. 131–132, cf. Marx, "Economic and Philosophic Manuscripts" in Karl Marx and Frederick Engels, *Collected Works*, volume 3 (London: Lawrence and Wishart, 1975), pp. 322–326 and Lawrence Wilde, *Marx and Contradiction* (Aldershot and Brookfield, Vermont: Avebury, 1989), pp. 53–56.
12. Fromm, *The Sane Society*, pp. 134–135.
13. Fromm, *To Have or To Be?*, p. 6.
14. Ibid., pp. 26–27. Fromm lists automobiles, television, travel, and sex as the main objects of consumerism.
15. Fromm, *The Sane Society*, p. 136; the conclusion fundamentally concurs with argument in the chapter on "The Culture Industry—Enlightenment as Mass Deception" in Adorno and Horkheimer's *Dialectic of Enlightenment*, published in 1944.
16. Fromm, *The Sane Society*, p. 137.
17. Ibid., pp. 152–162. The Park Forest community is strikingly similar to the community depicted in Gary Ross's 1999 film *Pleasantville*.
18. Fromm, *To Have or To Be?*, p. 35.
19. Fromm, *The Revolution of Hope*, p. 37.
20. Fromm, *The Sane Society*, pp. 164–165.
21. Ibid., p. 166.
22. Fromm, *To Have or To Be?*, pp. 187–188.
23. Fromm, *The Sane Society*, p. 148.
24. Fromm, *To Have or To Be?*, p. 148.
25. Ibid., p. 149.
26. Ibid., pp. 149–150.
27. Fromm, *The Sane Society*.
28. Fromm, *The Revolution of Hope*, p. 119.
29. Ibid., p. 118.
30. Ibid., p. 120.
31. Fromm, *The Sane Society*, pp. 345–348.
32. Fromm, *To Have or To Be?*, pp. 187–188.

33. Fromm, *The Revolution of Hope*, p. 121.
34. Aristotle, *Nichomachean Ethics*, Book One, (Harmondsworth: Penguin, 1976), p. 84.
35. Fromm, *The Revolution of Hope*, p. 121.
36. Fromm, *The Sane Society*, p. 332; *To Have or To Be?*, p. 176.
37. Fromm, *To Have or To Be?*, p. 176.
38. Fromm, *The Revolution of Hope*, pp. 120–121; *To Have or To Be?*, p. 177.
39. Fromm, *The Revolution of Hope*, p. 122.
40. Fromm, *To Have or To Be?*, pp. 180–181.
41. Herbert Marcuse, *One Dimensional Man* (Boston: Beacon Press, 1991), chapter 1; on the similarities of the approaches of Fromm and Marcuse see Lawrence Wilde, *Ethical Marxism and Its Radical Critics* (Basingstoke: Macmillan, 1998), chapter 4.
42. Marx uses this expression in "The Civil War in France"—see Karl Marx and Frederick Engels, *Collected Works*, volume 22 (London: Lawrence and Wishart, 1986), p. 329.
43. Roberto Mangabeira Unger, *Democracy Realized: The Progressive Alternative* (New York: Verso, 1998), pp. 19–20.
44. Fromm, *The Revolution of Hope*, pp. 123–124.
45. Fromm, *To Have or To Be?*, p. 176.
46. Fromm, *The Revolution of Hope*, pp. 128–129.
47. Ibid., pp. 129–130. From also quotes Alfred Marshall's call for healthier consumption.
48. John Stuart Mill, *Principles of Political Economy*.
49. Fromm, *The Revolution of Hope*, p. 133.
50. Fromm, *To Have or To Be?*, p. 187.
51. Fromm, *The Sane Society*, p. 333.
52. There is now a wealth of literature on this, but see in particular Richard Falk, *On Humane Governance: Toward a New Global Politics* (Cambridge: Polity Press, 1995).
53. Jon Burchell and Simon Lightfoot, *The Greening of the European Union?* (New York: Sheffield Academic Press, 2001).
54. Fromm, *The Revolution of Hope*, p. 124.
55. Fromm, *The Sane Society*, p. 346.
56. Ronald Inglehart, *The Silent Revolution: Changing Values and Political Styles Among Western Publics* (Princeton, NJ: Princeton University Press, 1997) and *Culture Shift in Advanced Industrial Society* (Princeton, NJ: Princeton University Press, 1990).
57. Bollier, *Citizen Action and Other Big Ideas: A History of Ralph Nader and the Modern Consumer Movement*, chapter one, pp. 2–3.
58. Fromm, *To Have or To Be?*, pp. 179–180.
59. Steve Yearley and John Forrester, "Shell, A Sure Target for Global Environmental Campaigning?" in Robin Cohen and Shirin Rai (eds.), *Global Social Movements* (Brunswick, NJ and London, 2000), p. 138.
60. Naomi Klein, *No Logo* (London: Flamingo, 2000), pp. 387–391.
61. Ibid., pp. 445–446.
62. Zygmunt Bauman, *Work, Consumerism and the New Poor* (Philadelphia and Buckingham: Open University Press, 1998), p. 24.
63. Ibid., p. 24.
64. Ibid., p. 25.
65. Ibid., p. 26.
66. Ibid., p. 28.
67. Ibid., p. 30, cf. Zygmunt Bauman, *Society Under Siege* (Malden, MA: Blackwell, 2002), p. 196.
68. Bauman, *Society Under Siege*, p. 183.
69. Erich Fromm, *The Anatomy of Human Destructiveness* (London: Pimlico, 1997), pp. 281–283.
70. Bauman, *Society Under Siege*, p. 185. The references are to Harvie Ferguson, *The Lure of Dreams: Sigmund Freud and the Construction of Modernity* (London: Routledge, 1996) and

"Watching the World Go Round: Atrium Culture and the Psychology of Shopping" in Rob Shields (ed.), *Lifestyle Shopping: The Subject of Consumption* (London: Routledge, 1992).

71. Bauman, *Society Under Siege*, p. 187.
72. Ibid., pp. 193–194.
73. Ibid., pp. 197–200.
74. Bauman, *Society Under Siege*, p. 188.
75. Zygmunt Bauman, *Postmodern Ethics* (Cambridge, MA: Blackwell, 1993), pp. 204–205.
76. Bauman, *Work, Consumerism and the New Poor*, pp. 29–30.
77. Conrad Lodziak, "On Explaining Consumption" in *Capital and Class* 72, Autumn 2000, p. 112. He quotes Bauman's *Intimations of Postmodernity* (London: Routledge, 1992); a fuller exposition can be found in Conrad Lodziak, *The Myth of Consumerism* (London: Pluto, 2002).
78. Lodziak, "On Explaining Consumption," pp. 116–117.
79. Ibid., p. 121.
80. Ibid., p. 132.
81. Bauman, *Society Under Siege*, p. 165.
82. Bauman, *Work, Consumerism and the New Poor*, p. 92.
83. Ibid., p. 41.
84. Ibid., pp. 87–89.
85. Ibid., p. 91.
86. Ibid., p. 93 and 75.
87. Ibid., pp. 95–98.
88. Bauman, *Society Under Siege*, p. 22.
89. Fromm, *To Have or To Be?*, p. 173.
90. Bauman, *Society Under Siege*, pp. 240–241.
91. James B. Twitchell, *Lead Us into Temptation: The Triumph of American Materialism* (New York: Columbia University Press, 2000).
92. Report in *The Independent on Sunday* (London), January 4, 2004, p. 24.
93. *The Truman Show*, directed by Peter Weir for Paramount Studios, United States, 1998.

Chapter Seven     Democracy

1. Erich Fromm, *Escape From Freedom* (New York: Henry Holt, 1994), p. 272.
2. Ibid., p. 270.
3. Ibid., p. 272.
4. Ibid., p. 273.
5. This was reflected in programmatic changes watering down the demands for the socialization of the means of production. See Stephen Padgett and William Paterson, *A History of Social Democracy in Post-war Europe* (London and New York: Longman, 1991), chapter 1; Lawrence Wilde, *Modern European Socialism* (Aldershot: Ashgate, 1994), chapters 2–5.
6. Erich Fromm, *The Sane Society* (New York: Henry Holt, 1990), pp. 186–191.
7. Joseph Schumpeter, *Capitalism, Socialism and Democracy* (New York: Harper and Row), 1962, chapter 21.
8. Ibid., p. 262.
9. Ibid., chapter 22.
10. Ibid., pp. 257–258.
11. Fromm, *The Sane Society*, pp. 190–191.
12. Ibid., p. 339.
13. Ibid., pp. 339–341.
14. David Truman, *The Governmental Process* (New York: Alfred Knopf, 1951); Robert Dahl, *A Preface to Democratic Theory* (Chicago: Chicago University Press, 1956).

15. Fromm, *The Sane Society*, p. 126.
16. Erich Fromm, *On Being Human* (New York: Continuum, 1998), p. 95.
17. Erich Fromm, *The Revolution of Hope: Toward a Humanised Technology* (New York, Evanston and London: Harper and Row, 1968), pp. 99–100.
18. Fromm, *The Sane Society*, pp. 241–243.
19. Fromm, *The Revolution of Hope*, p. 108.
20. See Theda Skocpol and Jill Ikenberry, "The Political Formation of the American Welfare State: An Historical and Comparative Perspective," in R. F. Tomasson (ed.), *Comparative Social Research*, 6 (London: Jai Press, 1983), pp. 87–148.
21. Fromm, *The Revolution of Hope*, p. 151.
22. Ibid., p. 153.
23. In the final report on the project, which can be found in the Erich Fromm Archive in Tübingen, Fromm comments that his own nomination should be disregarded as he was the author of the book and the originator of the idea. Fromm and McCarthy received 736 nominations. The only other people to receive over 100 nominations were Benjamin Spock, John Gardner, William Fulbright, Mrs. Martin Luther King, and Harry and Emilia Rathbun. The latter two were leading lights in the already functioning National Initiative Foundation in California and were nominated exclusively by their group.
24. Brandt Commission, *North–South: A Programme For Survival* (London: Pan Books, 1980). Willy Brandt was President of the Socialist International at the time. At one stage Fromm was a delegate of the American Socialist Party to the Socialist International.
25. World Commission on Environment and Development, *Our Common Future* (Oxford and New York: Oxford University Press, 1986).
26. Richard Falk, *On Humane Governance: Toward a New Global Politics* (Cambridge: Polity, 1995). The international steering committee comprised mainly of academic, many of them associated with Peace Institutes. The workshops drew in a wide range of sponsors and participants.
27. The Commission on Global Governance, *Our Global Neighbourhood* (Oxford: Oxford University Press, 1995).
28. Fromm, *The Revolution of Hope*, pp. 154–155.
29. Ibid., p. 157.
30. Ibid.
31. Ibid., p. 159.
32. From the file in the Fromm Archive in Tübingen.
33. Michael Maccoby, Introduction to Erich Fromm and Michael Maccoby, *Social Character in a Mexican Village* (New Brunswick and London: Transaction Publishers, 1996), p. xxi.
34. Erich Fromm, *To Have or To Be?* (New York: Continuum, 2002), pp. 181–182.
35. Ibid., pp. 180–183.
36. Ibid., pp. 189–191.
37. Fromm, *The Sane Society*, p. 269.
38. Ibid.
39. Ibid., p. 251; On Proudhon's view of human nature see David Morland, *Demand The Impossible? Human Nature and Politics in Nineteenth-Century Social Anarchism* (London: Cassell, 1997), chapter three.
40. Fromm, *The Sane Society*, pp. 284–285. He is quoting from Cole and W. Mellor, *The Meaning of Industrial Freedom* (London: Allen and Unwin, 1918).
41. Fromm, *The Sane Society*, p. 257.
42. Michael Bakunin, *Statism and Anarchy* (Cambridge and New York: Cambridge University Press, 1994), pp. 137–138.
43. Fromm, *The Sane Society*, pp. 259–261.
44. Ibid., p. 262.
45. Ibid., pp. 263–264.
46. Ibid., pp. 264–265.

47. Ibid., p. 257. The passage in question is from *The Economic and Philosophical Manuscripts* in Karl Marx and Frederick Engels, *Collected Works*, volume three (New York and London: International Publishers and Lawrence & Wishart, 1973), p. 295. The note in *The Sane Society* implies the passage is in *Capital*.
48. Marx and Engels, *Collected Works*, volume six, p. 504.
49. Fromm, *The Sane Society*, p. 265.
50. Ibid., p. 239. The emphasis is Fromm's.
51. Fromm is referring here to Luxemburg's attack on Lenin's party theory in "Organisational Questions of Social Democracy" (1904), sometimes entitled "Marxism or Leninism?," and also her constructive criticism of the Bolsheviks after the Russian Revolution of 1917, "The Russian Revolution" in Luxemburg, *Rosa Luxemburg Speaks.*, M-A. Waters (ed.), New York: Pathfinder Press, 1971, pp. 112–130 and 365–395.
52. The year after the publication of *The Sane Society* the Hungarian uprising was crushed by the Red Army, and although a popular protest movement in Poland succeeded in securing power for Gomulka, the system quickly reverted to being completely intolerant.
53. Fromm, *The Sane Society*, p. 248.
54. Ibid., pp. 358–359.
55. Quoted in W. Bonss, Introduction to Erich Fromm, *The Working Class in Weimar Germany*, (Leamington Spa: Berg, 1984), p. 20n.
56. Burston, *The Legacy of Erich Fromm*, p. 13.
57. Fromm, *The Sane Society*, p. 273.
58. Ibid., p. 268.
59. Ibid., p. 269.
60. Ibid., p. 323.
61. Ibid., p. 331 and 361.
62. Ibid., p. 363.
63. Ibid., p. 362.
64. Fromm, *To Have or to Be?*, p. 160.
65. Ibid., p. 202.
66. Fromm, *The Sane* Society, pp. 343–352.
67. Ibid., p. 352; cf. *To Have or To Be?*, pp. 201–202.
68. Fromm, *To Have or to Be?*, p. 170.
69. Ibid., pp. 174–175.
70. See John Dryzek, *Deliberative Democracy and Beyond: Liberals, Critics, Contestations* (Oxford and New York: Oxford University Press, 2000).
71. John Rawls, *Political Liberalism* (New York: Columbia University Press, 1993); Jürgen Habermas, *Between Facts and Norms: Contributions to a Discourse Theory of Law and Democracy* (Cambridge, MA and Cambridge: MIT Press and Polity, 1996).
72. Roberto Mangabeira Unger, *Democracy Realized: The Progressive Alternative* (New York and London, 1998).
73. Erich Fromm, Interview with Mike Wallace, American Broadcasting Association, 1958. The text is in the Fromm archive in Tübingen.
74. Unger, *Democracy Realized*, pp. 3–4.
75. Ibid., pp. 257–260.
76. Ibid., pp. 9–10.
77. Ibid., p. 165.
78. Ibid., p. 174 and pp. 207–208.
79. Fromm, *The Sane Society*, p. 346.
80. Fromm, Foreword to A. S. Neill, *Summerhill: A Radical Approach to Child Rearing* (1960), at www.erichfromm.de/làib_1/1960e.html.
81. Unger, *Democracy Realized*, p. 231.
82. Ibid., pp. 186–187.

83. Ibid., p. 138.
84. Ibid., p. 205.
85. Ibid., p. 144 and 207–208.
86. Ibid., pp. 136–137 and 174.
87. Ibid., p. 176.
88. Ibid., pp. 176–182.
89. Ibid., p. 123, 226–227.
90. Ibid., pp. 254–255.
91. Ibid., pp. 50–51 and 140–141.
92. Ibid., p. 50 and 134–135.
93. Ibid., pp. 150–162.
94. Ibid., p. 39 and 134.
95. Ibid., pp. 215–220.
96. Ibid., pp. 220–227 and 276–277.
97. Ibid., p. 20.
98. Ibid., pp. 77–78.
99. Fromm, *The Revolution of Hope*, pp. 144–150.
100. John Kenneth Galbraith, *The Culture of Contentment* (London: Penguin, 1993).
101. Richard Sennett, *The Corrosion of Character: The Personal Consequences of Work in the New Capitalism* (New York: W. W. Norton, 1998).
102. Ulrich Beck, *The Brave New World of Work* (Malden, MA and Cambridge: Blackwells and Polity, 2000), pp. 69–70.
103. Fromm, *The Revolution of Hope*, p. 150.
104. Ronald Inglehart, *The Silent Revolution: Changing Values and Political Styles Among Western Publics* (Princeton: Princeton University Press, 1977) and Inglehart, *Culture Shift in Advanced Industrial Society* (Princeton: Princeton University Press, 1990).

## Chapter Eight   One World

1. Erich Fromm, "A New Humanism as a Condition for the One World" in Fromm, *On Being Human* (New York: Continuum, 1998), p. 61. The lecture was delivered at Sherwood Hall in La Jolla, California.
2. Ibid., p. 65.
3. Ibid., p. 76.
4. Erich Fromm, *Man For Himself: An Inquiry into the Psychology of Ethics* (New York: Henry Holt, 1990), pp. 240–241.
5. Ibid., pp. 243–244.
6. Fromm, *On Being Human* , p. 63.
7. Erich Fromm, *Beyond the Chains of Illusion*: My Encounter with Mark and Freud (New York: Simon and Schuster, 1962), pp. 6–8.
8. Erich Fromm, *The Sane Society* (New York: Henry Holt, 1990), pp. 58–59.
9. Ibid., pp. 59–60.
10. Ibid., p. 196.
11. Ibid., p. 60.
12. Erich Fromm, *The Heart of Man: Its Genius for Good and Evil* (New York, Evanston, and London: Harper and Row, 1964), p. 78.
13. Terry Eagleton has done this in the case of Ireland in "Nationalism and the Case of Ireland" in *New Left Review* 234, 1999, pp. 44–61.
14. Ibid., p. 79.
15. Ibid.
16. Michael Billig, *Banal Nationalism* (London: Sage, 1995), particularly chapter five, "Flagging the Homeland Daily."

17. Pierre Bourdieu, *Language and Symbolic Power* (Polity: Cambridge, 1991). See also Bourdieu and Terry Eagleton, "Doxa and Common Life: An Interview" in Slovoj Zizek (ed.), *Mapping Ideology* (London and New York: Verso, 1994).
18. Erich Fromm, *The Anatomy of Human Destructiveness* (London: Pimlico, 1997), p. 276.
19. Fromm, *The Heart of Man*, pp. 88–90.
20. Ibid., pp. 106–107.
21. On the significance of the imagery of "motherland" in nationalist rhetoric see Ghassan Hage, *Against Paranoid Nationalism: Searching for Hope in a Shrinking Society* (London: Merlin, 2003), chapter three.
22. Fromm, *The Heart of Man*, pp. 90–91.
23. Ibid., pp. 91–92.
24. Erich Fromm, *May Man Prevail?: An Inquiry Into the Facts and Fictions of Foreign Policy* (New York: Anchor Books, 1964). Fromm engaged in a correspondence from 1952 with Democratic presidential candidate Adlai Stevenson on foreign affairs. It is no coincidence that this came to an abrupt end during the crisis, when Stevenson played a key role as United States Ambassador to the United Nations. The final letter to Stevenson is dated September 15, 1962, and reports on Fromm's visit to the Moscow Peace Conference. The letters are in the Erich Fromm Archive in Tübingen.
25. The text of the speech is unpublished but a copy is held in the Fromm Archive in Tübingen. Fromm was unable to deliver the speech as he had a heart attack shortly before the rally.
26. Fromm, *The Sane Society*, p. 333.
27. Erich Fromm, *To Have or To Be?* (New York: Continuum, 2002), p. 189.
28. Ibid., pp. 180–181.
29. Stephen Nathanson, "Nationalism and the Limits of Global Humanism" in R. McKim and J. McMahan (eds.), *The Morality of Nationalism* (New York: Oxford University Press, 1997), pp. 184–185.
30. Yael Tamir, *Liberal Nationalism* (Princeton, NJ: Princeton University Press, 1993), p. 95.
31. Ibid., p. 96.
32. David Miller, *On Nationality* (New York: Oxford University Press, 1997), p. 49.
33. Ibid., pp. 65–68.
34. David Miller, *Market, State and Community: Theoretical Foundations of Market Socialism* (Oxford: Clarendon Press, 1990), p. 245.
35. Miller, *On Nationality*, p. 154.
36. Ibid., pp. 64–65.
37. Erich Fromm, *Escape From Freedom* (New York: Henry Holt, 1994), p. 209.
38. Fromm, *To Have or To Be?*, pp. 139–144.
39. Ibid., pp. 141–142.
40. Ibid., p. 143.
41. Charles Taylor, "Nationalism and Modernity" in R. McKim and J. McMahan (eds.), *The Morality of Nationalism* (New York: Oxford University Press, 1997), pp. 40–41.
42. Richard Rorty, "The Unpatriotic Academy" in Rorty, *Philosophy and Social Hope* (London: Penguin, 1999), pp. 252–254. Billig exposes the latent nationalism in Rorty's position in chapter seven of *Banal Nationalism*.
43. I. Berlin, "The Bent Twig: A Note on Nationalism" in *Foreign Affairs* 51, 1972, cited in Tamir's *Liberal Nationalism*, p. 98; R. Rorty, *Contingency, Irony and Solidarity* (New York: Cambridge University Press, 1989), p. 191.
44. Miller, *On Nationality*, p. 184. Miller adds a second reason why internationalist humanism is misguided, namely that nationality has provided a successful vehicle for the realization of liberal goals, and is "the appropriate form of solidarity for societies that are mobile."
45. Rorty, *Contingency, Irony and Solidarity*, p. 198.
46. See David Held and Anthony McGrew (eds.), *Governing Globalization: Power, Authority, and Global Governance* (Cambridge: Polity, 2002).

47. Hans Küng, *A Global Ethic For Global Politics and Economics* (New York and Oxford: Oxford University Press, 1998).
48. Tamir, *Liberal Nationalism*, pp. 166–167.
49. Miller, *On Nationality*, p. 187.
50. John Tomlinson, *Cultural Imperialism: A Critical Introduction* (London: Pinter, 1991), p. 174.
51. Karl Marx and Frederick Engels, "Manifesto of the Communist Party" in *Collected Works*, volume six (New York and London: International Publishers and Lawrence & Wishart, 1976), p. 488.
52. Fromm, *Escape From Freedom*, p. 271.
53. Ibid.
54. Fromm, *To Have or To Be?*, pp. 180–181.
55. Peter Waterman, *Globalization, Social Movements and the New Internationalisms* (New York: Continuum, 2001), p. 237.
56. Fromm, *The Heart of Man*, p. 140.
57. See, for example, Daniele Archibugi and David Held (eds.), *Cosmopolitan Democracy: An Agenda For a New World Order* (Cambridge: Polity Press, 1995); David Held, *Democracy and the Global Order* (Cambridge: Polity, 1995); Richard Falk, *On Humane Governance: Toward a New Global Politics* (Cambridge: Polity, 1995); The Commission on Global Governance, *Our Global Neighbourhood* (Oxford: Oxford University Press, 1995). Two contributions in particular adopt an explicitly ethical stance not dissimilar to Fromm's— Andrew Linklater, *The Transformation of Political Community* (Cambridge: Polity, 1998); David Harvey, *Spaces of Hope* (Edinburgh: Edinburgh University Press, 2000).
58. John Holloway and Eloina Peláez, "Introduction: Reinventing Revolt" in Holloway and Peláez (eds.), *Zapatista: Reinventing Revolution in Mexico* (London and Sterling, VA: Pluto Press, 1998); see also Holloway's chapter "Dignity's Revolt."
59. For an excellent discussion of their significance for the development of a new internationalism see Massimo De Angelis, "Globalization, New Internationalism and the Zapatistas" in *Capital and Class* 70, Spring 2000; see also Paul Kingsworth, *One No, Many Yeses* (London: Simon and Schuster, 2003), chapter one.
60. Harry Cleaver, "The Zapatistas and the Electronic Fabric of Struggle" in Holloway and Peláez, *Zapatista: Reinventing Revolution in Mexico*.
61. See Immanuel Wallerstein, "New Revolts Against the System" in *New Left Review* 18, November–December 2002, pp. 36–37.
62. Fromm, *To Have or To Be?*, p. 201.
63. Ibid.

Chapter Nine    Conclusion: Radical Humanism and Human Solidarity

1. Erich Fromm, *To Have or To Be?* (New York: Continuum, 2002), pp. 156–157.
2. Ibid., p. 16.
3. I set to one side here his contribution to psychoanalysis. See Daniel Burston, *The Legacy of Erich Fromm* (Cambridge, MA: Harvard University Press, 1991) and Mauricio Cortina and Michael Maccoby (eds.), *A Prophetic Analyst: Erich Fromm's Contribution to Psychoanalysis* (Northvale, NJ: Jason Aronson, 1996).
4. See Lawrence Wilde, "A Radical Humanist Approach to the Concept of Solidarity" in *Political Studies* 52 (1), 2004, for a fuller critique of the positions of Rorty and Honneth.
5. Richard Rorty, *Contingency, Irony, and Solidarity* (Cambridge: Cambridge University Press, 1989), p. 192.
6. Norman Geras, *Solidarity in the Conversation of Humankind: The Ungroundable Liberalism of Richard Rorty* (New York and London: Pluto Press, 1995), pp. 89–90.
7. Axel Honneth, *The Struggle For Recognition: The Moral Grammar of Social Conflicts* (Cambridge: Polity, 1996), pp. 128–129.

8. See Andreas Kalyvas, "Critical Theory at the Crossroads: Comments on Axel Honneth's Theory of Recognition" in *European Journal of Social Theory* 2 (1), pp. 95–98. Although Kalyvas's critique is persuasive, he is as unwilling as Honneth to justify claims to solidarity on the basis of a shared human essence.

9. Alain Touraine, *Can We Live Together? Equality and Difference* (Stanford, CA: Stanford University Press, 2000), conclusion.

10. Iris Marion Young, *Justice and the Politics of Difference* (Princeton: Princeton University Press, 1990) p. 36.

11. The literature is immense, but see, for example, John McMurtry, *The Cancer Stage of Capitalism* (Sterling, VA and London: Pluto, 1999); William Greider, *One World Ready or Not: The Manic Logic of Global Capitalism* (New York: Simon and Schuster, 1997); John Madeley, *Big Business Poor Peoples: The Impact of Transnational Corporations on the World's Poor* (New York and London: Zed Books, 1999).

12. Sidney Tarrow, *Power in Movement: Social Movements and Contentious Politics* (New York and Cambridge: Cambridge University Press, 1998); Robin Cohen and Shirin M. Rai (eds.), *Global Social Movements* (New Brunswick, NJ and London: Athlone, 2000).

13. William Fisher and Thomas Ponniah (eds.), *Another World is Possible: Popular Alternatives to Globalization at the World Social Forum* (New York and London: Zed Books, 2003); Peter Waterman, *Globalization, Social Movements and the New Internationalisms* (New York and London: Continuum, 2001); Paul Kingsworth, *One No, Many Yeses: A Journey to the Heart of the Global Resistance Movement* (London: The Free Press, 2003).

14. For example, Greg Palast, *The Best Democracy Money Can Buy* (London and Sterling, VA: Pluto, 2002); Noreena Hertz, *The Silent Takeover: Global Capitalism and the Death of Democracy* (London: William Heinemann, 2001).

15. David Bollier, *Silent Theft: The Private Plunder of Our Commonwealth* (New York and London: Routledge, 2003); George Monbiot, *Captive State: The Corporate Takeover of Britain* (London: Macmillan, 2000).

16. Ronaldo Munck, *Globalization and Labour: The New Great Transformation* (New York and London: Zed Books, 2002), pp. 128–134.

17. Paul Kingsworth, *One No, Many Yeses*, pp. 219–220.

# SELECT BIBLIOGRAPHY

The complete works of Erich Fromm in German are published in 12 volumes as *Erich Fromm Gesamtausagbe* (Stuttgart: Deutsche Verlags-Antalt and München: Deutscher Taschenbuch Verlag, 2000). From 1938 on Fromm wrote his books and articles in English. Below are the books in English that have been used in the text, in the order in which they were first published. The year of original publication is in square brackets. The international bibliography of writings on Fromm, containing 4000 titles, is available from the Erich Fromm Archive (Ursrainer Ring 24, D - 72076, Tübingen, Germany) and on the website of the Erich Fromm Archive at www.erich-fromm.de.

*Escape From Freedom* (New York: Henry Holt, 1994) [1941].
*Man For Himself: An Inquiry Into the Psychology of Ethics* (New York: Henry Holt, 1990) [1947].
*Psychoanalysis and Religion* (Yale: Harvard University Press, 1978) [1950].
*The Forgotten Language: An Introduction to the Understanding of Dreams, Fairy Tales and Myths* (New York: Grove Press, 1957) [1951].
*The Sane Society* (New York: Henry Holt, 1990) [1955].
*The Art of Loving* (London: Thorsons, 1995) [1956].
*Sigmund Freud's Mission: An Analysis of His Personality and Influence* (Gloucester, MA: Peter Smith, 1978) [1959].
*Zen Buddhism and Psychoanalysis,* coauthored with D. T. Suzuki and R. De Martino (London: Souvenir Press, 1993) [1960].
*May Man Prevail?: An Inquiry Into the Facts and Fictions of Foreign Policy* (New York: Doubleday Anchor, 1964) [1961].
*Marx's Concept of Man* (Continuum: New York, 1992) [1961].
*Beyond the Chains of Illusion: My Encounter with Marx and Freud* (New York: Simon and Schuster, 1962).
*The Dogma of Christ* (New York: Henry Holt, 1993) [1963].
*The Heart of Man: Its Genius for Good and Evil* (New York, Evanston and London: Harper and Row, 1964).
*Socialist Humanism,* edited text (London: Allen Lane Penguin, 1967) [1965].
*You Shall Be As Gods: A Radical Interpretation of the Old Testament and its Tradition* (New York: Henry Holt, 1991) [1966].
*The Revolution of Hope: Toward a Humanised Technology* (New York and London: Harper and Row, 1968).
*The Crisis of Psychoanalysis: Essays on Freud, Marx, and Social Psychology* (New York, Chicago, San Francisco: Holt, Rinehart and Winston, 1970).
*Social Character in a Mexican Village,* coauthored by Michael Maccoby (New Brunswick and London: Transaction Books, 1996) [1970].

*The Anatomy of Human Destructiveness* (London: Pimlico, 1974) [1973].

*To Have or To Be?* (New York: Continuum, 2002) [1976].

*The Greatness and Limitations of Freud's Thought* (New York: Harper and Row, 1980).

*On Disobedience and Other Essays* (New York: Seabury Press, 1981).

*The Working Class in Weimar* (London: Berg, 1984).

*The Revision of Psychoanalysis* (Boulder, San Francisco, Oxford: Westview Press, 1992).

*The Art of Being* (London: Constable, 1993).

*The Art of Listening* (London: Constable, 1994).

*On Being Human* (New York: Continuum, 1998).

*Love, Sexuality and Matriarchy: About Gender* (New York: Fromm International, 1999).

# INDEX